THE JURISDICTION OF MEDICAL LAW

T0352757

Medical Law and Ethics

Series Editor
Sheila McLean, Director of the Institute of Law and Ethics in Medicine,
School of Law, University of Glasgow

The 21st century seems likely to witness some of the most major developments in medicine and healthcare ever seen. At the same time, the debate about the extent to which science and/or medicine should lead the moral agenda continues, as do questions about the appropriate role for law.

This series brings together some of the best contemporary academic commentators to tackle these dilemmas in a challenging, informed and inquiring manner. The scope of the series is purposely wide, including contributions from a variety of disciplines such as law, philosophy and social sciences.

Forthcoming titles in the series

Ethical and Regulatory Aspects of Human Genetic Databases
Edited by Bernice Elger, Nikola Biller-Andorno, Alexandre Mauron and Alexander M. Capron
ISBN 978-0-7546-7255-5

Bioequity – Property and the Human Body
Nils Hoppe
ISBN 978-0-7546-7280-7

Altruism Reconsidered
Exploring New Approaches to Property in Human Tissue
Edited by Michael Steinmann, Peter Sykora, and Urban Wiesing
ISBN 978-0-7546-7270-8

The Child As Vulnerable Patient
Protection and Empowerment
Lynn Hagger
ISBN 978-0-7546-7252-4

The Jurisdiction of Medical Law

KENNETH VEITCH
University of Sussex, UK

Routledge
Taylor & Francis Group
LONDON AND NEW YORK

First published 2007 by Ashgate Publishing

Reissued 2018 by Routledge
2 Park Square, Milton Park, Abingdon, Oxon OX14 4RN
711 Third Avenue, New York, NY 10017, USA

Routledge is an imprint of the Taylor & Francis Group, an informa business

First issued in paperback 2018

A Library of Congress record exists under LC control number: 2007023734

Notice:
Product or corporate names may be trademarks or registered trademarks, and are used only for identification and explanation without intent to infringe.

Publisher's Note
The publisher has gone to great lengths to ensure the quality of this reprint but points out that some imperfections in the original copies may be apparent.

Disclaimer
The publisher has made every effort to trace copyright holders and welcomes correspondence from those they have been unable to contact.

ISBN 13: 978-0-815-39791-5 (hbk)
ISBN 13: 978-1-138-62107-7 (pbk)
ISBN 13: 978-1-351-14624-1 (ebk)

Contents

For TJV, ISTV and WTT

Acknowledgements

I would like to thank various bodies and people whose assistance and support have been integral to the completion of this book. Firstly, I am grateful to the Law Schools of Cardiff University and the University of Sussex for their help in creating the conditions within which this book could be developed and completed. Secondly, I express my gratitude to the following people for their insights, constructive criticism, encouragement and guidance both in the course of writing this book and generally over the last several years: Jo Bridgeman, David Campbell, John Harrington, Bob Lee, Sheila McLean, Jonathan Montgomery, Derek Morgan, Sally Sheldon, Adam Tomkins and Scott Veitch. I am also very grateful to Alison Kirk and Emily Jarvis at Ashgate Publishing for their efficiency in seeing this book through to publication. Finally, I would like to thank three people without whose support this book would not have been written: my parents, for their assistance, encouragement and lifelong belief in the value of education; and my wife, Tee Tan, for her patience and willingness to make sacrifices. Thank you.

Introduction

One of the defining characteristics of medical law in recent years has been its inexorable expansion. From its relatively humble beginnings in the area of medical negligence, medical law has mushroomed to incorporate a variety of topics within its purview. Withdrawal of life-sustaining medical treatment; the rationing of public health care resources; access to artificial reproductive techniques; the regulatory implications of developments arising from research in molecular biology (especially in the field of human genetics): these are just a few of the many areas and issues that have come to form part of medical law's corpus over the last quarter century or so. The medical law textbook offers one of the most striking indicators of this seemingly incessant growth. Like the painting of Scotland's Forth Bridge, no sooner has the ink dried on the latest textbooks than the pace of events, and the arrival of new topics, compel their authors to embark anew on the next, invariably longer, editions. 'Keeping up' with, recording, and commenting upon the latest developments in legislation and the case law are constant endeavours – and sources of anxiety – in the medical law field.[1]

Accompanying this expansion in subject matter has been much reflection on the nature, or what might be called the constitution, of medical law – what defines it; which principles ought to constitute its essence; what distinguishes it from other legal sub-disciplines.[2] In other words, some academics have been concerned to map out the contours of medical law – attempting, in the process, to establish a legal sub-discipline whose practitioners and scholars can legitimately lay claim to exercise competence over a variety of disputes and issues arising not only in the field of medical practice but, increasingly, out of developments in biomedical science too. In this regard, an enduring topic of discussion and analysis in the literature has been the manner in which those who have the authority to make medical law – predominantly Parliament and judges – have exercised this power. Specifically, a large amount of

---

1 See, for example, the opening lines of Mason and Laurie's *Mason & McCall Smith's Law and Medical Ethics* (2006, v): 'Can it really be only three years since we last wrote a Preface to *Law and Medical Ethics*? ... The fact that a 7th edition has been called for is, in itself, an indication of the continuous, and apparently relentless, expansion of medical law as the framework of ethical medical practice – to such an extent that it is becoming increasingly difficult to write a generalised account of the subject within a book of manageable size.' It might also be noted that this expansion has a geographical dimension too, as illustrated, for instance, in the titles of Mason and Laurie's new chapter 'Health Rights and Obligations in the European Union' (Mason and Laurie 2006, Chapter 3) and Harrington's recent essay 'Globalisation and English Medical Law: Strains and Contradictions' (Harrington 2006).

2 This type of reflection is encapsulated in Morgan's basic question: 'What is medical law?' (Morgan 2001, Chapter 1).

critical academic energy has been directed towards what Sheldon describes as 'the medicalisation of law' (Sheldon 1997). Broadly speaking, this description denotes the deference that can be detected in substantive medical law towards the medical profession. Whether it be medical negligence, abortion law or questions regarding patient consent, for example, both the courts and the legislature have been consistently criticized for placing too much power in the hands of medical professionals either effectively to define certain issues (such as abortion) or to determine the legal standards to which those professionals are, themselves, held to account.

While the medicalization of law remains a significant feature of substantive medical law today, for a number of years now and perhaps influenced by the nature of the academic commentary just described, two aspects of this field have suggested a less deferential approach by the courts towards the medical profession. The first – an emphasis on the empowerment of patients – has become a staple feature, perhaps even the *raison d'être*, of medical law, with both academics and judges priding themselves on the promotion and enunciation of principles such as patient self-determination, patient autonomy and the right to choose. Power, we are told, has shifted decisively from the doctor to the patient and woe betide the medical professional who fails to appreciate this.

The second indication of the erosion of medical deference within the law manifests itself in the form of statements by some members of the judiciary in which they seek to promote a more proactive role for the courts in managing the increasing number of disputes and issues (especially those of an ethically controversial nature) coming before them. The following two quotations from the then Lord Chief Justice of England and Wales – Lord Woolf – are exemplary:

> The courts must recognise that theirs is essentially a regulatory role and they should not interfere unless interference is justified. But when interference is justified they must not be deterred from so doing by any principle such as the fact that what has been done is in accord with a practice approved of by a respectable body of medical opinion. (The Right Honourable The Lord Woolf 2001, 15–16)

> [T]he courts are nowadays, with increasing frequency, being asked to adjudicate on legal points bound up with fundamental and emotive questions of medical ethics ... The importance I attach to these cases is the fact that, although the expert evidence of doctors is most important on the ethical issues involved, the courts are final arbiters and not the doctors. (The Right Honourable The Lord Woolf 2001, 11 and 13)

And it is not only in the form of extra-judicial statements that suggestions for a more prominent role for the courts can be detected; the law reports contain similar, sometimes grander, proclamations. Thus, for instance, in the well-known case of the conjoined twins in 2000,[3] Ward LJ had this to say about the function of the courts: 'Deciding disputed matters of life and death is surely and pre-eminently a matter for a court of law to judge. That is what courts are here for' (*Re A (Children)* 2000, 987).

The foregoing narrative contains the seeds of the inspiration for this book. For it points to some interesting, though rarely explored, questions that go to the heart of

---

3   *Re A (Children)* (2000).

this relatively new field of law. Such questions include the following: Why is medical law expanding? Why are the courts increasingly becoming involved in settling, and being viewed as the natural fora through which to settle, conflicts and sensitive issues arising from medical practice and developments in biomedical science? Why have some academics been concerned to ruminate on the question, 'What is medical law?'? How are patients empowered by the courts? What does autonomy – the ethical value underlying claims to patient empowerment and often used rhetorically in the literature – actually mean? How do judges decide ethically controversial issues? Have they adopted the sort of proactive stance outlined above and, as we shall see, advanced by some prominent academics in this field? What might be some of the implications of the greater involvement of the courts in this area? These are the types of questions that will drive the discussion and analysis in this book.

Such questions can, it is suggested here, also usefully be understood to cluster around two themes – those of jurisdiction and power. As several legal scholars have noted, literally 'jurisdiction' (*juris-dire*) means the power 'to speak the law' (see, for example, Dorsett 2002 and Farmer 1996). It has been described as 'the right and power of a court to adjudicate concerning the subject matter in a given case' (*Black's Law Dictionary* 1990). As Dorsett has said: 'Jurisdiction can ... be conceptualised as a legal space, or sphere of competence. Thus, to have jurisdiction over a matter is to have the competence to make a determination with respect to that matter' (Dorsett 2002, 34). Additionally, though, jurisdiction is synonymous with the idea of territory. It points to a concern with determining boundaries and, in the legal field, with differentiating amongst bodies of law. Using property law as an example, Dorsett captures this when she says: 'In defining the boundaries of a substantive concept such as "property", we are also employing jurisdictional concepts. In asking "what is the province of property law, to what does property law apply, to what does it speak?", we are asking a jurisdictional question' (Dorsett 2002, 35). Those ideas underlying the notion of jurisdiction are directly relevant to part of the inquiry to be conducted in this book. Thus, for example, we will see how the academic inquiry into the constitution of medical law might be interpreted as an attempt to create a space or territory for this new subject called medical law – a subject that can be differentiated from other bodies, or sub-disciplines, of law in specific and identifiable ways. Similarly, in seeking to understand the reasons underlying the increasing role of the courts in this area, we will, essentially, be engaged in a jurisdictional inquiry – that is, how the courts have come to possess the competence to make determinations with respect to certain matters.

But the questions set out above also demand engagement with the issue of power. Of course, as is clear from the foregoing descriptions, jurisdiction is intimately bound up with the question of power. But rather than limiting the inquiry to how, for example, the courts have come to possess the power to adjudicate, this book is also concerned with the exercise and organization of that power. In particular, it will examine the manner in which judicial power is exercised and organized in a number of cases, especially those involving controversial ethical issues. To put it another way, one of the objectives of this book is to analyse how the courts assert their increasing jurisdiction in some prominent medical law cases. This type of inquiry is especially relevant at a time when, as noted, some members of the judiciary are keen to move away from the deferential stance traditionally adopted by the courts towards members of the medical profession. If this is no longer the principal way of asserting jurisdiction, then what has taken its place? If some judges are willing to be more proactive, then how, precisely, have they been so? What techniques have they used to assert their power, especially in cases involving ethically controversial issues? Whilst still relevant to medical law, the 'medicalisation of law' type of analysis fails to supply sufficient tools by which to understand the various ways in which courts assert and organize their power. To a degree, then, what is required is a reorientation of the traditional analysis of power within the medical law field. It is one of the purposes of this book to contribute to this undertaking. Finally, it is important to note that the book will also reflect on some of the actual and potential consequences, or implications, of the manner in which judicial power is exercised and organized in this area of law. In doing so, it will be possible to assess whether or not the greater involvement of the courts is beneficial.

At this stage, it will be useful to provide an example which illustrates the relevance of the foregoing themes. As the case referred to will be discussed and analysed in detail in a later chapter, it will only be dealt with very briefly here. We have already seen how, in *Re A (Children)* (2000), Ward LJ made a claim to jurisdiction on behalf of the courts. He effectively declared that the courts had, over and above any other institutions within society, the competence to determine contested matters of life and death. The 'matter' in this case involved a dispute over how to proceed in relation to conjoined twins who, unless operated on, would die within months. The problem, however, was that if an operation to separate them took place, only the physically stronger twin had a chance of survival, while the weaker one would definitely die. The conflict at the heart of the case was one between the medical team caring for the twins (who sought to operate to separate them) and the twins' parents (who, owing to their religious beliefs, could not agree to an operation which would effectively kill one of their daughters in order to allow the other to survive). Declaring the proposed operation to be lawful, the Court of Appeal held that the least detrimental alternative would be to separate the twins. The operation duly took place, the result being that the stronger twin survived, while the weaker one died.

As will be argued at greater length in Chapter 6, the manner in which the Court of Appeal proceeded to arrive at its conclusion was driven largely by what will in this book be called institutional requirements or exigencies. That is, certain features of legal reasoning – such as the need to discover in the existing body of the common law the relevant legal principle to be applied to the twins' case, and the duty of the courts to decide the cases brought before them, rather than refusing to do so on the basis that some of them might be too hard – impacted upon the way in which the Court exercised its power. One of the consequences of this was that the Court failed to do justice to the original conflict between the medical team and the parents. Rather than acknowledging that the idea of a least detrimental alternative simply had no meaning for the twins' parents, the Court proceeded to apply this principle to resolve the case, as it could not refuse to make a decision. As Ward LJ said: 'There has been some public concern as to why the court is involved at all. We do not ask for work but we have a duty to decide what parties with a proper interest ask us to decide' (*Re A (Children)* 2000, 987).

Given the nature of this case, an understandable temptation would be critically to analyse the Court of Appeal's ruling from the perspective of its relative ethical merits and deficiencies. Ethically, was it the right decision? Is it always better to save one life rather than losing two? Which principles from moral philosophy should hold sway in such an event? Whilst not unimportant, the suggestion here, and throughout this book, is that this mode of analysis is insufficient. It misses too much, and, by doing so, fails to offer an adequate understanding of how the courts assert their jurisdiction in ethically controversial issues arising from medical practice and developments in biomedical science. Specifically, analyses that concern themselves solely with questions of ethics offer no purchase on the role that such institutional exigencies play in determining the manner in which this jurisdiction is asserted. Moreover, the consequences that flow from the operation of those exigencies – one of which, as we have just seen, might be the effect on how moral issues and conflicts are constructed in the first place, and, thereafter, managed – remain obscured from view in analyses which deploy ethical reasoning as their critical tool.

The suggestion being made here, then, is that, in order to comprehend the increasing involvement of the courts in the medical law field, not only is it necessary to institute a partial reorientation of the analysis of power away from the target of the 'medicalisation of law' thesis; it is also essential to complement the existing, and dominant, critical form of analysis within the academic medical law literature – one based on ethics and the ethical supportability of court decisions and laws – with one whose critical eye is directed towards the more mundane, though by no means less important, institutional apparatus that structures aspects of how the courts function in this area. And this, essentially, is the overriding purpose of the book – to demonstrate the utility of this alternative methodological approach to the study of medical law. The precise ways in which this will be undertaken will become clear now as we turn to an outline of the chapters to follow.

Part I lays down the foundations of the book. Broadly speaking, the chapters in this Part are concerned with charting some aspects of the development of medical law. Chapter 1 looks at academic medical law and focuses on some of the literature that has been influential in shaping the development and nature of the subject. It is argued that aspects of this literature point to a concern with matters that can usefully be understood to revolve around questions of jurisdiction. For instance, the reflections on the nature of medical law (the 'What is medical law?' inquiry) referred to are interpreted as attempts to establish the boundaries or limits of the subject. They are efforts to determine what falls within the province of medical law and how this legal sub-discipline is to be differentiated from other areas of law, such as contract and tort. In other words, there is a real concern to establish the nature of the terrain or territory of medical law. Equally, it will be argued that it is possible to detect in this literature a desire for the creation of a space within which academics can develop the expertise that allows them to lay claim to speak with some authority about various controversial issues arising from medical practice and out of advances in, for example, human reproductive technology. Although, for the most part, academics have no power to adjudicate on the various disputes arising in this area, they nevertheless seek to construct a sphere of competence of sorts – that is, they claim some form of jurisdiction over such disputes.

Chapter 1 also attempts to pinpoint the specific techniques that some academics deploy to argue that law should develop jurisdiction over problems and disputes arising in the medical domain. Two principal mechanisms are identified: first, an emphasis on the position of the patient – that is, the need to empower patients and, thereby, diminish medical power; and, secondly, the desire to ensure that the ethical issues arising within medical practice are determined outside of the medical profession. Given that the importance of those mechanisms lies not merely in the role they play in structuring and defining academic medical law but also in how they are deployed in calls for the courts to become actively involved in determining such issues (that is, that those mechanisms are used as justificatory tools for the development of medical law generally), they will form the main focal points of the book.

Chapter 2 continues the analysis of the development of medical law by turning to consider some of the possible reasons underlying the growing involvement of the courts in this area. More specifically, this phenomenon is set against a backdrop of, on the one hand, some technological developments in medicine and biomedical science, and, on the other, various transformations in the social and political makeup of contemporary Western societies. Drawing upon work in the sociology of medicine and social theory, the argument advanced is that the more frequent resort to litigation as a means of settling disputes in this field can, at least to some degree, be explained by a shift in the types of values guiding social organization. Thus, much more emphasis is placed today on the individual, and his or her rights, agreements, choices and responsibilities, as the units of social arrangement. This state of affairs lends itself to a more prominent role for courts as the law is particularly good at treating people as individuals who are self-sufficient and the bearers of rights. Moreover, it will be noted how some transformations – particularly the dispersal of political power and decision-making from central institutions, including parliaments – have resulted in the courts becoming much more influential.

Chapter 2, however, has a further objective, which is to note some of the possible links between the central focal points of the book described above and those wider social and political transformations. So, for example, before proceeding in Part II to examine how the courts empower patients, it will be useful to reflect on how individuals generally are empowered today. Again, some literature in the field of social theory will assist in this endeavour as it allows us to note how individuals are not only encouraged to exercise their rights and choices but become responsible for the decisions they make too. The introduction of those themes of choice and responsibility are discussed in Chapter 2 in the context of the UK Government's recent proposals for improving the National Health Service and the state of the nation's health.

Part II of the book deals with the first focal point identified above – namely, the emphasis placed by both academics and the judiciary on the position of patients and the need to empower them. As a way of reflecting on this, Chapters 3 and 4 explore the ethical value of autonomy and its relationship with the common law in some medical law cases. One obvious reason for electing to concentrate on autonomy is that it is a, perhaps the, guiding value in medical law.[4] But despite 'the almost relentlessly increasing reliance on personal autonomy as the cornerstone of both medical ethics and medical law' (Mason and Laurie 2006, 6), there has been remarkably little by way of sustained reflection on it within the academic literature. Often autonomy is deployed, by academics and judges alike, in a rhetorical manner, presented as the consumer-friendly visage of medical law that will have the effect of saving patients from what is considered to be the dominance of medical professionals in the doctor–patient relationship. And yet, a more complicated picture lurks behind this façade. For in the process of converting the rhetoric into practice, something often jars. Patients may not get their way or they may do so only after substantial investigation and meticulous inquiry have taken place. In other words, the actual reproduction of patient autonomy within the common law is not as clear cut as some academic medical lawyers and judges make it out to be.

In an attempt to explain this state of affairs, Part II begins by describing some of the possible conceptual sources of the reliance on autonomy in medical law. Drawing especially on Kant's moral philosophy and some of Onora O'Neill's recent work on bioethics, it is suggested that different conceptions of autonomy exist. Thus, alongside the idea of autonomy as representing the atomistic individual who seeks to assert his or her right to self-determination by making whatever choices he or she wishes (what O'Neill calls 'individual autonomy'), exists a notion of autonomy that emphasizes the importance of responsibility and obligation (O'Neill's 'principled autonomy'). Whilst it is the former understanding of autonomy that has been most influential in medical law, it is argued that O'Neill's dual conception much more accurately captures the reality of how autonomy lives within the common law in this area.

Evidence for this argument is provided in Chapter 4 by way of reference to some prominent legal cases in several areas of medical law. Close analysis of those cases reveals how, in areas of medical law where the emphasis on patient empowerment is particularly keen, themes of obligation and responsibility are equally as important to the courts as their need to uphold the caricature of the atomistic, rights-bearing patient. Chapter 4 also reflects on what might lie behind the simultaneous presence of 'individual' and 'principled' autonomy in those cases. The argument advanced is that, in addition to an understanding of the ethical value of autonomy, there needs to be an appreciation of the role that legal institutional or structural features play in determining which conceptions of autonomy exist within the common law. For instance, there is evidence that the courts retain their traditional respect for medical professionals, and their standards and expertise, in the process of seeking to empower patients. This need to demonstrate professional respect, which manifests itself in the prominent role assigned to medics to assess whether patients have the mental capacity to make decisions about medical treatment, contributes to the presence of 'principled autonomy' within some of the cases referred to. This is because the examination of patients involved in such assessments can be as much to do with ascertaining whether the particular patient is acting responsibly (for example,

---

4   As Mason and Laurie say: '[A]utonomy is by far the most significant value to have influenced the evolution of contemporary medical law' (Mason and Laurie 2006, 6).

meeting unspecified standards of moral conduct) as it is with determining whether he or she can use and weigh treatment information in the balance when arriving at a decision (one of the conditions of the legal test for mental capacity). Similarly, the presence of individual autonomy in such cases can be explained by reference to various institutional features such as the desire of members of the judiciary to display the relevance of the common law in the face of the types of broader sociological changes discussed in Chapter 2. This results in great emphasis being placed on the importance of patients' rights to self-determination.

Part III addresses the second focal point of the book – the argument put forward by some academics that the ethical issues arising within medical practice must be determined outside of the medical profession, and, specifically, by law. This argument, which resonates with Lord Woolf's views set out above regarding the need for courts to be more proactive when dealing with cases involving 'fundamental and emotive questions of medical ethics', is tested by considering how judges have, in fact, responded to such cases. Focusing on litigation involving human rights challenges and issues of moral conflict, it is suggested in Chapters 5 and 6 that members of the judiciary have been reluctant to assert their jurisdiction over controversial ethical questions in such a proactive manner. Rather than grasping the opportunity to immerse themselves in discussions of the ethical ins and outs of those types of questions, or grounding their rulings in fundamental ethical principles, the cases discussed in Part III illustrate the conservative approach of senior members of the judiciary to such cases. This approach, it is argued, manifests itself in a concern to deploy traditional techniques of legal reasoning – including a respect for legal precedent and an adherence to the traditional functions of judicial review – as a way of resolving those cases. Thus, once again, it is possible to note the pull that institutional exigencies exert on judges and how these affect the manner in which they exercise their jurisdiction in some areas of medical law.

Thereafter, the discussion moves on to consider the consequences – both actual and potential – of the courts' involvement in cases arising out of medical practice and developments in biomedical science whose subject matter raises controversial ethical issues. As well as failing to replicate in practice the exhortations of some prominent academic medical lawyers, those implications range from failing to do justice to the moral conflicts at the heart of cases to the danger that the courts may contribute to, rather than help to alleviate, the democratic deficit that some academics, including the social theorist Ulrich Beck, argue is a significant feature of medical and scientific progress. In other words, if there is a need to create wide debate about the ethics of such progress, and the judiciary is reluctant to become involved in discussing the ethics of the issues coming before them, we must ask whether the courts can play any positive role in this process.

This completes the introduction to the book's substantive content and arguments. But before proceeding, it is worth saying something here about the scope, and limits, of the current project. In a book deploying the theme of jurisdiction, this seems appropriate! The first point to make relates to the book's title – *The Jurisdiction of Medical Law*. This is not intended to suggest that there is 'a' jurisdiction of medical law and it is the one described in this book. As noted above, 'jurisdiction' is deployed here as a way of capturing various phenomena – including the establishment of a legal sub-discipline called medical law and the nature of the courts' growing engagement in this area – that, it is suggested, are interesting and worthy of investigation. Nor is there any intention that what follows will encompass all the topics and issues traditionally associated with medical law. In other words, no claims are made regarding the relevance, or otherwise, of the arguments in this book to the entire field of medical law.

Secondly, this book differs from more traditional approaches to the subject as the discussion and analysis does not revolve around a particular area of, or issue within, medical law. Rather, cases from different spheres of medical law are used for the purpose of developing the book's arguments. In selecting the cases for discussion, every attempt has been made to use as examples prominent legal cases that, if the volume of commentary devoted to them in the academic literature is anything to go by, are commonly viewed as being significant in the development of medical law. An additional principle of selection is that the types of cases chosen had every chance of demonstrating that the claims made by some academics, whose work is discussed in the pages to follow, were justified. For instance, in keeping with the claim that law should be more proactive in dealing with ethically controversial issues, the 'conjoined twins' case, amongst others, presented the Court of Appeal with an excellent opportunity to engage in a discussion of the ethics of the dilemma before it. But, in that case, Ward LJ commented: 'This is a court of law, not of morals, and our task has been to find, and our duty is then to apply the relevant principles of law to the situation before us ...' (*Re A (Children)* 2000, 969). This disparity between the claims for a more interventionist judicial approach and what actually goes on in practice made this case a very useful one to investigate for the purposes of this book as it offered the possibility of reflecting on the reasons behind the existence of this discrepancy.

Thirdly, for the purposes of this book, it has not been necessary to describe and discuss all of those works that reflect on the nature of medical law. This is because the examples selected contain arguments about the purpose and constitution of medical law that, it is suggested, are sufficiently replicated, or taken for granted, in the general literature as to warrant examination as being defining features of this legal sub-discipline.

Finally, given that one of the main purposes of the book is to try to understand how the courts exercise their jurisdiction in the medical law sphere, the analysis will be confined to examples drawn from the common law. In other words, the book does not seek directly to discuss legislation in the field of medical law.

Given the foregoing, it might be suggested that the arguments made in this book will necessarily be of limited relevance to the medical law field generally. Of course, until further inquiries are undertaken, it is impossible to ascertain whether or not this is the case. All that can be said here is that determining the extent of the applicability of the arguments contained in this book is not its rationale; rather, its purpose is to *make* the arguments and illustrate the explanatory potential of an alternative methodological approach to the study of medical law.

PART I

Chapter 1

Jurisdiction and Academic Medical Law

Introduction

The argument advanced in this chapter is that some aspects of the academic medical law literature can usefully be interpreted through the prism of jurisdiction. This is especially true of academic writing that has sought to reflect on the nature of medical law, including what its function might be and how it ought to be constituted.[1] The relevance of jurisdiction in this context is principally twofold. Firstly, there is a discernable concern in this literature to determine the scope of the subject – which topics and areas, for example, should fall within its domain. Moreover, one detects a need to justify the existence of medical law as a separate legal sub-discipline – one that can be differentiated from more traditional legal subjects. In short, there is a desire to map out the territory or terrain of medical law, to determine, we might say, the province of medical law. Secondly, it is possible to investigate how some academic medical lawyers make the claim that law should develop jurisdiction over medical issues. What mechanisms do they deploy for this purpose? In order to illustrate this, reference will be made to some of Ian Kennedy's more reflective writings on medical law. It will be argued that the central features of his work – a concern to empower patients (and, consequently, disempower doctors) and the argument that ethical issues arising within medical practice must be determined outside of the medical profession – are not simply meant to improve current medical practice; they can also be thought to be one way in which the academic claims legal jurisdiction in this area (for the academic, the courts and the legislature). For the academic, this claim to jurisdiction is essential as it works to satisfy his or her desire to create a distinct subject within the legal academy that will act as a base from which he or she can claim to have the expertise to pronounce on controversial issues (especially ethical ones) arising in the course of medical practice. This affords legal academics the opportunity to develop a sphere of competence of sorts – that is, a jurisdiction – over those issues.

Some writing in academic medical law, however, is not merely intended to have effects within the law school. For some, its purpose is also to influence the nature of medical law in practice, especially within the courts. Thus, it is often intended that the stress placed in the literature on both patients' rights and the external determination

---

1 To some extent, this book is intended as an analysis of (some of) the conditions and principles underlying the emergence, and development, of the academic subject that has come to be known as medical law. This type of analysis exists in other areas of legal studies. In relation to the law of contract, for example, see Gilmore 1995 and Atiyah 1979 (especially Chapter 14).

of ethical issues arising from medical practice ought to be reflected in legal practice. While this chapter will touch upon the question of 'practical' legal jurisdiction, an inquiry into the extent to which the specific objectives of academics' arguments are, and can be, replicated in the courtroom will have to await future chapters. This will obviously demand a consideration of how members of the judiciary have defined their role in this emerging area of the common law. Anticipating this, towards the end of this chapter the observations of one academic (Jonathan Montgomery) regarding the potential difficulties of replicating the visions of some academic medical lawyers within the common law will be noted.

'What is Medical Law?' and the Question of Jurisdiction

> So how is the subject named medical law, or health care law, constituted? Does it have an identity? Is there agreement regarding its nature and boundaries? ... To be fair, it is doubtful whether a full account of the legal regulation of all aspects of health care and medical treatment can be given in one volume alone. (O'Donovan 1998, vii)

There has been no lack of reflection upon the nature of medical law in recent years.[2] The 'What is medical law?' type question has been raised by many of the influential writers in this field.[3] The question posed here is, why? What might be the reasons for asking such a question, and what can the answers that are given to it reveal about the preoccupations of those involved in this relatively new sub-discipline of law? The argument advanced here is that those answers illustrate concerns that are bound up with questions of jurisdiction.

The first, and perhaps most obvious, reason for seeking to define what medical law is relates to the attempt to determine the scope of the subject. In other words, the purpose of the question here might be thought to be directed toward identifying the nature of the actors and topics that ought to constitute the subject's focus of study. An example of this concern with scope can be seen in the first sentence of Jonathan Montgomery's book *Health Care Law*: 'The academic study of health care law is still a relatively young discipline and no consensus has yet been reached as to its proper scope' (Montgomery 2003, 1). Immediately, it is apparent that Montgomery refers to 'health care law' and not 'medical law'. In doing so, his purpose is not only to define the topics he considers form the focus of his subject but also to point out how these exceed the boundaries of what he understands to be 'medical law': '[T]he subject of health care law is wider than medical law. It embraces not only the practice of medicine, but also that of the non-medical health care professions, the

---

2   One example, which includes a discussion of the course medical law may take in the future, is Brazier and Glover 2000.

3   In doing so, those writers (some of whose work will be discussed in this chapter) provide a contemporary, and sub-disciplinary, reinforcement of Hart's famous observation: 'Few questions concerning human society have been asked with such persistence ... as the question "What is law?"' (Hart 1961, 1). Further examples can be found in other legal sub-disciplines. For instance, see Martin Loughlin's recent inquiry: 'The question is this: what is public law?' (Loughlin 2004, 1).

administration of health care services and law's role in maintaining public health' (Montgomery 2003, 3).

Thus, by defining health care law, Montgomery simultaneously defines what he considers the scope of medical law to be. The latter, he says, 'sees the clinical interaction between doctor and patient as the paradigm. This view influences both the content of the subject, individualizing its focus, and its underlying conceptual coherence, emphasizing the application of ethical principles' (Montgomery 2003, 1). According to Montgomery, while health care law encompasses this, it can be thought to extend beyond the boundaries of medical law.

This is all very straightforward and an eminently sensible way of defining the areas of focus that help delineate the boundaries of a subject of study. But, even at this most basic of levels, this concern with the scope and territory of subjects can usefully be understood as one involving the question of jurisdiction. As Montgomery observes, this need to map out boundaries is mainly a result of the relative novelty of both health care law and medical law as academic subjects within the legal academy. And it is this point about the novelty of medical law as an academic subject that forms the basis of the second possible reason why academics in this area feel compelled to pose the question: 'What is medical law?'.

The emergence of medical law as an academic subject has not been uncontroversial. But perhaps the most serious charge to have been levelled against it is captured by Derek Morgan in his observation that: 'The question "what is medical law?" is sometimes posed in a form that appears to assert that "medical law is not a subject"' (Morgan 2001, 3). He interprets this assertion as a charge not that medical law is not a subject *yet* – that is, that while it does not presently possess a sufficiently mature framework and conceptual basis to lay claim to independence in its own right, it might do so at some point in the future – but that it is nothing more (and presumably destined to be nothing more) than 'an amalgam of traditional categories of tort, contract and criminal law'[4] (Morgan 2001, 3). Morgan's interpretation is no doubt correct, especially when the assertion emanates from those whose legal education has been founded on the writings of Salmond, Chitty and Anson (to use Morgan's own examples). But this charge – that 'medical law is not a subject' – is also often levelled by those who *are* amenable to less turgid and prescriptive approaches to law and legal scholarship. Here, the criticism is less concerned with the need for mature legal frameworks than it is with the suggestion that medical law is not a sufficiently rigorous subject. Thus, for example, while questions of ethics have come to dominate medical law, at least in its academic form, this often manifests itself in the unreflective, wholesale adoption of ethical concepts such as justice and autonomy. The lack of rigorous analyses of such concepts within the literature leads to charges that the subject is most accurately, indeed perhaps only, characterized by its rhetoric and, as such, does not deserve to be taken seriously. Whether or not

---

4   This general charge that 'medical law is not a subject' has been noted, and refuted, by other writers in the field. See, for example, Sheldon and Thomson 1998b. While Sheldon and Thomson refer to 'health care law', the general tenor of the criticism they identify resonates with Morgan's analysis.

Morgan has this type of critic in mind too when responding to the general charge that 'medical law is not a subject', his reply is both robust and profound:

> I agree in part. Medical law is indeed not *just* a subject; it is also a responsibility. Whether medical law is a legal category in itself is beside the point. The framing of responses properly lying within medical law is part of an intellectual responsibility that lies at the heart of the academic obligation which, as John Fleming has otherwise observed, is to be 'sensitive to movement and direction ... [being] concerned with whence, whither and most important, with why'. (Morgan 2001, 3; emphasis in original; references omitted)

This broad understanding of medical law takes one far beyond Montgomery's concern with delineating its specific scope. Indeed, given the reference to 'responsibility', and despite his argument to the contrary, Morgan is perhaps more interested in answering the question: 'What is medical law *for*?'[5] (Morgan 2001, 6; emphasis added). And the interdisciplinary approach to the subject he sketches out is meant to suggest that the issues in this area cannot be contained within a prescriptive set of legal categories. Indeed, to characterize those issues as solely 'legal' ones misses, amongst other things, their 'important philosophical, ethical, sociological and political dimensions' (Morgan 2001, 5).

Morgan's reason for asking the question: 'What is medical law?', and the answers he offers to this, can be thought to concern the question of jurisdiction, but in a paradoxical sense. On the one hand, his characterization of medical law is designed to guard against any sense of clearly defined boundaries in this field. Thus, when discussing what he calls 'the context of medical law', he comments that: 'The *context* is illustrated by the failure of the traditional approach [to legal scholarship] to recognise either the scope or the terrain of medical law or its intellectual parameters' (Morgan 2001, 4; emphasis in original). Medical law is not simply about law; rather, the questions and issues with which it is concerned have 'philosophical, ethical, sociological and political dimensions' too. For Morgan, to ask what medical law is, is not primarily a question of the need to delineate boundaries – indeed quite the opposite. It points to the need to acknowledge that medical law transcends the traditional legal requirement for a clear and settled framework. If medical law has a definable feature at all, it might be thought to reside in the nature of the problems it seeks to address (problems arising from developments in medicine and biomedical science that engage questions of human values), rather than in the construction of clearly delineated legal boundaries.

On the other hand, Morgan's defence of medical law as a subject that undercuts the traditional need for legal boundaries can still usefully be understood in jurisdictional terms. This is because there is a need – indeed, 'an intellectual responsibility' –

---

5   Morgan argues that the question he is concerned with: 'What is medical law?' is very different to the question: 'What is medical law for?' But it would seem that the argument in Part One of his book – where he stresses the *purpose* of medical law and that the subject ought to contribute to the 'central task [of] biomedical diplomacy' – is directed towards answering this latter question. Medical law, he argues, is where we say 'who we are and who we want to become' and it has, in part, a responsibility in determining the values that we cannot give up in the age of rapid developments in biomedical science.

within the legal academy for the existence of a subject that, in order to devote itself to the study of those problems, does not, and cannot, conform to the idea of the law subject as based on traditional legal categories because it transcends such an idea and, indeed, the discipline of law itself. In other words, it is the multi-faceted and pressing nature of those problems (that, in Morgan's view, deny the possibility of clear boundaries) that creates the very need to carve out an identifiable space within the legal academy where they can be discussed and analysed by academics and researchers. This is necessary as it facilitates the construction of a sphere of competence or domain of expertise that allows those agents to claim to speak with some authority about those problems. If you like, the inquiry into the nature of medical law is, at least partially, an exercise in legitimation.[6]

Montgomery's and Morgan's reflections on the nature of their subjects can therefore usefully be understood in jurisdictional terms. But can this 'jurisdictional' characterization of academic medical law be applied more generally to the work in this field? In claiming that it can, we will now focus on two further aspects of Morgan's idea of medical law – a general concern for the individual and his or her rights[7] and the role of law in setting ethical standards in this area – that pervade most other reflections on the nature and objectives of the subject.[8] It will be argued that those aspects have played an integral role in defining much of the academic subject known as medical law. Specifically, they have been central in grounding the academic's claim that law should develop jurisdiction in this area. They have been deployed, at least partly, with the intention of creating and sustaining a foothold for law in the many problems and controversial issues emanating from medical practice and developments in biomedical science. In order to demonstrate this, the following section focuses upon some of the work of one academic – Ian Kennedy – who has promoted the idea of medical law as bound up with the rights of individuals and ethics.[9] Thereafter, the impact of these aspects of Kennedy's work on some other academic writing in this field will be discussed.

---

6   The following analysis of the relationship between legitimacy and the 'What is law?' type question might be thought to be relevant in the current context: 'There is not automatic legitimation of an institution by calling it or what it produces "law", but the label is a move, the staking out of a position in the complex social game of legitimation. The jurisprudential inquiry into the question "what is law" is an engagement, at one remove in the struggle over what is legitimate' (Cover 1985, 181; reference omitted).

7   It should be noted that Morgan's emphasis upon rights discourse here is concerned with what he calls 'negative rights'. Thus, he comments: '[M]edical law as a species of human rights law is valuable and significant if seen as and limited to a protection against harm (howsoever defined) and abuse, but limited in use and scope if seen in the form of a claim right' (Morgan 2001, 22). Negative rights, he argues, can be equated with rights to 'treat me gentle'. For present purposes, however, the important point to note here is that Morgan's understanding of the conceptual structure of medical law is, at least partly, defined by the language of rights.

8   It should be stressed that not all approaches to medical law in the literature are grounded in those two aspects. Notable exceptions are Jacob 1999 and Harrington 2002.

9   This idea of medical law can also be seen in the work of Sheila McLean. See, for example, McLean 1999.

Rights, Ethics and the Jurisdiction of Medical Law

Kennedy's thesis

The starting point for this inquiry must be Kennedy's essay 'What is a medical decision?', originally a paper delivered at the Middlesex Hospital Medical School in 1979 (Kennedy 1988b). As an aside, Kennedy prefaces his talk with the usual jousting between the medical and legal professions by pointing out that he is a lawyer, not a medic, and that some members of the audience may therefore disagree with what he has to say. Nonetheless, he says that he hopes that his approach will engender an ethos of 'mutual enquiry' between the two professions. Little did those medics in the audience know that Kennedy was about to challenge their exclusive jurisdiction over the making of the types of decisions that have become fundamental to defining the work they do.

Kennedy begins by saying that doctors make decisions about health and ill health. But what are these, exactly? At its most basic level, ill health, for example, may depend solely on an individual's physical condition; that is, if he or she deviates from the 'healthy' norm (also defined by members of the medical profession), this will warrant a designation of ill health. The notions of health and ill health may, however, be expanded to include individuals' mental conditions and their social well-being generally. This broad definition of health is, in fact, the one adopted by the World Health Organization in the Preamble to its founding Constitution: 'Health is a state of complete physical, mental and social well-being and not merely the absence of disease or infirmity' (World Health Organization 1948). Thus, if doctors have the 'unique competence' to make decisions about what constitutes health and ill health, that sphere of competence can, potentially, incorporate not only physical conditions but 'the management of our comfort and happiness, our social well-being' (Kennedy 1988b, 21).

At root, Kennedy's objection to this 'unique competence' is based on what he understands by the adjective 'medical'. In his view, this ought to be interpreted narrowly to include such technical matters as diagnosis, prognosis and the determination of the various treatment options available for a particular illness. However, as there are many non-technical aspects to the decisions that medical professionals make, these decisions cannot properly be described as 'medical'. Consequently, those non-technical aspects – which Kennedy says may include 'questions of morality or philosophy or economics or politics' (Kennedy 1988b, 24) – fall outside of 'the unique or special competence of a doctor' (Kennedy 1988b, 20). So, to take morality as an example, Kennedy argues that decisions about the quality of life of patients are moral decisions and, as such, engage moral principles that ought not to be determined exclusively by members of the medical profession. Rather, they are principles that emanate from moral debate within the wider world. Should this point remain unacknowledged, it would mean that the moral value systems of doctors, and not those of the wider world, would dictate which moral principles ought to apply in any given circumstance. To put it briefly, Kennedy argues that, given the multi-faceted nature of the decisions medical professionals are required to make, those decisions should not remain the preserve of doctors. The last paragraph of his essay outlines the direction in which he believes we ought to be moving:

> The other direction of the debate I am asking for calls for doctors to involve others in the dilemmas they face, to give up their closely guarded professional secrecy, and hence some of their *power*, and to indicate just what it is that they do and have to decide, so that we may all discuss it, and assist in deciding what is right. (Kennedy 1988b, 31; emphasis added; reference omitted)

How does Kennedy confront this issue of medical power, including what he argues is the medical profession's monopoly over the determination of which moral principles ought to apply to particular issues arising in medical practice? He does so by claiming that law should develop jurisdiction in this area: 'The ground rules must be set by society and must take the form of law. Law is the appropriate mechanism, both so as to convey the importance of the issue and also to indicate that no social mechanism other than law is adequate to the task' (Kennedy 1988a, 409). It would, however, be naïve to assume that this call for the development of legal jurisdiction merely involves the promotion of a more proactive role for the courts and the legislature.[10] Implicitly, it also amounts to an assertion that, within the legal academy, there ought to exist a subject, the teachers and researchers of which can lay claim to possess expertise in developing moral principles and standards that will assist in keeping a check on medical power, and, thus, to play a part 'in deciding what is right'. Moreover, and as Hope has noted, this vigilant function has been extended in Kennedy's work to incorporate critical reflection on the extent to which the judiciary is succeeding in questioning the purported moral expertise of doctors[11] (Hope 1991). Once more, presumably the medical law academic's assessment here will be based on moral principles and standards over which he or she professes to have some expertise. Thus, by arguing that law has a proper role to play, Kennedy not only stresses the need for practical involvement by members of the judiciary and legislature; he is also intent on carving out a field of academic work for himself and others (which will provide both a vehicle for the development of his and their views as to what is right, morally speaking, and a base from which to claim to exercise authoritative critical scrutiny of the law's performance in this field).

If Kennedy's call for the development of legal jurisdiction in this field is clear, what means does he deploy to justify his argument? To put it differently, what is it

---

10 It should be acknowledged, however, that this is an integral aspect of such exhortations. As Mason and Laurie note, the argument that law should assume responsibility for the resolution of issues in this area can be detected in much of the academic literature: 'Medical lawyers spend much of their time calling for the courts to take responsibility away from the medical profession and to assume it themselves' (Mason and Laurie 2006, 46).

11 This aspect of Kennedy's approach can be found in the writing of others in this field. For instance, in the course of arguing that the most suitable mechanism for curbing the excessive power of the medical profession is the law, McLean comments that the problem to date has been the latter's deference to the former: '[The law] has proved unwilling, unable or inefficient when asked to adjudicate on or control issues which are at best tangentially medical' (McLean 1999, 2).

about law that Kennedy believes makes it a particularly useful mechanism for curbing medical power and delineating the moral principles and standards that society ought to impose on the practice of medicine? The answer is its traditional association with rights – specifically, human rights. Designating medical law as a subset of human rights law allows Kennedy to make several significant claims, which, cumulatively, it is suggested, are designed to contribute to the entrenchment of legal jurisdiction in this area.[12] Firstly, one of the ways in which Kennedy proposes curbing what he sees as the excess of medical power is by emphasizing the importance of the position of the patient in the doctor-patient relationship. Owing to its language of rights, he suggests that the intervention of law would be particularly useful in helping to redress this pressing imbalance of power:

> [R]esort to the language of rights assists in the attempt to develop law which redresses the disequilibrium of power between doctor and patient. To argue that patients have rights ensures that they will be taken seriously as partners in the enterprise of health. (Kennedy 1988a, vii)

Secondly, the focus on human rights allows Kennedy to claim for law that location external to medicine where 'society's' moral standards and principles can legitimately be delineated and applied to specific problems in this area. This is because human rights for Kennedy do not merely connote individual 'claim' rights, or, indeed, legal rights; rather they also refer to:

> certain broad over-arching legal *as well as* ethical principles against which any proposed legal measure must be tested and approved. And, when I talk of human rights here, I would make it clear that I refer not only to those rights declared in international Conventions or set down in the Constitutions or Charters of particular nations, but also those inchoate rights which are the product of reasoned moral analysis. (Kennedy 1988a, 385–6; emphasis in original)

In other words, Kennedy's idea of human rights stresses not only their legal basis in various documents but also that they are broad *moral* or *ethical* principles that emanate from 'reasoned moral analysis'. Consequently, by characterizing medical law as a subset of human rights law, he advocates for law a role that will include ascertaining the nature of those ethical principles and inchoate rights by which medical practice ought to be judged.

Finally, the subsumption of medical law under human rights law allows Kennedy to argue that medical law is a legitimate subject in its own right as, in contrast to much of English law generally, it benefits from a sound conceptual framework (human rights). As he puts it:

> I have for some time been urging that if medical law is to find its identity (or justify its existence) it needs to break out of the traditional English approach to legal categories.

---

12 Kennedy is not alone in characterizing medical law as a part of human rights law. See, for example, McLean 1999. Brazier and Glover have also used the discourse of human rights to define the essence of medical law: 'Fundamental issues of the boundaries of human rights are the central concern of what we will style medical law' (Brazier and Glover 2000, 371).

These are almost universally fact-based or contextual. Fact situations are shovelled under the heading of, for example, tort, or contract, or property almost as if by accident ... The search for an underlying conceptual framework is ignored as an empty exercise, something for idle hands ... In my view this general challenge to English law can be met as regards medical law by stating that medical law is a part or sub-set of human rights law. It is the contextual application of the over-arching framework of human rights. Obviously, there is a lot more work to be done.[13] (Kennedy 1988a, vii)

Thus, not only is the equation of medical law with human rights law meant to point to the specific roles that law in this area ought to perform (the empowerment of patients, for example); its deeper purpose is, as Kennedy says, to justify the very existence of the subject. The discourse of human rights lends conceptual rigour to medical law and, thereby, facilitates the claim to its distinctive, and deserved, identity.

Kennedy's thesis and the claim to jurisdiction

Kennedy's thesis is directed towards redressing the imbalance of power he believes exists between medical professionals and their patients, and ensuring that the moral standards and principles by which medicine is practised are determined externally to it. But, as noted, his suggestion as to the manner in which this ought to be carried out – through the medium of law – can be thought to be an instance of claiming jurisdiction for the legal academic, the judge and the legislator alike. Moreover, while his use of rights and human rights discourse to characterize medical law is the mechanism through which he seeks to empower patients and have standards set externally, this discourse also acts as the means by which medical law is to be justified as a sub-discipline of law and its claim to authority progressively realized. Thus, the promotion of patients' rights may be viewed not simply as an attempt to improve their lot; equally, the existence, and awareness, of such a discourse ensures that the disgruntled among them will seek redress through the law, thereby entrenching its role and claim to authority. Similarly, the declared need to have the moral principles and standards against which the practice of medical professionals is to be judged determined externally, does not lead Kennedy to consider the various possible ways in which this might be accomplished. Rather, through the deployment of human rights discourse, the argument is advanced that only the law can be entrusted with such a significant task. Again, what matters here is not only, or even primarily, the nature of the specific reform that Kennedy advocates (standards must be set externally to medicine); rather, it is also the need to ensure that law, and law alone, will perform this function.

Thus, from one angle, it might be thought that, rather than Kennedy purely being interested in empowering patients and guaranteeing that moral principles emanate from outside the medical profession, those very points of focus – together with his

---

13 This reliance on human rights to provide the conceptual basis of medical law is also evident in the following statement in Andrew Grubb's *Medical Law* (of which Kennedy was co-author for the first two editions): '[W]e see medical law as having some conceptual unity. The unifying legal theme is, to us, human rights. In our view, therefore, medical law is a subset of human rights law. That is what provides its intellectual coherence' (Grubb 2001, 3).

desire to ensure that medical law has a sound conceptual framework – are also the products of his objective of claiming jurisdiction for law in this area. Moreover, the rhetoric of medical law as human rights law sounds important and ominous enough to ground the academic's claim to a legitimate stake in an increasingly popular game – debating and 'resolving' the ethical issues and problems arising not only from the practice of medicine, but from developments in biomedical science too.

If this reflects the specific manner in which Kennedy seeks to develop legal jurisdiction over matters arising in the medical sphere, how might we characterize this jurisdictional claim more generally? What, in other words, can be thought to constitute its central components? In the course of the foregoing discussion, the claim to jurisdiction has been characterized as having both a professional aspect (in so far as Kennedy seeks to carve out roles for the academic, the judge and the legislator) and a close relationship with the specific issues and problems that arise in the course of medical practice.[14] In the remainder of this section, those two features shall be discussed briefly by drawing on work from other disciplines.

In 1979 Philip Strong wrote an article in which he critically analysed the thesis of medical imperialism advanced by some medical sociologists (Strong 1979). Like Kennedy, those sociologists were concerned with what they identified as the medicalization of social problems and the social world generally. Medicine's net had been cast particularly wide and this was becoming a cause of some concern. What is interesting about Strong's analysis of the sociological critique of medical imperialism is its reflexive character. Rather than viewing this critique as an objective and disinterested account of the colonizing tendencies of the medical profession, Strong argues that, to some degree at least, it in fact serves to further such sociologists' own professional ambitions and desires (here, in the form of instituting a social, as opposed to a medical, model of health). Indeed, he observes that the imperialistic trait criticized by those medical sociologists is characteristic of professions generally:

> [T]he aspect of life which professions seek to control is not restricted to their original remit; rather, it is in the nature of professions to seek to expand their empire, to redefine others' problems in their own terms and to discover wholly new ones for which they alone can provide solutions. (Strong 1979, 199)

This analysis is useful in explaining a significant underlying cause driving Kennedy's thesis.[15] The claims he makes regarding the need for legal jurisdiction find their common root in the inbuilt tendency of professions to expand their territories and attempt to colonize hitherto 'foreign' sites. Moreover, this propensity to jurisdictional creep works not only to further Kennedy's declared objectives (such as the empowerment of the patient), but also to satisfy the sorts of professional

---

14 It should be noted that the terms 'profession' and 'professional' are employed loosely here, rather than in any technical, sociological way. Consequently, the question of whether legal academics form part of the legal profession is not discussed. The equation of academics with a 'profession' is simply meant to denote a field over which they claim some expertise.

15 Indeed, in 1984 Strong described Kennedy's work in the following terms: 'Kennedy's much acclaimed Reith lectures were little more than legal imperialism in populist clothing' (Strong 1984, 354). Kennedy's Reith lectures were published in Kennedy 1981.

needs and ambitions outlined earlier – such as the desire to develop a sphere of academic research the practitioners of which can lay claim to expertise in respect of the controversial issues, problems and dilemmas arising from contemporary medical practice. As Hope, in the course of discussing Kennedy's book of essays on medical law, *Treat Me Right*, perceptively observed: '[Lawyers have] a vested professional interest in exerting control over medicine' (Hope 1991, 250).

If we are to understand the claim to legal jurisdiction in this area fully, though, we must also take seriously Strong's identification of the close relationship between the imperialistic nature of professions and what he calls 'problems'. This point is usefully drawn out in the context of health care law and ethics in an article by Loes Kater et al., and it is to a brief discussion of this that we now turn (Kater et al. 2003).

Kater et al. use the idea of jurisdiction as a method of gaining some purchase on why the Dutch definition of euthanasia has taken its current form. They begin with the observation that the concept of medical ethics is no longer a simple set of standards that exists within medicine for the purpose of assisting medical professionals to perform their jobs. Instead, the authors define medical ethics as 'an arena of moral issues in medicine, rather than a specific discipline' (Kater et al. 2003, 669). This change in the nature of medical ethics has opened up that arena to the interest of other disciplines, including what they call health care ethics and health law.[16] It is by tracing the influence and interaction of those two disciplines in the arena of medical ethics that Kater et al. argue it is possible to understand how the Dutch definition of euthanasia has come to exist. Fundamentally, they suggest that this is the result of a 'complex jurisdictional process'.

It is the theoretical bases upon which Kater et al.'s inquiry rests that are of interest here. These are drawn from the work of two authors – Andrew Abbott and Joseph Gusfield. Abbott developed his notion of jurisdiction in the context of a history of the relations between professions and argued that this history could be thought of as 'a history of jurisdictional disputes'. According to Kater et al.:

> [Abbott argued that] [p]rofessions grow when there are *niches* for them to grow into; they change when other professions threaten their control of particular kinds of work. Technology, for example, can reshape professional work. New technologies create opportunities for jurisdiction. Professions establish, defend and exercise claims of jurisdiction. (Kater et al. 2003, 671)

While it is obvious that academic medical lawyers are not threatening to compete with medical professionals in the sense of carrying out operations and the like, Abbott's argument still retains some relevance to the development of legal jurisdiction over issues arising in medicine. As Kater et al. explain, it is generally acknowledged that one of the main driving forces behind the emergence of disputed ethical issues and problems in medicine has been developments in medical technology. The controversial nature of these issues clearly creates a 'niche' into which existing and

---

16 Kater et al. use 'bioethics' as an umbrella term to describe that field – and its various professions – that has emerged within which debate about ethical issues in medicine takes place. In their reading, health care ethics and health law form part of bioethics.

new professions can grow, and the academic lawyer is merely one of many who has seized this new and exciting opportunity. Indeed, one need look no further than Kennedy's *Treat Me Right* for evidence of this move to claim legal jurisdiction over such issues and problems. Like most medical law textbooks, Kennedy's volume is littered with discussions, and proposed resolutions of, a host of ethically sensitive issues, including sterilization, whether disabled babies should be kept alive, and the medical treatment of children. This focus on issues or problems is further developed in Gusfield's work.

Whereas Abbott suggests that analyses of jurisdictional disputes ought to begin from a focus on the particular professions involved, Gusfield's starting point is the specific problem over which jurisdiction is being claimed (Gusfield 1981). His book concerns how certain issues – in his case, drink-driving – become public problems. One aspect of this is what he calls 'the ownership of public problems':

> [I]n the arenas of public opinion and debate all groups do not have equal power, influence, and authority to define the reality of the problem. The ability to create and influence the public definition of a problem is what I refer to as 'ownership.' The metaphor of property ownership is chosen to emphasize the attributes of control, exclusiveness, transferability, and potential loss also found in the ownership of property ... Owners can make claims and assertions. They are looked at and reported to by others anxious for definitions and solutions to the problem. They possess authority in the field. Even if opposed by other groups, they are among those who can gain the public ear. (Gusfield 1981, 10)

Kennedy's work might be thought to display elements of Gusfield's description. Thus, Kennedy himself has been in positions that have allowed him to 'gain the public ear' – first, as a professor of medical law (through, for example, presenting the prestigious Reith lectures); and, secondly, and very prominently, in his capacity as Chairman of the Bristol Royal Infirmary Inquiry (Kennedy 2001).[17] And, to a large extent, he has used both roles not simply to influence the manner in which specific, 'medical' problems should be defined or redefined (using mainly the discourse of rights and human rights), but to publicly identify and define the nature of what he believes to be a much more profound problem – that is, the problem of the culture of professional medical practice *per se* – including its perceived aloofness and its unwillingness to share power.[18] In doing so, Kennedy does not, of course, 'own' the problem of the culture of medical practice in Gusfield's sense, since he has not single-handedly created the public definition of that problem. Nonetheless, he clearly makes claims and assertions in respect of this problem and is 'looked at and reported

---

17 It would be a mistake to think that Kennedy is the only academic medical lawyer to have been in a position in which to influence both the definition of specific issues in this area and possible future policies in relation thereto. Others include Sheila McLean (see McLean 1997) and Margaret Brazier (see Brazier 1998).

18 Dingwall and Hobson-West note Kennedy's overarching criticism of medicine in his Bristol Inquiry Report: '[T]he final report repeats his earlier criticisms of medicine for persistent paternalism, hierarchy, excessive clinical freedom, undermanagement and lack of accountability, and urges that it should become more open, accountable, quality-oriented and patient-centred, using National Health Service employment discipline to achieve these goals' (Dingwall and Hobson-West 2006, 40).

to by others anxious for definitions and solutions to the problem'. Moreover, his is an authoritative voice, and his definition of the precise problem (that of the culture of professional medical practice *per se*) contributes to, and helps sustain, the public definition of a still wider problem, which is the perceived untrustworthiness of professionals and experts generally in contemporary society. By so doing, Kennedy ensures that his long-held views about how to address this problem in the context of medicine are taken seriously, and, indeed, lead to the reform of aspects of medical practice.

Summary

The need to curb medical power and to stress that decisions made by members of the medical profession involve aspects that do not fall within doctors' unique competence, leads Kennedy to argue that the various ethical issues and problems that arise in the course of medical practice ought to be defined in terms of human rights. By doing so, he facilitates three possibilities, all of which are directed towards establishing legal jurisdiction in this area: first, that patients should have rights; secondly, that moral standards and principles ought to be set beyond the boundaries of the medical profession; and, finally, that law ought to be integral to the realization of the first two possibilities.

It has been suggested, however, that it should not be thought that this claim to legal jurisdiction only affects the courts and the legislature. Rather, Kennedy's thesis might also be theorized as an attempt to establish a new subject – medical law – within the legal academy. This is because his claim that the issues and problems arising from medical practice ought to be defined in terms of human rights has sought to present medical law as a distinctive and legitimate subject within the law school, having a firm conceptual basis and, thus, a degree of order. Indeed, it could be said that this concern with establishing academic jurisdiction in this area exists in a symbiotic relationship with the desire to advance the cause of the patient and to ensure that standards are set externally to medicine. For, by promoting those latter two aspects, Kennedy simultaneously facilitates the advancement of his vision of a new subject, the guardians of which can legitimately lay claim to possess the expertise and authority to pronounce upon various issues. The suggestion that a concern for patients and the ethical issues arising from medicine ought properly to be matters of legal interest promotes Kennedy's interest in establishing an academic subject that claims jurisdiction over a variety of matters arising in the course of medical practice.

The Effect of Kennedy's Jurisdictional Claims

Kennedy's thesis and, especially, his identification of rights and ethics as the guiding features of medical law, have had an impact on this field of academic research. One of the purposes of this section is to offer two examples which illustrate this. The first endorses Kennedy's outlook; the second replicates his emphasis on the need for law in this area to be based on ethical principles. At the end of the section, the focus will turn to a recent article by Jonathan Montgomery, in which he presents a compelling, if ultimately traditional, response to the type of approach to medical law advanced by Kennedy and others in the field.

Michael Davies' Textbook on Medical Law

Michael Davies' *Textbook on Medical Law* is a fine example of the influence that Kennedy's thesis has had on shaping academic reflection on the nature of medical law. This is illustrated in Chapter 1 of Davies' book – entitled 'The Nature of Medical Law' – where he sets out his idea of medical law:

> Medical law is concerned with the responsibility of members of the medical profession for their actions. It is also about human rights, moral viewpoints, ethical concepts, economic demands on society and duties owed ... Medical law, which leads from medical ethics, is the mechanism for 'doing the right thing' in a vast array of medical circumstances. A good medical law is an ethical law. This book, as well as being a description of medical law, is an analysis of whether the various laws are 'good' ones. One must decide what it means to be ethical. (Davies 1998, 1–2)

For Davies, then, medical law incorporates a variety of aspects, including ethics, rights and economics. His wide description of the subject is in keeping with his argument that attempting to provide a definition of medical law is a relatively fruitless endeavour given that it always results in the over- or under-inclusion of different topics. Nonetheless, he goes on to say: 'The link between medical ethics and its practical expression in law *is the essence of defining* medical law' (Davies 1998, 3; emphasis added). Like Kennedy, then, ethics, specifically medical ethics, is central to Davies' idea of medical law. And, again like Kennedy, this question of ethics is one that properly falls within the lawyer's sphere of competence. As he (Davies) comments: '[T]he first question for the medical lawyer [is]: What ought to be done?' (Davies 1998, 5). The subject, then, is about finding answers – ethically tight resolutions to often controversial dilemmas. The apogee of achievement in this area would be to have laws that are good, ethically speaking. And it is the prospect of such an achievement that ought to drive the work of the medical lawyer.[19]

How, according to Davies, is one to judge what amounts to a 'good' law – that is, a law that 'does the right thing'? To begin with, one must decide what the moral course of action ought to be. Where the practice of medicine is concerned, he asserts that this depends on whether one chooses utilitarianism or deontology as one's starting point – a choice, he says, that will be 'dependent on the myriad personal influences on one's life' (Davies 1998, 5). Say, then, we choose utility and we discover that a proposed action is morally wrong; what should the law's response be? Davies argues that this depends on the extent to which a law prohibiting the act would limit personal liberty – again, a judgment that presumably depends on one's moral deliberations. This, then, is Davies' idea of medical law – ultimately, particular laws are to be analysed for their moral rightness and wrongness on the basis of our

---

19 This idea of medical law as 'good ethics' is shared by other academics in this field. See, for example, Mason and Laurie 2006, Chapter 1.

personal convictions and the extent to which a law would infringe personal liberty. It is against this background that he asserts 'that a fundamental aspect of doing the right thing is to respect the individual' (Davies 1998, 13). Specifically, there are certain human rights against which medical law can be measured for the purpose of ascertaining whether particular laws are 'good' ones.

There is little doubt that Davies places rights at the heart of what he thinks medical law should aspire to. The pervasiveness of human rights and rights discourse, he argues, is not to be found in medical law, but it ought to be. What is interesting, though, about his emphasis on rights is how they are deployed in the performance of the same two separate functions that Kennedy envisaged for them. Thus, in one sense, rights come to operate in what might be described as a quantitative manner. Here, they fall within a number of classical dichotomies – such as doctor–patient; paternalism–autonomy; duties–rights. In this formulation, rights seem to mean that more patients' rights are needed to counter what Davies sees as the law's excessive emphasis on the position of the doctor, paternalism and duties. Patients need to be thought of as individual rights-holders who are powerful enough to counter the traditional paternalistic approach associated with medical practice.

The second function of Davies' reliance on rights is to be found in his use of the term 'human rights'. Here, rights are intended to function as specific ethical markers against which the content of medical law ought to be judged. And while it is often difficult to distinguish clearly between human rights and rights in the first sense – for the former are often couched in claim terms too – Davies seems to be going beyond this here by arguing that human rights are ethical standards that can be used to measure the 'goodness' of medical law(s). Again, this idea of medical law as deeply associated with a human rights discourse that advances a set of ethical principles which law ought to uphold perfectly replicates Kennedy's description, and suggested function, of human rights.

Sheldon and Thomson's Feminist Perspectives on Health Care Law

In Chapter 1 of their edited collection – *Feminist Perspectives on Health Care Law* – Sheldon and Thomson set out the components of their feminist approach to health care law (Sheldon and Thomson 1998b). Starting from the claim that health care law must be viewed as a discrete discipline within the legal academy, it is clear that while their vision of the subject does not replicate Kennedy's thesis of medical law exactly, it nonetheless relies heavily upon two aspects of this. Firstly, like Kennedy, Sheldon and Thomson identify the law's deference to the expert opinions of members of the medical profession as a 'unifying feature' of their idea of health care law. Discovering ways in which to address and reform this 'medicalisation of law' – as Sheldon has called it (Sheldon 1997) – is, as in Kennedy's thesis, a definitive aspect of their approach to health care law.

Secondly, and as a means of distinguishing this new subject, Sheldon and Thomson stress the need for health care law to possess some underlying coherence. Though not deploying the discourse of human rights, they follow Kennedy by using the language of ethics – in their case, 'ethical precepts' – to provide the foundation for their feminist approach to health care law: 'One common concern [of the essays in this volume] is with the (lack of) realisation of the ethical principles which according to the above citation from Kennedy, are supposedly at the core of health care ethics and law: justice, dignity and, most importantly, autonomy' (Sheldon and Thomson 1998b, 9). Thus, while in some important respects the analyses of particular ethical principles to be found in the essays in Sheldon and Thomson's collection – and feminist approaches to medical law and health care law generally – differ from those in more traditional works such as Kennedy's,[20] the underlying structure upon which the feminist approach to the subject is built (ethical principles or precepts), and, significantly, by which it defines its specific sphere of competence, is identical to that found in more orthodox treatises.

Jonathan Montgomery's response to the Kennedy-type approach

In a recent article, Jonathan Montgomery argues that the rise in use of market concepts (including choice and consumerism) in health care law threatens what he calls 'the moral basis of medical practice' (Montgomery 2006). In his view, the prevalence of such concepts may result in 'the demoralisation of medicine' – that is, their presence could force moral debate outside of the boundaries of medicine, thereby weakening the moral values that underpin sound health care practice.[21] In order to combat this worrying trend, Montgomery calls for health care lawyers to defend a robust idea of 'a common moral community'. This would seem to equate to what he calls 'a system of values within healthcare' and points to the need to establish an integrated model of the health care professional – that is, one in which technical skill and moral reasoning are indivisible. By establishing 'a legal context in which professional morality could flourish', health care law and lawyers could promote this model, and, thereby, contribute to the broader objective of recovering some of the trust in the health care professions that has ebbed away in recent years.

As well as trying to restore trust in the health care professions, Montgomery's argument can be read as a critique of, and response to, the approach advocated by Kennedy and others, including Davies. He refers to this approach as 'the dominant view':

> Traditionally, legal scholars have attacked the reluctance of legislators and the judiciary to wrestle from the grip of doctors the authority to determine ethical issues. The dominant view has been that this was a failure to recognise the fact that society has a stake in these matters and that legal non-intervention was an abdication of responsibility that undermines

---

20 One example would be the relational idea of autonomy advanced in the feminist literature. In contrast to the atomistic conception of the self upon which much orthodox reflection within the medical law field (and, indeed, within legal and political theory more generally) is founded, the 'relational' approach stresses the socially embedded nature of human beings. Examples of the relational approach to autonomy within the medical law and health care law fields include: Stychin 1998 and Jackson 2001 (Chapter 1). For discussions of this within feminist legal scholarship generally, see Nedelsky 1989 and Lacey 1998 (Chapter 4).

21 As well as the uncoupling of medicine and morals, Montgomery's idea of 'the demoralisation of medicine' also encompasses the effect of this uncoupling on those working in the health care professions.

the rule of law. However, the integration of medical and moral decision making into a collaborative enterprise can also be seen as a more effective defence against the forces of demoralisation than the separation that the orthodox approach implies. (Montgomery 2006, 185)

In other words, one of the ways in which the demoralization of medicine might occur is by arguing that ethical issues be removed from the province of the doctor, who, in the dominant view, is seen simply as a technician. Another is through the emphasis that the orthodox approach places on the rights and choices of patients as a way of ensuring that the powers of health care professionals are confined to their technical competences. To put it briefly, by advocating an interventionist role for law that seeks to place patients' rights and the legal determination of ethical issues at its core, some medical lawyers (both academics and those in practice) are in danger of contributing to the demoralization of medicine.

Montgomery does not suggest that a system of values for health care cannot be advocated by law. Rather, it is in his characterization of the function of law in this area that the crucial difference between his own view and that of the dominant thesis lies. In his opinion, law should be facilitative (stressing the importance of the ethics and values of the health care professions) rather than proactive (taking over the determination of ethical issues and promoting patients' rights), and it is through the former approach that morality can usefully be re-established in health care law.

Montgomery's argument might be thought properly to fit the jurisdictional theme advanced here. This is because, like the other authors discussed in this chapter (including Kennedy), his inquiry can be viewed as an attempt to map out the proper function of health care law (in both its academic and practical forms). Thus, he reflects on questions such as: What role should the legal academic play in this field?; If the judiciary has the power to hear, and adjudicate on, controversial ethical issues and problems, how should it organize this power? Should it seize the initiative to determine those issues and problems, developing its own toolbox of ethical principles, or should it defer to the ethical standards and resolutions of those working in the health care professions? So, while his answers to these questions differ from Kennedy's entirely, the nature of Montgomery's underlying inquiries is, to a large degree, indistinguishable from that conducted by advocates of 'the dominant view'.[22] Moral values; the issue of professional authority and which of two professions – the legal or the health care – should have the power to determine the various ethical issues and controversies arising from medical practice; the objective of legal academic work in this field – all are intimately connected to determining the nature of health care law and how legal jurisdiction in this area should be exercised.

---

22 Montgomery's own vision of health care law might be described as 'the pre-dominant dominant view' – that is, the legal (judicial) view of medical practice to be found in many of the early medical negligence cases, such as *Bolam v. Friern Hospital Management Committee* (1957). As Montgomery notes, his approach to the subject is very similar to that of Jacob (see Jacob 1999) – someone who places great emphasis on the 'classical', or 'Hippocratic', model of medicine.

Despite those similarities with the dominant view, Montgomery's article also points in a different direction, an appreciation of which is crucial if we are to acquire a fuller understanding of medical law and, specifically in the current context, the nature of the courts' involvement in this area. This direction demands a shift in the nature of our inquiry. Thus, rather than simply inquiring as to the '*ought*' of power (for example, which profession – the legal or the health care – ought to determine controversial ethical issues), Montgomery hints that it is also necessary to address the '*how*' of power.[23] In other words, some of his arguments point to the need to analyse the actual workings or practices of the common law in this area. In the language of this book, this might translate into an inquiry into the nature of the common law's jurisdiction over contested ethical issues and problems arising from the practice of medicine and developments in biomedical science. This would involve questions such as the following: How does the judiciary assert this jurisdiction? How does it exercise and organize its power? How do judges manage the ethical principles that some legal academics suggest ought to guide it when making decisions in this area? How do they deploy legal reasoning in this field, and what are some of the consequences of the manner in which they do so? Whilst Montgomery does not pursue this focus upon the practices of the common law in any great depth, he does raise the possibility of such a line of inquiry. As this aspect of his article will be discussed more fully later in the book (especially in Chapter 6), at this stage only a brief indication of how he points in this direction need be given.

Firstly, referring to Kennedy's summary of the ethical principles (such as autonomy, consent and truth-telling) that he argues lend medical law its coherence, Montgomery comments: 'I have long been critical of this approach for its failure to explain how medical law has really worked' (Montgomery 2006, 207). He goes on to explain that what he means by this is that, rather than the development of medical law having taken place through the explicit recognition of such principles, it has traditionally functioned on the understanding that an acknowledgement that medicine is a moral practice would allow those principles to flourish. Whether or not one agrees with this assessment, the important point is that Montgomery stresses the need to focus on the manner in which the common law actually works in this field.

Secondly, addressing the claim made by some legal academics that, by becoming actively involved in resolving ethically contentious disputes, the courts can reflect deeply embedded societal values, Montgomery identifies a potential difficulty with this: '[A] new type of case is emerging that actually *obscures such value conflicts* and in which the translation of conflict into the discourse of law *excludes moral debate rather than enables it to be addressed*. If this type is to become the norm, then, once again, more law turns out to mean less morality' (Montgomery 2006, 190; emphasis added). One of the reasons for this, he says, is the tendency by members of the judiciary to focus on issues of legal technicality – such as questions of statutory interpretation and legal precedent – to the exclusion of the substantive

---

23 This chapter has, of course, addressed a central feature of the 'how' of power – that is, how legal academics in this field have gone about establishing and defending a role for law in regulating medical practice. In other words, it has looked at how they have sought to create medical law (as both an academic subject and a discrete sub-discipline of legal practice).

ethical arguments. Whether or not one agrees that this emerging judicial trend is favourable is, at the moment, irrelevant. What it is important to stress, though, is that, in a field largely obsessed with sound ethical principles, tight ethical arguments and justifiable resolutions to controversial ethical dilemmas, this crucial observation has been consistently overlooked. The aspirational character of much of the legal academic commentary in this field – together with the need to stress the significance of ethical principles as a means by which to distinguish medical law as a subject in its own right – has meant that the more mundane, but nevertheless fundamental, business of inquiring into the actual working practices of the common law, and the consequences of the manner in which these operate, has remained unfulfilled.

To summarize, then, both Davies, and Sheldon and Thomson, can be thought to be taking up the challenge of Kennedy's thesis – the former by endorsing it completely; the latter by accepting Kennedy's assertion that certain fundamental ethical principles provide the structure upon which the subject is both based and distinguished from other legal sub-disciplines. To this extent, and like Kennedy, those academics can be thought to be engaged in issues involving the question of jurisdiction. There is an attempt to constitute new subjects – whether medical law or health care law – and justify their existence by differentiating them from other fields of law. And, although Montgomery's recent reflections contain elements that coincide with the themes addressed in the work of Kennedy and the other academics considered in this chapter, he implicitly points to an aspect – the way the common law actually functions – that, in keeping with the approach adopted in this chapter, suggests the need to shift the focus of analysis away from the question of which ethical principles the law ought to uphold and onto an inquiry into the concrete legal practices and tests through which the courts assert their jurisdiction over matters arising in the course of medical practice. It is not the purpose of such an inquiry to suggest that ethics and ethical principles form no part of the common law in this area. Rather, the objective will be to demonstrate how the operation of various techniques of legal reasoning can affect traditional assumptions regarding the role of ethics and the meaning of ethical principles within medical law.

Conclusion

In this chapter, it has been argued that features of some of the academic medical law literature can usefully be understood to revolve around questions of jurisdiction. There are two aspects to this. The first concerns the mapping out of the scope of the subject and the need to stress that it deserves its place within the legal academy. In other words, academics defend their attempts to carve out, and sustain, a space for a legitimate new subject – medical law – whose conceptual foundations and specific field of competence can clearly be distinguished from other, more traditional, legal subjects such as contract, tort and criminal law.

The second aspect relates to the manner in which some academics can be thought to make the claim to legal jurisdiction. In Kennedy's case, it was the discourse of patients' rights and a concern to ensure that ethical issues were resolved externally to medicine that performed this function. It was suggested that these might be thought not only to be intended to have effects at the level of medical practice but could also be understood as underpinning Kennedy's claim to legal jurisdiction – academic, as well as judicial and legislative – in this area. From the academic point of view, those features create the foundations from which the researcher and teacher can claim authority and expertise to pronounce upon various issues and problems arising not only from the practice of medicine, but also, increasingly, from developments in biomedical science. This attempt to develop legal jurisdiction is meant to convey to medicine and science that they can no longer expect to exercise exclusive control over the consequences of their practices.

Part of Montgomery's analysis suggests a line of inquiry – a focus on the actual workings and practices of the common law in this area – that will be taken up later in the book (in Chapters 4 to 6). In order to do so, the choice has been made to focus on two features that, as already illustrated, have been central to the claims made by some academics for the development of legal jurisdiction – they are the need to empower patients and the claim that the law ought to be involved in determining ethical issues, ethical standards and social values. In so far as the first of these is concerned, the focus will solely be upon what has arguably become the most important ethical value in medical law – autonomy. In relation to the second area, the discussion will be organized around the relationship between the common law and, on the one hand, human rights and, on the other, moral conflict. The basic intention of the analysis is to focus on the manner in which the common law manages and asserts its increasing power in the field of medical law, and to consider what some of the consequences of this might be. Before embarking on this analysis, however, it will be useful to place the emergence, and increasing prevalence, of medical law within a wider sociological and political context. This is the subject of the next chapter.

Chapter 2

Medical Law in Context

Introduction

This chapter continues the effort to trace some aspects of the development of medical law by setting these within a wider explanatory framework. This methodology facilitates two possibilities. Firstly, it offers the opportunity to think through some of the possible reasons underlying the increasing involvement of the courts in resolving various conflicts and issues arising in the domain of medical practice. What movements and changes, whether technological, sociological or political, might explain the growing jurisdiction of the courts in the medical law sphere? Secondly, it allows us to locate the two main focal points of the book – the empowerment of patients and the claim that law should be the institution that determines the ethical issues arising within medical practice – against a broader background, thus providing an understanding of the types of social and political transformations against which contemporary medical law operates. So, for example, if the empowerment of patients is of concern not only to academics, but also to the courts, before analysing how this plays out in practice in legal cases, we can ask how the individual within contemporary Western society is empowered. It is important to stress that by proceeding in this manner it is not intended to suggest that what goes on in practice in the courts can simply be taken to replicate general societal shifts. This would be to neglect the role that particular legal institutional dimensions play in determining how the courts function. Nonetheless, the sociological type of inquiry allows for reflection on how some changes in the underlying structure of society might relate to aspects of medical law. Moreover, it offers the possibility of identifying contemporary themes and ideas – discussed and developed especially in work in the field of social theory – that, it is hoped to demonstrate in future chapters, assist in understanding the practice of the courts in some areas of medical law.

Shifting Modes of Governmentality: From Medicalization to Legalization

How might we account for the increasing involvement of the courts in a number of issues and problems which, had they arisen in the past, would have fallen to be discussed and resolved within the province of medicine? Why, as Ward LJ's claim in *Re A (Children)* (2000) with respect to medical disputes involving questions about the continued existence of human life suggests, are courts of law increasingly coming to be viewed as the preferred mechanism through which to settle disputes arising in the domain of medical practice? What might be the conditions responsible for the emergence and steady growth of medical law? These are the types of questions with which the discussion in this section will be concerned. Drawing on the work of Dingwall and Hobson-West in the field of medical sociology, it will be suggested that their identification of a movement from medicalization to legalization (or, as they put it, 'the substitution of legalisation for medicalisation as the paramount mode of governmentality' [Dingwall and Hobson-West 2006, 41]) provides, in general terms, a useful framework for thinking through the expansion of medical law. Before turning to their work, however, it is worth considering the role that some technological developments, and their applications in the field of medicine, have played, and continue to play, in creating the types of conflict which law increasingly manages.

Technological developments and their possible implications

The first examples fall within a category of what might be termed medico-technological advances. Peter Singer provides a useful account of two related developments – the medical redefinition of death in the 1960s and the emergence of the ventilator – that had significant consequences for what he calls our 'traditional ethic' (that is, the sanctity of life principle) (Singer 1994). The invention of the mechanical ventilator or respirator in the 1950s was intended to replace the function of the brain stem (which makes breathing and heartbeat possible) and, thereby, maintain the lives of individuals long enough for them to make a full recovery from their illnesses. While it undoubtedly had this effect for some, others continued to live without recovering consciousness. As this process could continue indefinitely, the question arose as to the value of maintaining ventilation in such circumstances.

By the 1960s, questions surrounding organ transplantation, especially that of the heart, were becoming pertinent to discussions regarding artificial ventilation. In order for the heart to be transplanted successfully, it needed to be removed as quickly as possible after death. The many irreversibly unconscious individuals receiving ventilation in hospitals then came to be seen as potential sources of life-saving organs for others awaiting transplant surgery. The problem, however, was that the removal of an irreversibly unconscious individual's heart would amount to murder. In Singer's view, it was this obstacle, together with the futility of providing ventilation to such individuals that, in 1968, led to the recommendation by the Harvard Brain Death Committee that the definition of death be altered from one of the cessation of breathing and circulation to that of irreversible cessation of all brain function.[1] Those falling within the latter category – the functioning of whose organs could be maintained artificially by means of ventilation – could therefore simultaneously be declared dead and provide a source of organs for transplantation to those who needed them. Thus, while the ventilator could be useful in helping patients to recover, this

---

1   Others have been less willing to make this causal link between potential organ transplantation and the re-definition of death. See, for example, Lamb 1990. It should be noted, though, that Lamb does make a loose connection between the two: 'By the late 1960s an increasing rate of organ transplantation and greater successes in resuscitation provided a background to the need for greater philosophical clarity concerning what it meant to be dead' (Lamb 1990, 33).

outcome was by no means guaranteed. For those placed on it, the guiding principle of action was the hope of recovery. Should it not prove successful for the patients themselves, it could nevertheless at least provide another possible avenue of cure for other patients. In other words, this development in medical technology created the potential for an enlarged scope of therapeutic practice through those who, until very recently, had been patients themselves.

The second category of progress in medicine – or, as it should more accurately be called here, biomedical science – has become much more embedded in public consciousness recently, particularly as a result of intense media coverage and speculation. But if public awareness of the potential medical applications of research in molecular biology (especially research into the molecular structure and function of human genes) has been a relatively recent phenomenon, the origins of this category of medical progress extend much further back.[2]

Hans-Jörg Rheinberger explains that molecular biology was established in the decades between 1940 and 1970 (see Rheinberger 2000). This area of science is concerned with research into the molecular structure of biological living systems, and its purpose is to understand how life processes, at their most basic level, work. During these years, some molecular biologists became involved in researching the molecular structure and function of human genes, with many non-scientists hoping that the research would lead to the application of concrete knowledge for the purpose of therapeutic ends in the field of medicine. Their hopes began to be realized because, at the beginning of the 1970s, gene technology and genetic engineering, or, as it is also known, applied molecular genetics, started to develop rapidly. Today, genetic testing, gene therapy and pre-implantation genetic diagnosis are just some of the many developments that have arisen as a result of research conducted by molecular biologists into the structure and function of human genes.

According to Rheinberger, technological development in human genetics will have consequences for the manner in which we come to view medicine in the future:

> With gene technology, informational molecules are constructed according to an extracellular project and are subsequently implanted into the intracellular environment. The organism itself transposes them, reproduces them, and 'tests' their characteristics … [T]he organism as a whole advances to the status of a locus technicus – that is, to the status of a space of representation in which new genotypic and phenotypic patterns are becoming probed and articulated. This technique is of potentially unlimited medical impact. For the first time, it is on the level of *instruction* that metabolic processes are becoming susceptible to manipulation. Until that point was reached, medical intervention … was restricted to the level of metabolic *performance*. (Rheinberger 2000, 25; emphasis in original)

In other words, human genetic technology will be capable of making organisms work to express pre-planned objectives that have been programmed molecularly. As

---

2   For an interesting history of the pivotal role played by the Laboratory of Molecular Biology in Britain in the development of molecular biology generally, see de Chadarevian 2002.

Rheinberger comments, the aim is to re-programme metabolic actions in order that cells may alter the way in which they function, resulting, for example, in perceptible differences in an organism's physical expression (its phenotype). Such a possibility differs from medicine's traditional ability which was restricted to improving metabolic performance, not altering its inherent function. This technological capability is not, of course, confined to therapeutic possibilities surrounding inherited disease since there is also, at least potentially, a host of genetic characteristics which may be manipulated to coincide with specific desired objectives.

What are some of the implications of such developments in medicine, medical practice and biomedical science? Firstly, they obviously help people either to recover from illness or to prevent its onset in the future. The purpose of the ventilator, for example, is to replace the vital functions of the body long enough to allow patients to recover and breathe unaided. Secondly, such advances allow certain patients to benefit the health, or sustain the life, of others. The respirator, for instance, provides the opportunity for the organs of those who cannot be helped to be transferred to those who can. It can also allow for the creation of human life itself by artificially maintaining the breathing of pregnant women long enough for their babies to be delivered.[3] Medical technology therefore enlarges the scope of therapeutic agents to include *patients* – or, more accurately, those patients who cannot be helped – as well as doctors. A recent court case – where human genetic technology allowed for the creation and implantation of an embryo with genetic material that might save the life of an existing sibling of the future child – illustrates the extent of the shift in potential therapeutic sources that has resulted from developments in technology.[4] Here, human life is brought into existence in order to cure human life. People are now being created in order to provide cures for the sick. In a sense, however, those who are created are themselves patients in that their genetic material is, in some circumstances, selected to ensure that, at least in one respect, they will not themselves become patients in the future.[5] In other words, they constitute a new type of patient – one who 'exists', and is 'cured', *before birth*.

Thirdly, developments in medical and biomedical technology, and especially the manner in which they are portrayed through various institutions (such as the media), have the ability to transform traditional understandings of human life, death, health and illness. The respirator, for example, clearly has implications for the medical definition of death and alters the status of the patient who cannot be helped; but it does much more than this. It changes social and cultural perceptions of what it means to have a life, and thereby challenges societies' traditional sensibilities

---

3 The case of Marion Ploch is indicative of this possibility. See Singer 1994, 12–16.

4 See *R. (on the application of Quintavalle) v. Human Fertilisation and Embryology Authority* (2003a). This case is discussed in more detail in Chapter 6.

5 This is not so in all cases. See, for example, the case of Mr and Mrs Whitaker in which the future child was not at risk from hereditary disease but was primarily needed to act as a donor of tissue of a specific type to the couple's son. The Human Fertilisation and Embryology Authority refused to grant a licence for the necessary pre-implantation genetic diagnosis to be carried out. The Authority has since changed its policy in respect of such cases – see <http://www.hfea.gov.uk/cps/rde/xchg/SID-3F57D79B-914B9364/hfea/hs.xsl/1046.html> (accessed 21 January 2007).

surrounding questions of life and death. Despite the existence of a medical definition of death, the actual operation of the respirator defies a human tendency toward the need for perceptual clarity in such circumstances. To be told that someone we have known for years is dead when they continue to breathe, or even give birth, not only unsettles our ideas about life and death, but can also distort the perceptions of that person's identity that have developed in our minds over the course of those years. The respirator can work in such a way as to leave an indelible impression of an individual's life in our memories. We might say that the respirator and the medical definition of death not only have the potential to change the status of patients who are beyond assistance, but can also affect how their identities and lives are remembered by those who knew them.

Developments in human genetics research and its associated technologies will also have implications for traditional perceptions of life, death, health and illness. The discovery in 1953 of the structure of deoxyribonucleic acid (hereinafter 'DNA') by James Watson and Francis Crick ensured that much research would follow into the genetic constitution of human beings, and that human understanding continued the trend of locating the sources of disease in increasingly minute elements of human life. This latter aspect is evident from Rheinberger's illustration above of the nature of the changes that will be brought about by progress in human genetic technology (hereinafter 'HGT'). In particular, it seems that this will have implications for medicine in terms of HGT's power to alter normative perceptions of health and illness. While the drugs that led to the eradication of disease in the middle of the twentieth century sought to restore self-regulation to the internal processes of the bodies of human beings – what Rheinberger calls 'metabolic performance' – the possibility that HGT will allow for the external instruction of metabolic processes will produce changes in settled understandings of what amounts to health and disease. In other words, the products that develop from research in human genetics will not simply seek to restore living beings to a state where their vital norms can once again fluctuate in conjunction with alterations in their environments; rather, what is also likely to become prevalent are attempts to alter vital functions through re-programming the activity of cells for specific purposes. Nikolas Rose has described the possible effect this will have on the function of medicine:

> This opens up the normativity of life for experimentation and manipulation: the therapeutic maximization of 'quality of life' in the name of normality. Medical judgement about life becomes infused with values that are indeed statistical and social rather than vital and organic. The judgements of probabilities and of risks that have become central both to experimental and clinical practice inescapably connect to the judgements of value that are placed upon different forms of existence and the logics of treatment they mandate. What is normality at the level of the genetic code? … Much of our current medical politics is situated in the conflicts and tensions between different modes of normativity and normality. (Rose 1998, 165)

In other words, medicine will no longer be limited to re-establishing the health of individuals. Indeed, the point is that our traditional understanding of health will demand to be rethought as the possibilities of HGT become clearer. Given technology's ability to alter the function of metabolic processes, or to choose the genetic constituency of embryos *in vitro*, the identification of what amounts to health, of what is the healthy norm, of the nature and purpose of therapeutic treatment (in other words, what is therapy, what is treatment, and what are they for), becomes a much more uncertain endeavour that, as Rose rightly points out, admits of broader social judgments about the types of people societies wish to exist.

It is clear, then, that developments in medicine, molecular biology (specifically, human genetics) and their associated technologies have had, and will continue to have, wide-ranging consequences, including transformations in traditional understandings of human life, death, health and disease.[6] Above all, though, the simple point to be noted is that settled perceptions of those categories have been, and are being, rendered problematic; the thresholds between them are no longer susceptible to clear demarcations, resulting in a situation in which the presence of blurring is all too apparent. Inevitably, conflict will result from such a situation, and this is the final consequence of technological advances within the fields of medicine and the life sciences to be noted here. Discussing the potential impact of developments in human genetics, Mitchell Dean observes:

> The capacity to manipulate our mere biological life, rather than simply to govern aspects of forms of life, implies a bio-politics that contests how and when we use these technologies and for what purposes. It also implies a redrawing of the relations between life and death, and a new 'thanato-politics', a new politics of death. (Dean 2004, 16)

Dean's use of the word 'politics' (in both its 'bio' and 'thanato' formulations) is useful as it accurately captures the contestation and conflict produced as a result of the ever growing technological ways in which human life can be manipulated. The presence of this conflict has resulted in the courts coming to be viewed as important sites where the controversies and disputes arising in the field of medicine can be played out and managed. The withdrawal of artificial nutrition and hydration from patients in a permanent vegetative state;[7] the question of whether to provide ventilation to seriously ill babies;[8] the diagnosis, and selection, of embryos for the purpose of creating healthy human beings[9] – all are illustrative of the types of conflict that ensue from the application of technological developments in the field of medical practice. The result has been the steady growth in the courts' jurisdiction over such conflicts.

But while such technological developments clearly contribute to the creation of the types of conflict which courts increasingly arbitrate, they do not, on their own, explain why law is coming to be seen as the preferred institution through which those

---

6   As Ulrich Beck has said: 'What is socially considered "health" and "disease" loses its pre-ordained "natural" character in the framework of the medical monopoly and becomes a quantity that can be produced in the work of medicine. "Life" and "death" in this view are no longer permanent values and concepts beyond the reach of human beings. Rather, what is considered and recognized socially as "life" and "death" *becomes contingent in and through the work of medical people themselves*' (Beck 1992, 210; emphasis in original).

7   See, for example, *Airedale NHS Trust v. Bland* (1993).

8   See, for example, *Re Wyatt* (2005).

9   See, for example, *R. (on the application of Quintavalle) v. Human Fertilisation and Embryology Authority* (2003a).

conflicts and issues arising in the domain of medical practice are to be regulated. In order to address this question more fully, it will be useful now to turn to Dingwall and Hobson-West's essay (Dingwall and Hobson-West 2006).

Shifting modes of governmentality

Dingwall and Hobson-West argue that the challenge to medicine today can best be understood as part of a broader shift from medicalization to legalization – what they describe as a shift in the mode of governmentality. They define this latter term as relating to 'the interlocking systems of values and institutions constitutive of the ordering of a society' (Dingwall and Hobson-West 2006, 41). Consequently, what they say we are witnessing today is not merely a challenge by law to medicine in the narrow sense, for example, of the courts regulating aspects of doctors' practices or procedures; more fundamentally, a shift in the values and institutions underpinning the very manner in which authority is exercised, and society ordered, is underway. Viewed in this light: 'The fundamental challenge to medicine is not from law but from the governmentality that favours law as its operative strategy' (Dingwall and Hobson-West 2006, 57).

This 'governmentality that favours law as its operative strategy' – that is, legalization – denotes a society in which the individual and his or her particular interests, rights and agreements constitute the definitive values. Individual autonomy and self-reliance, rather than dependency and community, are the guiding principles of social organization and Dingwall and Hobson-West argue that this state of human relations is ripe for 'the colonial aspirations of law' because: 'Law casts human beings as self-sufficient individuals, intentional actors and guardians of their own interests' (Dingwall and Hobson-West 2006, 54). The consequence of this is that not only does law come to be treated as the preferred means by which to settle disputes and seek redress of one's grievances, but, in the very process of acting in such a capacity, the institution of law plays a crucial role in reinforcing and perpetuating the type of social organization that calls it into play in the first place. In other words, rather than simply being used as the most obvious location for the expression of individuals' rights and interests, law's burgeoning authority means that it plays an integral role in constructing and maintaining the social order – and the idea of human relations as based on rights and contract – of which it is a part.

Medicalization, on the other hand, and at least after the creation of the National Health Service in the UK in 1948, was one aspect of a different mode of governmentality – that is, one which 'reache[d] out to embrace the population in a moral community, a holistic vision of a welfare society' (Dingwall and Hobson-West 2006, 55). This was the era of social medicine which, amongst other things, was defined by the importance of community and the protection of the less fortunate members of society (in this case, the sick). The coincidence of those values with the broader ethos of the welfare state meant that medicine and medical professionals occupied a central and authoritative role in the overall ordering of society.[10] Thus,

---

10 Some would argue that, despite the retrenchment of the welfare state, the medical profession still plays an integral role in the organization of society today. See, for instance,

according to Dingwall and Hobson-West, it would be incorrect to conceive of medicalization as an attempt by medical professionals to colonize various areas and aspects of social life; rather, it is to be better thought of 'as one aspect of the governmentality of social democracy where "the imperfections of the market are … tempered by measures of social reform based on the values of an enlightened bourgeoisie"'[11] (Dingwall and Hobson-West 2006, 53; reference omitted).

Dingwall and Hobson-West point to several examples in the medical field which underline the displacement of medicalization by legalization in contemporary Western societies. Increasing resort to litigation for the purpose of seeking individual redress of one's grievances; the erosion of trust in the doctor–patient relationship; the willingness to challenge medical professionals' opinions; the contractualization of health care services – all indicate the decline of medicalization as the dominant mode of governmentality and the corresponding emergence of legalization in its place. The institution of law therefore comes to play a central role in managing the uncertainty and disorder produced by the retreat of medicalization. In doing so, however, it also contributes to the maintenance of a new type of social order and organization (a new mode of governmentality) – one defined by self-reliance and the assertion of individual rights and interests.

To sum up, medicalization and legalization are not, for Dingwall and Hobson-West, primarily terms or notions associated with imperialism, colonization or jurisdiction – if, by these terms is meant one field actively seeking to displace another by taking over its issues and problems. Thus, it is not a matter of law attempting to colonize medicine and adopt its issues as its own that defines legalization. Rather, the threat to medicine by law lies in law's compatibility with the types of values and idea of human relations accompanying changes in the social, economic and political make-up of contemporary Western societies. It is suggested that this compatibility has played an important part in the rise in litigation to be witnessed in the field of medical law. Unlike some academic medical lawyers, the courts have not, on the whole, actively sought jurisdiction over the issues and disputes that arise in medical practice. In other words, they have not tried to colonize medicine and, if you like, steal its problems. Nonetheless, the increase in litigation arising from, amongst other

---

Beck 1992 (especially Chapter 8). Even so, this role is played out against a background of changed values, the most significant of which is, as Dingwall and Hobson-West's idea of legalization captures, the emphasis placed on the individual – both in terms of increased choice *and* responsibility. Moreover, and as will become apparent shortly, Beck notes the importance of the courts in what he calls today's 'risk society'.

11 As noted in the previous chapter, the traditional meaning of medicalization is associated with medical imperialism – the tendency of medicine to colonize various spheres of everyday life. Strong, who discusses this feature of medicalization, and the corresponding colonization attempts of other fields (including law), notes how their relative success is, ultimately, dependent on structural changes within society: '[I]n conclusion, although clinical rule seems likely to be increasingly shared, which branches of the academy partake in that rule will be heavily determined by much broader changes in the polity and economy of individual countries' (Strong 1984, 356). While he did not elaborate on this latter point, Dingwall and Hobson-West have clearly taken it up in their article. For a useful overview of traditional and contemporary understandings of medicalization, see Ballard and Elston 2005.

things, the shift in the mode of governmentality from medicalization to legalization has inevitably resulted in the courts coming to have jurisdiction over such issues and problems. It is this jurisdiction, and the manner in which it is asserted by the courts, that will form the focus of the remaining chapters. In conclusion, we can say that both technological developments and the changing mode of governmentality identified by Dingwall and Hobson-West have contributed to the emergence of the courts as important sites where the various disputes, issues, and problems arising in the field of medicine are managed.

Whilst the foregoing discussion provides an explanation of how the courts have come to acquire jurisdiction over matters arising within medicine, there remains the question of how they assert their authority or power. This latter feature will be addressed in the remaining chapters of the book by examining how the courts have responded, on the one hand, to claims that patients should be empowered and, on the other, to exhortations that judges should adopt a more proactive stance towards the many ethical issues involved in cases coming before them. In the remainder of the present chapter, it will be useful to preface this study by locating it against a more general sociological and political backdrop. As well as offering a glimpse of the types of themes and arguments to follow in the remainder of the book, it is hoped that this approach will enable the reader to note some of the linkages (albeit loose and never complete) between medical law in the courts and more general social and political transformations. It will also provide an opportunity to begin to think through the potential effects of law's involvement in issues of conflict and controversy. The next section will discuss the prevalence of ideas of individual choice and responsibility in contemporary Western societies; the final part of the chapter will concentrate on the implications for democracy of 'progress' in medicine and the life sciences and what role, if any, the courts might play in enhancing the level of debate about such 'progress'.

Choice and Obligation in Liquid Modernity

Underlying Dingwall and Hobson-West's discussion of the shift from medicalization to legalization is the recognition of a transformation in the forms of social life, order and organization in contemporary Western societies. This transformation – which, in very broad terms, involves a reduction in the role of the welfare state (and the erosion of the values upon which it was founded) and an increasing focus on the individual and practices of self-regulation – and its consequences have been documented and analysed by many influential writers.[12] In this section, only one element of this shift – the increasing prevalence of ideas of individual choice and responsibility – will be noted. Thereafter, it will be shown how those ideas are infiltrating both health care and developments in medicine and biomedical science.

'Ours is ... an individualized, privatised version of modernity, with the burden of pattern-weaving and the responsibility for failure falling primarily on the individual's

---

12 Examples include the work of Zygmunt Bauman – see, for instance, Bauman 2000 and 2005; Loïc Wacquant (Wacquant 2001); Nikolas Rose (Rose and Miller 1992 and Rose 1999b); and Peter Wagner (Wagner 1994).

shoulders. It is the patterns of dependency and interaction whose turn to be liquefied has now come' (Bauman 2000, 7–8). At the heart of Zygmunt Bauman's analysis of our contemporary social condition – which he calls liquid modernity – lies a concern with the consequences of the latest episode of the disintegration of the 'solids' (that is, those 'bonds which interlock individual choices in collective projects and actions'). With the erosion of 'solid' group structures such as classes, individuals' destinations are less pre-determined today. Of course, one consequence of this is that individuals are released from the fetters accompanying such structures. They become free to construct their own ends and goals, their own identities, their own life projects. Choice becomes one of the key notions of liquid modernity. In a society of consumers, individuals assert themselves, indeed define themselves, by means of the choices they make.[13] This culture of choice and individual self-assertion, Bauman argues, also has consequences for the nature of ethical and political discourse, which is transformed from discussions about the 'just society' into the language of 'human rights' – 'the right of individuals to stay different and to pick and choose at will their own models of happiness and fitting life-style' (Bauman 2000, 29).

This shift to the central role adopted by the individual in liquid modernity has, though, a less appealing flip side – that of 'individualization'. This notion, which Bauman adopts from Ulrich Beck's work (see Beck 1992), denotes the fact that with the progressive erosion of 'solid' structures individuals become *obliged* to construct their identities and life projects – identities and projects which were previously defined for them by those structures. Moreover, and significantly, individuals become responsible for how well, or not so well, they perform this task of construction. Should they fail, responsibility for this failure rests squarely on their own shoulders. One might call it the privatization of blame. It is, for example, not the fault of the ruling authorities for the inability of an individual to secure employment; rather, it is their own failings (whether a lack of initiative or reluctance to work, for example) that are the cause. Or, as Bauman says in respect of another of his examples: '[I]f [individuals] fall ill, it is assumed that this has happened because they were not resolute and industrious enough in following their health regime' (Bauman 2000, 34). In other words, the reality of individual self-sufficiency and self-reliance renders all failures (including those which are socially produced), and successes too, the responsibility of the relevant individuals.

Two points can be noted from this brief description of part of Bauman's work. The first is the close relationship between freedom of choice and individual responsibility in conditions of liquid modernity. Individuals are not only free to choose; they are compelled to do so, and, additionally, to accept responsibility for the choices they make, together with the consequences flowing from these. As Bauman puts it: 'In the land of the individual freedom of choice the option to escape individualization and to refuse participation in the individualizing game is emphatically *not* on the agenda' (Bauman 2000, 34; emphasis in original). The second concerns the gap between the right of individual self-assertion in theory and the ability of individuals to make that right meaningful in practice. The existence of the latter is dependent on forces – such

---

13 Bauman has argued that 'the absence of routine and the state of constant choice … are the virtues (indeed the "role prerequisites") of a consumer' (Bauman 2005, 25).

as the resources societies make available to assist those who find it difficult to stand on their own two feet – beyond the control of any particular individual. The general point to be noted is that the existence of a right to self-assertion in practice is largely contingent on the setting within which the claim to that right is asserted. The specific dimensions of the institutional setting, for example, will play a prominent role in the extent to which the theoretical right is practically meaningful.

Having sketched out one account of the transformation currently underway from a society based on the kind of collective values underpinning Dingwall and Hobson-West's notion of medicalization to one driven by an emphasis on individual choice and responsibility (which would constitute the sorts of values underlying their idea of legalization), we can now see, by reference to two examples, how those latter notions – of choice and responsibility – are infiltrating, and increasingly coming to define, the discourse surrounding health care.

In a recent White Paper, the UK Government outlined its plans for further improvements to the National Health Service (hereinafter 'NHS') (Department of Health 2004a). In his Foreword to the Paper, the then Prime Minster – Tony Blair – sets out the need for, and the nature of, the changes required to the country's health service:

> A system devised for a time of rationing and shortages cannot be right for a century when the public expect high-quality products, better services, choice and convenience … [There is a need] to reshape the health service around the needs and aspirations of its patients … [T]his requires us to put power in the hands of patients rather than Whitehall. (Department of Health 2004a, 3)

The then Secretary of State for Health – John Reid – expands on the Government's objectives as follows:

> Our vision is one where the founding principles underlying the NHS are given modern meaning and relevance in the context of people's increasing ambitions and expectations of their public services. An NHS which is fair to all of us and personal to each of us by offering *everyone* the same access to, and the power to choose from, a wide range of services of high quality, based on clinical need, not ability to pay. (Department of Health 2004a, 6; emphasis in original)

What is clear from this, and the Prime Minister's statement, is that the proposed changes are driven mainly by a desire to introduce the language and ethos of consumerism and the market into a health care system founded, as the Secretary of State notes, on the welfare notion of equality in need. Thus, throughout the Paper, one encounters numerous references to 'personal choice' ('patient choice will be a key driver of the system'), patients' 'right to choose', care which is 'personal and tailored to the individual'.[14] So, for example, when seeking treatment patients will have the right to choose from at least four or five different health care providers, and will be able 'to call the shots about the time and place of their care'. As the Paper notes, one of the consequences of this ability to choose will be the need for NHS

---

14 As Bauman has noted: 'Choice is the consumer society's meta-value, the value with which to evaluate and rank all other values' (Bauman 2005, 58).

staff 'to work more flexibly in a way that best responds to patients' needs'. The internet will supplement this move towards personal choice by allowing patients to access their own 'personal *HealthSpace*' where they will be able to view their health records and convey their personal preferences regarding their care.

It is obvious, then, that, in the Government's view, the provision of decent or even high-quality care and products in one's local GP surgery and hospital is no longer an adequate measure of a successful NHS. Rather, success is now also dependent on whether patients have the ability to choose between different providers of the same (high-quality) product. Moreover, the beneficial effects of health care services for patients' health are not, in themselves, indicators of a good health service; rather, they must be supplemented by working to ensure 'the personal experience of patients as individuals'. One might think that visiting a hospital, or the doctor's surgery, is enough of an experience for patients, without worrying about whether, over and above the desired restoration of, or improvement in, their health, they are obtaining some kind of enjoyment or memorable day out. But it is the whole package that counts. A trip to the hospital now needs to reflect other types of consumer experiences, such as going shopping or buying a car. It is not just buying a piece of clothing, for instance, that is important; rather, it is having the ability to choose from a range of options that constitutes the real source of pleasure. As Bauman says: 'Goods acquire their lustre and attractiveness in the course of being chosen; take the choice away, and their allure vanishes without trace' (Bauman 2005, 59). The same might be said of health care providers and products – they are really not very appealing unless one has the ability to choose between them. Again, as Bauman notes, the inherent problem of the services of the welfare state in a consumer society is that, even if what they offered was of a high standard, they 'would still be burdened with the fundamental flaw of being exempt from allegedly free consumer choice – a flaw that discredits them beyond redemption in the eyes of converted and devoted, "born again" consumers' (Bauman 2005, 59). It is this 'flaw' that the proposals in the Government's White Paper are geared towards correcting.

This desire to convert patients into customers and consumers, which defines the essence of the Government's White Paper, can only heighten the possibility of more work for the courts. Litigation is likely to be one of the consequences of the inexorable drive to embed a consumer mentality within the NHS. In addition to clinical negligence claims, which have been a staple of the medical law scene for decades, and those based on defective medical products, recourse to the courts might expect to take the form of claims founded on lack of choice between health care providers, or, perhaps more plausibly, lack of a sufficient number of providers of high-quality services from which to choose between; lack of access to particular types of medicines which, while available privately, may not have been considered financially justifiable by the National Institute for Health and Clinical Excellence (the body that, amongst other things, determines which medicines are to be available through the NHS); the lack of a GP to see me at 4 o'clock in the morning for a routine check-up because this is the most convenient time for me; and, who knows, even the failure to provide me with the type of personal experience I expected when I visited hospital for my operation. This latter type of claim may be fanciful, but the underlying point is clear – the introduction of a consumer culture into a publicly funded health service with finite resources is a recipe for the type of litigation that is symptomatic of Dingwall and Hobson-West's 'legalisation'.

Accompanying this stress on patient choice has been a drive towards the responsibilization of patients and individuals. In other words, there has been a marked tendency to promote the idea that individuals should become more responsible for their health care, thereby reducing pressure on NHS services. On the one hand, this trend has arisen in the context of long-term medical conditions, such as diabetes, heart disease and depression. Patients suffering from such conditions are to be enabled 'to take greater control of their own treatment' (Department of Health 2004a, 35) – something which is to occur through the Expert Patients Programme. The idea is that, through training designed to teach such patients how to manage their conditions, they become 'expert patients' who need not call on doctors or other health care professionals for assistance. As one such patient, quoted in the White Paper, comments of the Programme: 'I have learnt that I need to take responsibility for my health instead of leaving it all to the GP' (Department of Health 2004a, 37).

On the other hand, it can be argued that this ethos of responsibility defines the current Government's drive to improve the health of the nation generally. In its recent White Paper – *Choosing Health: Making Healthy Choices Easier* (Department of Health 2004b) – the Government seeks to set in place the mechanisms which will, in the Prime Minister's words, 'enable [people] to choose health'. It is not, he says, a case of the State intervening in individuals' lives and forcing them to become healthy. Rather, the State's involvement is designed to facilitate the possibility of individuals choosing to lead healthier lifestyles than they currently do. It is, he says, entirely down to the individual whether he or she wishes to 'make the healthy choice'. There is no need to discuss all the various ways in which the Government proposes to effect such a change. Rather, it is the nature of the relationship between individual choice and responsibility underlying the Government's proposals that is relevant here.

As with the Government's plans for improving the NHS (outlined above), the notion of 'choice' lies at the heart of its proposals for improving public health. But unlike the former, the latter suggest the need for individuals to choose responsibly. As noted, choosing the healthy option is not to be forced on individuals by the State; it is, rather, to be fostered through a variety of different means – such as advertising, retailing, the media, changes in employment practices, local government and industry. The idea would seem to be to create a culture of health and a web of healthy environments within society from which it would be very difficult for individuals to extricate themselves and choose anything but the healthy option. In other words, choice, and especially the freedom to choose the non-healthy option, becomes increasingly difficult – not only as the options available will tend, with time, to be healthy ones, but also, and perhaps more importantly, because choosing the non-healthy option will be viewed as irresponsible, a morally aberrant act that flouts the healthy norm and tends to say something about the character of the individual making the choice.[15] So, despite the Government's rhetoric of individuals retaining

---

15 We can already witness this phenomenon in the pariah status increasingly, though often implicitly, assigned to smokers.

the opportunity to opt out of making the healthy choice, the reality is that the healthy option will, increasingly, be the only responsible course of action to adopt.

This is a classic example of the nature of contemporary political power described by Nikolas Rose and Peter Miller:

> Political power is exercised today through a profusion of shifting alliances between diverse authorities in projects to govern a multitude of facets of economic activity, social life and individual conduct. Power is not so much a matter of imposing constraints upon citizens as of 'making up' citizens capable of bearing a kind of regulated freedom. Personal autonomy is not the antithesis of political power, but a key term in its exercise, the more so because most individuals are not merely the subjects of power but play a part in its operations. (Rose and Miller 1992, 174)[16]

The type of government envisaged in the proposals for improving the health of the nation today is what Rose and Miller would refer to as governance 'at a distance' (see also Rose 2001). Two features of this are noteworthy. First, the political authorities use not the might of the State, but various other mechanisms (in our example, techniques such as advertising) for the purpose of securing their objectives – here, a healthy nation.[17] Those mechanisms encourage and persuade individuals to exercise their choices in accordance with prevailing ideas of what is normal or good or healthy. This process, however, and this is the second feature of governance at a distance, relies on the capacities of individuals to act freely. In other words, political power here operates through freedom (or, as Rose and Miller put it, 'individuals can be governed through their freedom to choose' [Rose and Miller 1992, 201]). Individuals internalize, and reproduce, the standards and objectives of authorities who are distant from them. Their freedom to choose is positively nurtured but in such a way that the choices made are responsible ones – that is, they conform to the goals of the political authorities. Governing here is a subtle, almost imperceptible, process. It produces individuals who regulate themselves by freely choosing objectives that coincide with those of the State. As Rose has said of the governmentality of the 'enabling state': 'This entails a twin process of autonomization plus responsibilization – opening free space for the choices of individual actors whilst enwrapping these autonomized actors within new forms of control' (Rose 1999a, xxiii).

As well as characterizing the Government's approach to improving public health, this notion of 'regulated freedom' has also been noted by some social scientists

---

16 Rose and Miller's reflections on political power build on Michel Foucault's idea of governmentality. See Foucault 2000b.

17 Other institutions implicitly assist in ensuring that the Government's objectives have a good chance of being realized. Witness, for instance, the recent spate of television programmes in the UK – such as Channel 4's *You Are What You Eat* – that, by focusing on individuals whose diets (and weights) are extreme, are not only designed to entertain through ridicule, but also to shock the viewer into choosing to live more healthily in the future. And it is worth noting that, at the same time as such programmes castigate those who are seduced by the marketing strategies of fast-food companies, they seek to promote an altogether more 'healthy' form of consumption – the purchase of the various products and books of those who present the programmes. See, for instance, McKeith 2004, and her food range at <http://www.mckeithresearch.com/shopping-shop.php> (accessed 21 January 2007).

writing on the biomedical applications of developments in the life sciences. Rose's work itself is a useful example (see Rose 2001). Discussing the central role that professionals, such as genetic counsellors and reproductive experts (the 'gatekeepers to tests and medical procedures' or the 'new pastors of the soma'), play in guiding patients as they mull over what decisions to make, Rose comments:

> These new pastors of the soma espouse the ethical principles of informed consent, autonomy, voluntary action and choice, and non-directiveness. But in the practices of this pastoral power, such ethical principles must be translated into a range of micro-technologies for the management of communication and information. These blur the boundaries of coercion and consent. They transform the subjectivities of those who are to give consent or refuse it, through discursive techniques that teach new ways of rendering aspects of oneself into thought and language, new ways of making oneself and one's actions amenable to judgement. (Rose 2001, 9–10; reference omitted)

In other words, because such professionals implement techniques of communication that seek, for example, to persuade individuals to reflect on, and even transform, the way in which they think about themselves and their responsibilities, in reality individual choice becomes mediated. Moreover, Rose's statement illustrates the importance of context on how ethical principles such as autonomy come to acquire meaning in practice. In this case, it is impossible to understand those principles fully without also comprehending the practices of pastoral power. The rhetoric of the language of consent, choice and autonomy masks how those ethical principles are mediated as a result of the techniques and requirements of particular practices.

Summary

Two basic points should be noted from the discussion in this section. The first is the interplay between individual choice, rights and self-assertion on the one hand, and individual responsibility, obligation and regulation on the other. Individuals are simultaneously empowered and responsibilized. They have the freedom to choose, but exercise that freedom responsibly. Rose has referred to this as 'responsibilized choice' and 'autonomization plus responsibilization'. Additionally, the power of authorities in contemporary Western societies is inextricably bound up with individuals. But this is not in the sense of the State either overtly repressing individuals or granting them unlimited freedom to do as they please. Rather, power, it might be said, uses, and operates through, freedom; it subtly works on the conduct of individuals so that they come to act responsibly – that is, in accordance with broader social objectives and prevailing conceptions of normality.

The second point is that the meanings of all those key notions associated with individual empowerment today – choice, rights, self-assertion and autonomy – cannot be understood apart from the institutions and contexts within which they are promoted. This demands an appreciation, and analysis, of the workings and practices of such institutions – what, for instance, their internal requirements are, and how the various interests of the actors within the institution are managed. Only then, it is suggested, can those notions be understood adequately.

As we will see in Chapters 3 and 4, those two points are relevant when attempting to understand how the idea of patient autonomy acquires meaning in some medical law cases.

Medicine, the Judiciary and Sub-politics

Accompanying the increasing importance attached to the individual and his or her rights, choices and responsibilities is what Ulrich Beck has described as 'a systemic transformation of the political' (Beck 1992, Chapter 8). In general terms, this involves the dispersion of political power and decision-making from their traditional location in central political institutions, including parliament and government, to what Beck calls sub-political sites. As two such sites – the judiciary and medicine – are relevant in the current context, it is worth describing Beck's view of how these fit within this contemporary transformation of the political. The purpose in doing so is to set the scene for the discussion and arguments which appear in Chapters 5 and 6.

According to Beck, the realization of democratic and constitutional rights by parliaments throughout the twentieth century has, paradoxically, led to the erosion of parliamentary power and the displacement of parliament as the centre of political decision-making. One reason for this is that citizens, armed with their newly acquired rights, no longer view their role as obedient observers of the dictates of the executive and parliament. Rather, by deploying those rights as a means by which to challenge and monitor decisions of the state and its public bodies, a new mode of political participation emerges in the form of citizens' interest groups and new social movements created to promote particular issues. And rather than challenges and rights claims being pursued solely through the centralized political channels, the law also becomes an important vehicle for attempts to secure various interests, thereby ensuring that the courts become sites of sub-politics. Judicial review actions, through which individual citizens and groups challenge the lawfulness of controversial decisions made by the executive or public bodies, open up the possibility for the politicization of judicial decision-making. Moreover, judges are increasingly called upon not only to uphold citizens' basic rights, but also to 'flesh out' the meaning of the fundamental freedoms they are designed to protect. This greater involvement of the judiciary leads to 'the courts becom[ing] omnipresent monitoring agencies of political decisions' (Beck 1992, 194). The courts are sites of a political process that exists independently of parliament.

Beck argues that medicine constitutes a site of sub-politics too. What distinguishes the decisions made in the field of medicine from those in parliament, however, is that the former, despite being contentious, are not subject to the traditional requirements of democratic politics, such as 'knowledge of the goals of social change, discussion, voting and consent' (Beck 1992, 184). Beck suggests that progress in medicine, and the social consequences of its practical applications, lack legitimation as they cannot be debated in advance by parliamentary bodies or the public because those implications are necessarily only visible after the event. There is, for instance, no way of knowing, and thus no way of debating or discussing, the consequences of the applications of human genetic technology until they occur. But by that stage discussion, scepticism and debate can merely amount to 'an *obituary* for decisions taken long ago' (Beck 1992, 203; emphasis in original). It is, however, also the social structure of medicine that undercuts the possibility of public discussion, debate and consent regarding the decisions taken by medical professionals. As Beck says:

> Medicine alone possesses in the form of the clinic an organizational arrangement in which the development and application of research results to patients can be carried out and perfected autonomously and according to its own standards and categories in isolation from outside questions and monitoring. In this way, medicine as a professional power has secured and expanded for itself a fundamental advantage against political and public attempts at consultation and intervention. In its fields of practice, clinical diagnosis and therapy, it not only controls the innovative power of science, but is at the same time its own parliament and its own government in matters of 'medical progress'. (Beck 1992, 210)

Beck's own suggestion as to how to control unfettered medical and scientific adventurism, without curtailing necessary research in those fields, involves a combination of 'strong and independent courts', 'strong and independent media' and mechanisms of professional self-criticism within medicine and human genetics, amongst other practices.

As will become clear in Chapters 5 and 6, aspects of those parts of Beck's work just described are relevant to thinking through the courts' role in certain medical law cases. Specifically, it is possible to witness an increase in recourse to the courts by, on the one hand, individuals seeking to have their claims to basic rights (especially human rights) upheld and, on the other hand, interest groups seeking judicial review of decisions which they argue endorse unethical applications of cutting edge research in the field of human embryology. In other words, there is recent evidence within medical law of the use of the courts in precisely the kind of way Beck describes – that is, as a sub-political site. Moreover, some academic work within medical law has sought to promote a more central and interventionist role for the courts in controlling and managing the disputes arising from medical practice and the application of techniques derived from research in biomedical science. We have already seen how Ian Kennedy defines medical law as a sub-set of human rights law, with the courts having the task of upholding those rights – and the ethical values upon which they are based – in the face of what he perceives to be medical dominance. Others have taken up Beck's suggestion of the need for strong and independent courts by arguing that the judiciary can make a positive contribution to redressing the democratic deficit he identifies at the heart of medical sub-politics through providing strong moral judgments in ethically controversial cases which will enhance ethical debate about medical and scientific progress (see Lee and Morgan 2001). What all those authors have in common, then, is an aspirational view of the role that courts can, and ought to, play in response to the sub-politics of medicine.

Whilst Beck's identification of the transformation of the political usefully contributes to our understanding of the conditions responsible for the rise in litigation in the area of medical law, he stops short of analysing how, if at all, courts have performed the 'strong and independent' role he suggests is necessary. Similarly, the aspirational view of the courts' role to be found in some of the academic medical law literature has tended to be advanced without any detailed investigation into the nature of the judicial response in cases involving controversial and contentious ethical issues in this area. Thus, if we are to assess the contribution (if any) of the courts to checking unfettered medical power and raising debate about the consequences of progress in medicine and biomedical science, it is necessary to move the inquiry on, and begin to address how courts actually function in those types of cases. How have the courts managed claims by individuals seeking to uphold their fundamental (human) rights? Have the courts embraced the controversial disputes in this field by actively discussing the moral conflicts that lie at their heart and seeking to resolve these through the deployment of ethical reasoning? Do judges contribute to ethical debate about medical progress? The argument advanced here is that it is only by addressing such questions – questions whose common theme is the manner in which the courts exercise their jurisdiction in the area of medical law – that it becomes possible to reflect on both how courts are 'strong and independent' (how, we might say, using Beck's terminology, the courts are sub-political) and what the possible effects of how they function are back upon the various claims made for the importance of a strong judiciary – such as the need to enhance debate and, thereby, to help to redress the democratic deficit within medicine and science. If, as Beck argues, the social structure of medicine is, at least partially, responsible for the problems surrounding medical progress, then any corresponding attempt to ascertain how successful the judiciary can be in helping to alleviate those problems would, it would seem, need to consider the effects of what might be called the operations of the structural characteristics of the common law and judicial reasoning. This part of the analysis will occur in Part III of the book. It is, however, worth prefacing this with a brief mention of one of the potential problems with legal involvement in the management of controversial issues generally.

This problem concerns what is known as the expropriation of conflict, the essence of which is described by Gunther Teubner as follows: '[H]human conflicts are torn through formalization out of their living context and distorted by being subject to legal processes' (Teubner 1987a, 7–8). This process, and its accompanying dangers, have been usefully noted by Thomas Mathiesen:

> [J]urisprudence contains a peculiar potential to transform political questions of conflict into *apparently* neutral, technical and professional questions ... In parts this happens by the jurist's raising the fundamental legal question of whether there exists a 'legal authority' or 'legal basis' for given actions; in short, whether the actions are legal. Thereby the debate is transformed from being a clearly political debate – for and against a political standpoint – to being an exchange of opinions concerning the *apparently* neutral and unpolitical issue of whether legal authority or basis 'exists' ... [T]he debate is 'lifted' from the political to the professional-juridical level, the professional-juridical level being regarded as superordinate and therefore more 'elevated'. (Mathiesen 2004, 17; emphasis added)

Similarly, we might expect that with the more prominent role of the courts in regulating and managing conflicts and disputes arising in the field of medicine, the nature of those conflicts will be transformed in the course of their subjection to the exigencies of the common law – such as the search for legal precedent and the application of the rules of statutory interpretation as means of determining the lawfulness of proposed actions. Indeed, one might even anticipate the dissipation of the contested nature of such disputes as they are subsumed under the calming features of legal categories. Thus, rather than promoting, and contributing to, ethical debate, such a state of affairs would tend to suggest that the courts' involvement might have the opposite effect – diminishing the prospects of legal assistance in redressing the democratic deficit created by progress in the fields of medicine and the life sciences.

Furthermore, it is significant that Mathiesen refers to the '*apparently* neutral and unpolitical issue of whether legal authority or basis "exists"'. For, if it is the case that the effect of the courts' developing jurisdiction in this area is to depoliticize (or, perhaps more accurately in the current context, demoralize) conflict, then this effect, and the legal mechanisms by which it is produced, can, in themselves, be cast as contentious features that one might think ought to be subject to debate. Thus, even though it does not appear, nor is necessarily intended, as such, the conversion of conflicts into technical questions of legal authority and lawfulness may be described as controversial or political, but, perhaps somewhat paradoxically, because of law's ability to *de*politicize or *de*moralize the nature of the conflict that originally called the courts into play in the first place. In other words, rather than contributing to the solution of the types of problems identified by Beck and others, the involvement of the courts may threaten to exacerbate them.

All of this points to the need to address the manner in which the courts assert their jurisdiction in the field of medical law. To put it another way, it is imperative to focus on the question of judicial power in this area, the manner in which it is exercised, and, especially in light of the types of objectives and functions advocated for law by some academics, the nature of the consequences that flow from its operation.

Conclusion

No doubt many more reasons than the ones set out in this chapter could be offered for the emergence and steady expansion of the courts' involvement in the field of medical law in the UK. It is hoped, however, that the sociological and political contexts described here not only serve to illuminate some of the dynamics against which medical law operates, but also assist in identifying the types of issues, themes and areas of focus to be discussed in the remainder of the book. It is the themes of individual self-determination (including the 'right to choose') and responsibility that will be relevant in Part II, as consideration now turns to the relationship between medical law and the ethical principle that has largely been deployed to emphasize the importance of the patient – namely, autonomy.

PART II

Chapter 3

Autonomy:
Kant, Bioethics and Medical Ethics

Introduction

In Chapter 1 it was argued that some academic medical lawyers deploy two mechanisms through which they make their claim to legal jurisdiction over issues arising in medical practice. This part of the book is concerned with the first of these – that is, a focus on the position of patients and their need for empowerment. More specifically, the analysis will revolve around the main ethical value – autonomy – that is used to support this stress upon patients and to justify the argument that the law should recognize and uphold patients' rights.

One of the most striking ironies of the academic medical law field is that, while autonomy has featured prominently in academics' arguments, there has been very little sustained discussion of it in the literature.[1] The importance of autonomy in medical law has been accompanied by the unimportance of the need for detailed reflection upon its meaning. This is, no doubt, a result of what is taken to be the largely self-evident nature of autonomy within academic medical law. The very obviousness of its meaning has rendered detailed inquiry of it superfluous. This, in turn, is linked to the underlying objective of some academics – that is, to empower patients and diminish the power of doctors. In the pursuit of this goal, autonomy, like the language of patients' rights and self-determination, has become a rhetorical device.

Chapter 4 will address the relationship between autonomy and the courts in the area of medical law. The present chapter will concentrate on identifying, and discussing, some of the possible *conceptual* sources of the emphasis placed on autonomy in the academic medical law literature.[2] There are three reasons for

---

1 For a recent attempt to redress this state of affairs, see Brazier 2006. It should be noted that there has also been some analysis of autonomy in the feminist literature in the medical law field. References to this literature can be found in footnote 20 of Chapter 1. Whilst valuable, these analyses will not be considered further in this book. This is because the objectives here are to focus in some detail on the possible conceptual sources of a particular type of autonomy advanced in some of the more mainstream academic medical law literature and to note the role that certain institutional factors within the law play in determining how autonomy is taken up within the common law (something the feminist literature does not discuss).

2 It should be clear from the discussions in Chapters 1 and 2 that there are also other reasons behind the uptake of autonomy within the medical law field. On a different point, it should be noted that only one work from each of the areas of bioethics and medical ethics is discussed in this chapter. Obviously, this is not to suggest that these works constitute the

focusing on these conceptual foundations. The first – the dearth of such analyses – has already been mentioned. The second is to identify the manner in which, and the purposes for which, a particularly influential moral philosophy – that of Immanuel Kant – has been taken up in the academic medical law literature. Specifically, it will be argued that the use of his moral philosophy to justify the strong notion of individual autonomy advanced in the medical law field is unjustified. This is because Kant puts obligations, and not rights, at the heart not only of his moral philosophy, but, by implication, of his concept of autonomy too. Finally, and perhaps most importantly, the detailed analysis of the work of Kant, and others, undertaken in this chapter is intended to demonstrate the limitations inherent in conceptual arguments about ethical values. One such limitation is that those arguments do not necessarily assist in any attempt to understand how, and why, those values exist within different institutional settings. Translated into the current context, this means that the conceptual arguments about autonomy referred to here (and the general ethical theories of which they form a part), whilst useful, do not provide adequate tools by which to fully comprehend the relationship between autonomy and the common law in some prominent medical law cases. This is because those arguments and theories revolve solely around questions of ethics – that is, their purpose is to offer advice as to how to act ethically. But if, as the following chapter seeks to demonstrate, the question of how patient autonomy exists in legal cases involves other, non-ethical dimensions or concerns too, then theories offering merely ethical injunctions will fail to grasp fully the various contours of the relationship between autonomy and the common law in the medical law sphere. It should be stressed that this is by no means to dismiss the works discussed in this chapter as irrelevant to an understanding of autonomy in medical law. Indeed, it will be argued that the ethical arguments and theories set out here contain elements – such as the idea of autonomy as involving obligation and responsibility – which, as will become clear in the next chapter, assist in comprehending the relationship between autonomy and the common law. The point, then, is that while this 'ethical' literature contributes to the endeavour to acquire a fuller appreciation of the place of patient autonomy within the common law, it is also an insufficient means by which to do so.

The Moral Philosophy of Immanuel Kant

The framework of Kant's ethical theory[3]

It is worth stressing at the outset that, like all ethical theories, Kant's work is concerned with assessing what amounts to ethical action. His theory is dedicated to offering

---

entire ambit of reflection on the meaning of autonomy within those fields. Rather, the analysis concentrates on them because of the influence they have had within the medical law sphere.

3   Kant's work on ethics is mainly contained in his *Groundwork of the Metaphysics of Morals* and *Critique of Practical Reason*. See, respectively, Kant 1997 and Kant 1949. The more practical application of his theoretical ideas on ethics is contained in *The Metaphysics of Morals*. This includes writings on specific moral duties and practical questions of political morality. For a detailed discussion of *The Metaphysics of Morals*, see Gregor 1963. In this

criteria which, if complied with, will lead to individuals doing the 'right' thing. His *Groundwork of the Metaphysics of Morals* is the search for what he calls 'the supreme principle of morality' (4:392). He begins by speaking of 'common cognition' or the manner in which we ordinarily think of morality. If someone does the 'right' thing for the 'right' reason, this, according to Kant, demonstrates what he calls a 'good will'. This will is crucial as it represents a significant component in Kant's attempt to construct a theory of morality which can be justified objectively by the delineation of *a priori* principles. In order to assess whether an action is morally 'good', Kant says that we must look to the reason given, or the motive, for performing that action. In other words, what is the principle or, in Kant's phraseology, the 'maxim' according to which an individual acts? Having identified this, it becomes necessary to establish a method by which we can distinguish between the morality of different maxims, and this is where the objectivity of Kant's ethical theory becomes important. There are a number of points to be made here.

The concept at the root of Kant's ethics is that of practical reason, and it is this that ought to produce a good will: '[R]eason is given to us as a practical faculty ... reason's proper function must be to produce a good will in itself and not one good merely as a means ... This will must indeed not be the sole complete good but the highest good and the condition of all others ...' (Kant 1949, 58).

As reason is an objective entity, its applicability is not dependent on the satisfaction of individuals' preferences or passions. In other words, if an action is to be considered moral, it will be the extent to which it is in accordance with reason that will be crucial and not the fact that it represents the desires or inclinations of the individual concerned. It is also important to note the emphasis Kant places on the immanence of the good will as a measure of morality. This will is to be good 'in itself' and not dependent for its authority on either some higher, external standard of reason or the nature of an action's consequences. Having noted these points, the following question remains: How do we establish if a particular individual's maxim or principle or reason for acting accords with practical reason? Here, Kant introduces the importance of the concept of duty into his ethical theory.

Duty is intimately bound up with the maxims individuals choose to act upon, something which is evident from one of Kant's propositions of morality: 'An action done from duty does not have its moral worth in the purpose which is to be achieved through it but in the maxim by which it is determined' (Kant 1949, 61). This does not, however, seem to move things forward – it merely adds duty to the other objective concepts (reason and the good will) that are crucial from the point of view of assessing the morality of individuals' actions. In relation to duty, for example, the circularity of Kant's 'we should do our duty for no other reason than for duty's sake' is palpable.

---

section, reference will be made to both the *Groundwork* and the *Critique of Practical Reason* in order to construct an outline of Kant's ethical theory. In relation to the *Groundwork*, the analysis will draw on Korsgaard 1997. Throughout this section on Kant's moral philosophy, references in the form 4:123, for example, are to the German Academy's edition of Kant's works. Those references, which appear in Korsgaard 1997, are retained here.

What, however, does it mean to do one's duty, or to act in accordance with duty? In Korsgaard's reading of Kant, it means that individuals 'choose' to act on the basis of a particular maxim because they think that 'that is what [they are] required to do' (Korsgaard 1997, xiv). It is, therefore, obligation or imperative that lies at the heart of Kant's concept of duty. As such, the maxims on which we 'choose' to act take on what Kant describes as the 'form' of a law. He calls this law 'the practical law', and suggests that, if we feel compelled to do our duty, this demonstrates respect for that law:

> [A]s an act from duty wholly excludes the influence of inclination and therewith every object of the will, nothing remains which can determine the will objectively except the law and subjectively except pure respect for this practical law. This subjective element is the maxim that I should follow such a law even if it thwarts my inclinations. (Kant 1949, 61–2)

This idea of obligation or imperative results in Kant's overriding concept of the categorical imperative. There are several formulations of this, the most recognizable of which is the following: 'I should never act in such a way that I could not will that my maxim should be a universal law' (Kant 1949, 63). Korsgaard mentions that Kant equates the test of whether an individual can universalize his or her maxim to a 'thought experiment'. What needs to be asked is this: '[C]ould [you] will your maxim to be a law of nature in a world of which you yourself were going to be a part[?]' (Korsgaard 1997, xviii). It is important to stress, however, that, in order for an action to be moral, there is no choice to be made between or among competing maxims because, in Kant's words, 'the unconditional command leaves the will no freedom to choose the opposite' (Kant 1949, 79). And there is 'no freedom to choose the opposite' because the individual is subject to respect for the practical law and, hence, to respect for duty and reason. As Kant puts it: 'To duty every other motive must give place, because duty is the condition of a will good in itself, whose worth transcends everything' (Kant 1949, 64). The categorical imperative therefore tells us how to act morally.

How do Kant's discussions of 'respect for persons' and autonomy sit in relation to his first practical principle of the will, namely universality – the ability of individuals to will that their maxims be universal laws? His reflections on 'respect for persons' begin with the following statement: '[S]uppose there were something the *existence of which in itself* has an absolute worth, something which as *an end in itself* could be a ground of determinate laws; then in it, and in it alone, would lie the ground of a possible categorical imperative, that is, of a practical law' (4:428; emphasis in original). According to Kant, this absolute or intrinsic worth is something to be found only in human beings. Unlike something that has a price, for example, the intrinsic worth of human beings has no equivalent that can be substituted in value. As such, human beings are ends in themselves and we ought to respect both ourselves and others as rational beings who can make decisions about their own lives. There results from this a further formulation of the categorical imperative: 'Act so as to treat every rational being, whether in yourself or in another, never as a means only but also always as an end.'[4]

The crucial point to note about Kant's idea of 'respect for persons' is that it is integrally linked to the categorical imperative. Thus, while we ought to respect the decisions others make, those decisions must still rest on the basis of a maxim that is capable of universalization. In other words, individuals' actions will not necessarily be moral simply because we ought to respect those individuals as ends in themselves. As Kant says: 'The above three ways [universality, human beings as ends in themselves, and the autonomy of the will (which will be discussed next)] of representing the principle of morality are at bottom only so many formulae of the very same law, and any one of them unites the other two in it' (4:436).

Kant's concept of autonomy, then, is only important to the extent that it forms a further component in his search for the 'supreme principle of morality'. Thus, it can be viewed as the final stage (after universality and his argument that human beings are ends in themselves) in the triumvirate of practical principles of the will.

Kant comes to the conclusion that 'the will of every rational being [is] a will giving universal law' (4:431). Thus, the will is not merely subject to the law but, simultaneously, gives the law to itself. This is the 'autonomy of the will' – a concept that both constrains and frees the rational agent. As Douzinas and McVeigh have said: 'Kantian autonomy makes modern man the subject of the law in a double sense, he is the legislator (the subject that makes the law) and the legal subject (who obeys the law on condition that it has participated in its legislation)' (Douzinas and McVeigh 1992, 5). Autonomy, in Kant's view, is self-determination in the sense that rational beings determine the law for themselves. In other words, they impose a moral law on themselves, a law which must control their desires, passions and inclinations. However, he sees the essence of autonomy as residing in his first principle of morality: 'The principle of autonomy is ... to choose only in such a way that the maxims of your choice are also included as universal law in the same volition' (4:440). In that way, the autonomous will becomes synonymous with morality itself:

> *Morality* is ... the relation of actions to the autonomy of the will, that is, to a possible giving of universal law through its maxims. An action that can coexist with the autonomy of the will is *permitted*; one that does not accord with it is *forbidden*. A will whose maxims necessarily harmonize with the laws of autonomy is a *holy*, absolutely good will. (4:439; emphasis in original)

Kant's concept of autonomy is not intended to allow individuals to act in whatever manner they see fit. His reference to the exclusion of inclinations and desires from his theory of ethical action is evidence enough of this. Indeed, if individuals wish to act ethically, they must act in accordance with the 'autonomy of the will',

---

4　What is striking about this formulation is the word 'only'. It is often assumed that Kant's 'respect for persons' rests on the importance of ends to the exclusion of means. But it would seem from this formulation of the categorical imperative that humanity is capable of being used as a means to (at least) some types of ends. As nothing rests on this point in the current context, it shall not be pursued further.

or, what amounts to exactly the same thing, in accordance with the principle of universalization.

Autonomy in Kant's ethical theory is therefore bound up with obligation and imperatives – one must act in accordance with practical principles of the will. Autonomy of the will is equivalent to the ability to universalize one's maxims and, thus, to Kant's conception of morality *per se*. It can be said, then, that autonomy in Kant's ethical theory means self-determination or self-government through the observation of universal laws. Similarly, we ought to respect persons and the decisions they make provided that they satisfy the condition of universalizability. This point about universalizing maxims will be taken up again shortly.

Clarifying Kantian autonomy

In order to draw out the essence of Kant's concept of autonomy, it will be helpful to contextualize the foregoing discussion. To do this, reference will be made to Onora O'Neill's recent book, *Autonomy and Trust in Bioethics* (O'Neill 2002). O'Neill's work is particularly relevant here given its disillusionment with arguments that seek to advance a strong idea of individual autonomy on the back of Kant's ethical theory.

The main objective of O'Neill's book is to demonstrate how some conceptions of autonomy – namely Kant's – and trust are compatible and reconcilable. The precise manner in which she develops this argument is not relevant here. What is of interest, though, are the importance of the distinction she draws between what she calls 'individual' and 'principled' autonomy, and the significance of this in respect of her area of interest – ethical action. How are we to act ethically in the fields of medicine, science and biotechnology? This is the question to which O'Neill's reconciliation of certain concepts of autonomy and trust is geared to finding answers.

In her view, individual autonomy and individual rights have become the guiding ideas in bioethical and, specifically, medico-ethical discourse. She notes that autonomy, in this context, is posited as a feature of individuals in that it is taken to mean either independence from something or, at the least, a capacity for independent decisions and action. Thus, it relates either to some notion of what Isaiah Berlin called 'negative liberty' (see Berlin 1969, 118–72) or to ascertaining the degree to which an individual is capable of being independent – usually through assessing the state of his or her mind. O'Neill says that claims by bioethicists to found their notion of individual autonomy on the moral philosophy of Kant (amongst others) are misplaced. The reason for this is that Kant's concept of autonomy has nothing to do with persons, and as such, cannot be used as the basis for claims in bioethics to individual autonomy and individual rights.[5] Rather than creating an avenue for individuals to act freely on the basis of whatever reason or, to use Kant's term, maxim they wish, his concept of autonomy is about creating an ethical world constructed

---

5 O'Neill is slightly quick to make her point here. If respect for persons, autonomy and universability are internally related in Kant's ethics, then autonomy does have something to do with persons. Nonetheless, this is only relevant to the extent that it relates to Kant's overriding concern to identify ethical obligations and principles.

on the basis of obligations and principles derived from practical reason and the will. This is what O'Neill calls 'principled autonomy'. She argues that Kant never refers to the autonomous self, autonomous persons or autonomous individuals. Rather, and as already noted, he talks, for example, of the autonomy of the will. As O'Neill says: 'For Kant, autonomy ... is a matter of acting on certain sorts of principles, and specifically on principles of obligation' (O'Neill 2002, 83–4). The focus of his autonomy:

> was on a distinctive constraint or requirement, a test that shows which principles are universalis*able*, or *fit to be universal laws*. As Kant sees it, individuals can choose to act on principles that meet or that flout the constraints set by the principle of autonomy, but have reasons to act only on those principles that meet those constraints. (O'Neill 2002, 84; emphasis in original)

Thus, ethical action will be action in conformity with principles derived from the will, duty and practical reason.

What underpins Kantian autonomy is the fact that action, in order to be principled – that is, for its principles or maxims to be universalizable – must be based on coherent and non-contradictory reasoning. If I can will a principle that could be acted on by others, this principle must rest on such reasoning. Kant gives deception as an example of this. He asks us to imagine an individual who needs to borrow money. The individual knows that he or she will not be able to repay this but, nevertheless, gives a false promise to the contrary. Kant argues that such an action breaches the categorical imperative because it is impossible for the individual to will that his or her maxim (to make false promises) should become a universal law. In Kant's view, the reason for this stems from the fact that such a maxim cannot, without contradiction, be universalized because, if it were, we would begin to witness the decline of trust in societies and, eventually, the demise of promising itself.

Some reflections on 'principled autonomy' and Kant's ethical theory

The first point to note is that Kantian autonomy cannot justifiably be used as a basis for claims advocating the centrality of individual autonomy, where these encompass arguments in favour of rights to choose how to act for any, or no, reason at all. O'Neill's discussion of individual and principled autonomy demonstrates this comprehensively. And, given that Kant's 'respect for persons' and autonomy (of the will) are internally related – because they are components of his objective of creating a general ethical theory – then the former, also, cannot act as a justification for individual autonomy. Kant's ethical theory is concerned with assessing the degree to which individuals' actions and choices can be considered to be ethical; it is about obligations and not rights.

This realization has implications for the medical law field. In this field, Kant's thought usually finds expression in the presentation of the competing ethical stances of deontology and utilitarianism. While the latter is concerned with the consequences of proposed actions, Kant's moral philosophy teaches us that such actions will be right or wrong in themselves, whatever the consequences. More specifically, it is his imperative that we respect persons by treating them as ends in themselves and never merely as a means to others', or our own, ends that has been highlighted as especially important in the medical law literature. Ian Kennedy's discussion of the centrality of consent as an ethical doctrine in medical law is indicative of this: 'It [consent] flows from the Kantian imperative of respect for others, respect for each person as a person in his own right. One of the crucial consequences is that we should respect each person's autonomy, his power to reach his own decisions and to act on them. Consent is one aspect of respect for autonomy' (Kennedy 1984, 456). While this statement is unremarkable, others writing in this field have noted how Kant's moral philosophy has, in medical law, come to ground claims to the type of individual autonomy and individual rights that O'Neill rightly argues is alien to his philosophy (see, for example, Harrington 1996, 350–51, and Mason and Laurie 2006, 5). It is the atomistic, rights-bearing individual that has dominated both the academic medical law literature and, at least ideologically (as will be demonstrated in the following chapter), the courts over the last quarter century or so. In part, at least, it is argued that this is a consequence of the energy devoted by some academics to ensuring that the law is deployed as a means of transferring power from members of the medical profession to patients. The polarization of those two groups, which is inherent in such arguments, results in the patient being posited as an individual rights-holder, in conflict with the doctor, free from the shackles of any obligations, and having the power to choose as he or she wishes.[6]

It is only now, however, that the potential consequences of such an incarnation of the patient, and the skewed use of the principle of autonomy to support it, are dawning on academic medical lawyers (see, for example, Brazier 2006). This is largely due to the realization that this characterization of the patient, together with the language of patients' rights, choice and consumerism – so integral to the UK government's programme of privatizing public services – are incompatible with a National Health Service (hereinafter 'NHS') founded on social welfare, rather than market, principles.[7] Such a culture of choice and rights leads patients to expect that their demands for access to publicly funded health care will be met in full. But this assumption fails to take account of the demands of others who have equal, or more deserving, claims to treatment. This nascent culture of placing unlimited demands on the limited funds of a public health care system, the effects of which are beginning to appear in the courts too,[8] could not be further from Kant's concept of autonomy – a concept which stresses restraint, obligation and responsibility, rather than the satisfaction of unfettered choice and desire. It is this notion (and the teachings of his moral philosophy more generally), rather than the individual rights-holder type of patient that his ethical theory has been erroneously deployed to support in the

---

6   Not all reflections on the nature of the doctor–patient relationship proceed on this basis. For an alternative formulation – based on a fiduciary approach – see Harrington 1996.

7   For an excellent analysis, and critique, of the UK government's privatization of the NHS, see Pollock 2004.

8   A very useful discussion of this emerging aspect of medical law, and its implications for the nature of the subject, can be found in Montgomery 2006.

medical law field, that more closely reflects the original collective ethos upon which the NHS was built.

The second observation on principled autonomy regards the argument about principles and non-contradiction set out above. As his example of deception suggests, Kant's ethical theory was directed towards setting out some overarching principles and obligations within which the conduct of individuals had to fall if it was to be deemed to be ethical. But the test of coherence as the crucial gauge of what amounts to ethical principles and obligations would seem to require some pre-existing assumptions. Thus, if one considers the reasoning behind Kant's rejection of suicide as an ethical act – '[A] nature whose law it would be to destroy life itself by means of the same feeling whose destination is to impel toward the furtherance of life would contradict itself and would therefore not subsist as nature ...' (4:422) – it can be said that this is certainly coherent in its argument; it is indisputable that it logically follows. But, crucially, it assumes that man's destination is always 'toward the furtherance of life'. Indeed, that Kant finds it necessary to use suicide as an example is ample proof that this is not, in fact, the case. His response to this would seem to be to deny it outright – for the nature of human beings is just not that.[9] This confidence in his own ability to identify ethical principles and obligations is summed up well by Alasdair MacIntyre:

> Kant is not of course himself in any doubt as to *which* maxims are in fact the expression of the moral law; virtuous plain men and women did not have to wait for philosophy to tell them in what a good will consisted and Kant never doubted for a moment that the maxims which he had learnt from his own virtuous parents were those which had to be vindicated by a rational test. (MacIntyre 1985, 44; emphasis in original)

Given her reliance on Kant's concept of autonomy, it is possible to detect a similar sort of confidence in O'Neill's arguments. This can be seen, for example, in her rejection of arguments that seek to employ individual autonomy as a basis for gaining access to artificial reproductive techniques. Rather than making it a matter of rights, she contends that it must be thought of in terms of certain obligations and principles. There is no doubt in her mind what these should be: first, the initial decision to reproduce will be 'irresponsible' unless the child is to be born to people who 'can reasonably offer adequate and lasting care and support' (O'Neill 2002, 62); secondly, O'Neill sets out the categories of people who 'cannot reasonably intend or expect to be active and present throughout a childhood' (O'Neill 2002, 62). These include the chronically ill or addicted, the very young or very old and the incapable or uncommitted.

---

9   Hegel was the first to point out what he called the 'empty formalism' of Kant's ethical theory. He meant by this that there needed to be something more than the absence of contradiction for Kant's theory to hold sway. To take the earlier example of deception – Hegel would have argued that the demise of promising would not, in itself, be contradictory in so far as Kant's categorical imperative was concerned. Rather, it would only be contradicting the assumption that promising ought to exist. And, in order to establish that promising should exist, Kant would have required something more in his ethical theory. See Hegel 1942, § 135.

The reason for outlining this aspect of the work of Kant and O'Neill is to note a couple of the consequences of the confidence in their own ability to identify sound ethical standards and principles that ought to apply in different contexts. One implication of this is O'Neill's failure to see the need to explain what she means by such loaded adjectives as 'incapable' and 'uncommitted'. Similarly, while stressing that certain exceptions (such as 'habits of civility' and 'white lies') are permitted to the otherwise unethical practice of deception, what is notable is her lack of discussion of the meaning and boundaries of these – what are 'habits of civility' and just how many 'white lies' are to be permitted before our tolerance begins to wane? Given the importance she places on the *meaning* of autonomy, O'Neill's omissions may seem somewhat surprising. Nonetheless, this confidence results in a comfortable silence. The impression given is that there is no need to explain those terms because 'we' just know who the incapable and uncommitted are, and 'we' have a good idea of who falls within the chronically ill and the addicted. It would seem that the pursuit of ethical clarity demands that difficult questions regarding the meanings of certain assumptions are kept to a minimum.

Another consequence of this confidence is the failure to recognize that institutions, and their specific dynamics and requirements, may affect the manner in which autonomy operates in practice. For present purposes, the fundamental problem with O'Neill's reliance on principled autonomy is that it can offer no purchase on those institutional dimensions. This is because the objective of Kant's ethical theory is to outline the ways in which the conduct of rational agents can be assessed for its moral worth; it has nothing to say about the role of institutions. In the current context, the exclusive focus on ethics and ethical theory cannot fully grasp the relationship between autonomy and medical law as it has nothing to say about how autonomy exists within, and is affected by, the institutional practices of the common law.

Summary

One important observation that arises from the foregoing discussion of Kant's ethical theory and O'Neill's work is what might be described as the double-edged nature of Kantian autonomy. Thus, on the one hand, the fact that his autonomy is bound up with obligation and responsibility might be thought to be useful in the context of, for example, the NHS. In other words, before making demands on a publicly funded health care system, I ought to consider other patients who may have an equal, or more urgent, need to access its finite funds. On the other hand, this idea of principled autonomy subtly demands of individuals that they conform to certain standards of moral behaviour or conduct before their requests are granted. One might say that it imposes on them a responsibility to display the desired traits of the model moral citizen. This normalization and responsibilization of individuals is clear from O'Neill's discussion of who should, and should not, be permitted access to artificial reproductive techniques. You must, for example, be a 'capable' and 'committed' individual – terms whose precise meanings are not only capable of many interpretations, but are also determined solely by those in positions of authority. It is this cleavage inherent in the nature of Kantian autonomy – the fine line that exists between its usefulness in certain contexts and its ability, in others, to be deployed as a mechanism by which to measure the extent to which individuals conform to desired moral norms – rather than its unjustifiable use to ground claims to individual rights, that might, it is suggested here, be of more assistance in comprehending some aspects of the relationship between autonomy and the common law in the field of medical law. But while this feature of Kant's moral philosophy and O'Neill's work may help illuminate how autonomy exists within medical law, it should be stressed that their work generally cannot help to clarify the relationship between autonomy and the institutional dimensions within the common law because it is merely concerned with how individuals can act ethically.

The following section will consider another possible source of the central role that autonomy has come to play in medical law. This source is the work of two of the most fervent proponents of bioethics – Beauchamp and Childress. While bioethics concerns the moral aspects of the life sciences and health care, their discussion of autonomy is helpful here as it identifies some of the practices that have come to surround the operation of this notion within medical law.

Bioethics – Beauchamp and Childress

For many, Beauchamp and Childress's *Principles of Biomedical Ethics* has become the foundational text of contemporary bioethics (Beauchamp and Childress 2001). As Susan Wolf has commented: 'The four principles offered in the book have become the most familiar litany recited in bioethics: autonomy, beneficence, nonmaleficence, and justice' (Wolf 1994, 400). Wolf has, however, criticized bioethics generally for its reluctance, until recently, to acknowledge and confront issues of, *inter alia*, gender, race and ethnicity – factors which manifest themselves in the clinic. She suggests that one of the main reasons for this has been 'the field's early embrace of a liberal individualism largely inattentive to social context. This has not only made individual autonomy the pivotal value in bioethics, but has generally led to an overly simplistic vision of what autonomy and liberty entail' (Wolf 1994, 402). The following subsections will focus on what Beauchamp and Childress have to say about autonomy and its meaning, both generally and, more specifically, in the context of bioethics. The intention is not necessarily to test the validity of Wolf's critique (although there may be some incidental comment on this in what is said), but, rather, to outline the nature of Beauchamp and Childress's concept of autonomy and to locate it within the framework of their overall thesis. The latter aspect will be set out first and then the analysis will turn to their thoughts on autonomy.

General ethical framework

Beauchamp and Childress's starting point is what they call 'the common morality'. They define this as follows: 'The common morality contains moral norms that bind all persons in all places; no norms are more basic in the moral life ... The common morality ... comprises all and only those norms that all morally serious persons accept as authoritative' (Beauchamp and Childress 2001, 3). Examples of norms of the common morality, they say, would include: 'do not lie', 'do not steal property' and 'respect the rights of others'.

They go on to argue for the importance of principles to their thesis as these give expression to 'the general values underlying rules in the common morality' (Beauchamp and Childress 2001, 12). Specifically, they stress the centrality of the four principles mentioned by Wolf: autonomy, beneficence, nonmaleficence and justice. The choice of those principles is justified as follows:

> The four principles derive from considered judgments in the common morality and medical traditions both of which form our starting point in this volume ... Both the choice of principles and the context ascribed to the principles derive from our attempt to put the common morality and medical traditions into a coherent package. (Beauchamp and Childress 2001, 23)

Having identified the four principles, Beauchamp and Childress go on to stress their *prima facie* nature: that is, an obligation or principle ought to apply unless it conflicts with another that is its equal or outweighs it. *Prima facie* obligations, however, are to be distinguished from actual obligations. The latter relate to the action to be taken in specific circumstances. Where, for example, two obligations conflict, the individual with responsibility for deciding must choose which one should apply in the circumstances. In order to do this, he or she must weigh the competing obligations and come to a conclusion that demonstrates '"the greatest balance" of right over wrong' (Beauchamp and Childress 2001, 14). In the authors' view: '[J]ustified acts of balancing entail that good reasons be provided, not merely that an agent is intuitively satisfied' (Beauchamp and Childress 2001, 18). They try to reduce the incidence of intuitive judgments by delineating certain conditions that must be complied with when balancing, and choosing between, *prima facie* norms. One of these conditions stipulates that 'better reasons' must be given for acting on what is considered to be the dominant norm or obligation rather than on its competing counterpart. Finally, their acknowledgement that, sometimes, it will not be possible to identify an overriding norm or obligation should be noted. In such a situation, all they ask of the individual making the decision is that he or she 'make[s] judgments conscientiously in light of the relevant norms and the available and relevant evidence' (Beauchamp and Childress 2001, 22).

In addition to 'the common morality', Beauchamp and Childress outline their method or model of 'moral justification', something which requires only the briefest of mentions. They rely on John Rawls's work to advocate a method of 'reflective equilibrium' (see Rawls 1971). In their view, this notion allows for a coherence of moral beliefs and values because:

> Whenever some feature in a moral theory that we hold conflicts with one or more of our considered judgments [or firm moral beliefs], we must modify one or the other in order to achieve equilibrium ... The goal of reflective equilibrium is to match, prune, and adjust considered judgments in order to render them coherent with the premises of our most general moral commitments. (Beauchamp and Childress 2001, 398)

At the end of their book, Beauchamp and Childress bring together the ideas of 'common morality' and 'reflective equilibrium' (or what they call 'the coherence model of justification'). As a result, they claim that this allows them 'to rely on the authority of the principles in the common morality, while incorporating tools to refine and correct unclarities and to allow for additional specification of the principles' (Beauchamp and Childress 2001, 403).

Having outlined their broad ethical framework, Beauchamp and Childress's thoughts on autonomy, and its place within that framework, will now be discussed.

The principle of 'respect for autonomy'

At the beginning of their discussion of this principle, Beauchamp and Childress set out what they believe autonomy, in the broad sense of the word, means:

> Personal autonomy is, at a minimum, self-rule that is free from both controlling interference by others and from limitations, such as inadequate understanding, that prevent meaningful choice. The autonomous individual acts freely in accordance with a self-chosen plan, analogous to the way an independent government manages its territories and sets its policies. (Beauchamp and Childress 2001, 58)

They focus their attention on what they call 'autonomous choice'. Unlike inquiries into the 'autonomous person', which involve assessing individuals' 'capacities of self-governance' (that is, whether individuals are competent to, or capable of, 'adequate decision-making' or autonomous choosing – something which depends, for example, on their ability to understand information and provide reasons for their decisions), they argue that autonomous choice refers to the nature of people's actions when they make decisions. Beauchamp and Childress approach 'autonomous action' or 'autonomous decision making' (synonyms for 'autonomous choice') in terms of 'normal choosers who act: (1) intentionally, (2) with understanding, and (3) without controlling influences that determine their action' (Beauchamp and Childress 2001, 59). They go on to set out the elements that must exist before an individual's action can be deemed to be autonomous. What is required is:

> [A] substantial degree of understanding and freedom from constraint, not a full understanding or a complete absence of influence ... A person's appreciation of information and independence from controlling influence in the context of health care need not exceed, for example, a person's information and independence in making a financial investment, hiring a new employee, buying a house, or selecting a university. Such consequential decisions must be *substantially* autonomous, but not necessarily *fully* autonomous. (Beauchamp and Childress 2001, 59–60; emphasis in original)

The creation of the conditions of autonomous choice, and thus autonomous choice itself, is viewed by Beauchamp and Childress as an obligation on the part of doctors and other health care professionals. These groups are obliged to 'disclose information, to probe for and ensure understanding and voluntariness, and to foster adequate decision-making' (Beauchamp and Childress 2001, 64). It is only by undertaking these obligations that the right to autonomous choice can become a reality. On the other hand, doctors and health care professionals are under no obligation to respect the autonomy of those who lack the capacity for autonomous action, such as 'infants, irrationally suicidal individuals, and drug-dependent persons'.

A number of observations can be made in respect of Beauchamp and Childress's work. The first concerns the sustainability of their attempt to separate the ideas of the autonomous person and autonomous choice. The latter, which they say is so important, would seem to be intimately related to, and indeed dependent on, the existence of the former.[10] For example, the existence of autonomous choice is, at least in part, conditional upon ensuring that patients understand the information provided to them, which, in turn, is really a question about their ability to understand information – whether or not they have competence or, what is the same thing, are autonomous persons. This difficulty of distinguishing between autonomous choices and persons matters because it affects the nature of our understanding of Beauchamp and Childress's principle of respect for autonomy. Specifically, it directs us to the fact that doctors and health care professionals have important rights, as well as obligations, where this principle is concerned. Thus, in addition to the obligation, for example, to disclose information to patients, those groups have the right to determine the degree to which patients have understood that information. If they fail to display a substantial degree of understanding they will be deemed incapable of acting autonomously and, presumably, have failed to exhibit the understanding necessary to be treated as an autonomous person (as the latter depends on acting with understanding). Those groups have the right to determine who is, and is not, a 'normal chooser' for the purposes of ascertaining whether or not a patient is an autonomous person; similarly, and to take their own example, they have the right to decide whether or not individuals seeking to end their own lives are rationally or irrationally suicidal. The right to categorize patients in this way matters as it is, at least in part, upon such categorizations that the existence of Beauchamp and Childress's principle of respect for autonomy depends.

The flip side of such rights is that, before the principle of respect for autonomy can come into play, patients have obligations to meet the standards of understanding, normality and rationality (to take the foregoing examples) that doctors and health care professionals stipulate are necessary for the purposes of being an autonomous person and demonstrating autonomous action. Moreover, they have such obligations despite the fact that those standards may not necessarily be defined in advance. Who, they might legitimately inquire, are these 'normal choosers'? What does it take to be a rationally suicidal individual? Presenting the principle of respect for autonomy as intimately bound up with patients' rights (Beauchamp and Childress say that 'Autonomous choice is a *right*, not a *duty* of patients' [Beauchamp and Childress 2001, 63; emphasis in original]) conceals the role that patients' obligations play in determining whether or not that principle is relevant.

---

10 Beauchamp and Childress themselves appear to acknowledge the difficulty of any attempt strictly to separate the two: 'Competence in decision-making is closely connected to autonomous decision-making, as well as to the validity of consent' (Beauchamp and Childress 2001, 69).

The second observation is that while the meaning of autonomy in Beauchamp and Childress's work differs from that to be found in Kant's moral philosophy, the two are nevertheless similar in one important respect. Unlike Kant's approach to autonomy, Beauchamp and Childress's understanding of this notion does not rest on an assessment of the ethical quality of individuals' actions or choices. Thus, in order for individuals to act autonomously, it is not necessary for them to act morally. How individuals act, or the reasons why they choose to act, are, from a moral point of view, irrelevant, provided they act autonomously – that is, with sufficient understanding and freedom from outside control. While, in the current edition of their book, this point is implicit in Beauchamp and Childress's argument, it can be seen clearly in a previous one:

> It ... does not follow from the fact of an action's being autonomous that it is morally acceptable or morally principled. One can reject morality or act against morality and still act autonomously. Autonomy is compatible on the one hand with immorality and on the other hand with moral authority and tradition. (Beauchamp and Childress 1989, 71)

Ostensibly, then, autonomy is divorced from questions of morality here.[11] Rather, and as has already been seen, the existence of autonomy depends on compliance with what might be called technical, non-ethical tests, such as tests for mental competence and those setting out standards of information disclosure to patients. Assuming these tests are met, autonomous choice will exist, and patients will, subject of course to the other competing ethical principles, be allowed to proceed as they wish. On the one hand, by allowing for patients' desires and passions to be satisfied whatever these are and irrespective of the consequences, this position directly contradicts Kant's moral philosophy. On the other hand, though, it has just been seen how these technical tests can be interpreted as creating obligations on patients, obligations that are bound up with meeting standards – of normality, rationality and understanding – whose determination cannot easily be divorced from questions of morality. Thus, despite the difference between Kantian autonomy and Beauchamp and Childress's autonomous choice – a difference O'Neill would describe as one between, respectively, 'principled' and 'individual' autonomy – both versions appear to open up the possibility of assessing the degree to which individuals conform to certain (though often unspecified) standards of moral behaviour or conduct or character. It should be noted that this possibility, and the influence it may have on determining the relevance of the principle of respect for autonomy in any particular case, is not obvious from Beauchamp and Childress's work, mainly because the process of arriving at a decision regarding autonomous choice is held out to be objective, neutral and 'doctor' or 'health care professional' focused.

The final observation revolves around the question of professional authority. At root, Beauchamp and Childress's book can be interpreted as a charter or template which professionals (that is, doctors, other health care professionals and medical researchers) can use to negotiate the ethical issues and dilemmas which confront them in the course of their work. It is a text that is intended to tell them how to act

---

11 Of course, the overarching principle – that of respect for autonomy – is held out by Beauchamp and Childress as being an ethical one.

ethically – how, for example, they should weigh competing ethical principles in the balance and arrive at justifiable decisions. It places obligations on those professionals to do their best, for example, to create the necessary conditions for the existence of autonomous choice. But by doing all this, their book is an exercise in the creation of an enormous degree of power and its placement in the hands of one professional sector or body. One example of this has already been noted – that is, how the existence of the principle of respect for autonomy is, at least partially, dependent on various professional assessments of patients. But this authority also exists at the broader level of resolving conflicts between competing ethical principles. Thus, it will be recalled that the professional with responsibility for making such decisions must justify his or her resolution by providing 'good reasons', rather than proceeding on the basis of intuition. What reasons would suffice? If the identification of an overriding principle is impossible, the judgment must simply be made 'conscientiously'. What does this mean and entail? All this is not meant to be a criticism of the professionals themselves. Rather, the intention is to highlight how Beauchamp and Childress's focus on the principle of respect for autonomy, and the obligations of health care professionals generally, while seeking to improve the position of patients, also has the effect of embedding the power of those professionals.

The final section of this chapter will contrast Beauchamp and Childress's approach to autonomy with that which can be derived from the work of two medical ethicists, John Keown and Luke Gormally. It will be argued that the meaning of patient autonomy is implicitly developed in the latter's work in a manner which owes more to Kant than to the work of Beauchamp and Childress.

Medical Ethics – Keown and Gormally

Keown and Gormally's argument

Keown and Gormally criticize the Consultation Paper *Who Decides?* (hereinafter 'the Paper'), published in December 1997 by the Lord Chancellor's Department (Keown and Gormally 1999; Lord Chancellor's Department 1997).[12] The Paper's subject matter is the proposed legislation by the Law Commission covering decision-making on behalf of adults who are assessed as being 'mentally incapacitated'.[13] Focusing on the provisions in the Paper relating to health care, they argue that: '[T]he legislative proposals underrate the value of human life, overrate the value of individual autonomy, and undermine the respect due to all the mentally incapacitated

---

12 It should be noted that the journal Keown and Gormally's article appears in does not use page numbers. Consequently, the references provided are simply to page numbers in the downloaded document.

13 This legislation has, after a long period of consultation, now been passed in the form of the Mental Capacity Act 2005. At the time of writing, this statute is not yet in force. 'Mental incapacity' or 'mental incompetence' are interchangeable terms that have arisen in the fields of bioethics, medical ethics and medical law to describe individuals who have been assessed as being unable to consent to, or refuse, medical treatment that it is believed will benefit them.

in virtue of their fundamental equality-in-dignity' (Keown and Gormally 1999, 1). For them, there is a characteristic of human beings which is universal and ought to be the starting point for any discussion about the treatment of mentally incapacitated patients:

> It is necessary to begin with the recognition that every human being, however immature or mentally impaired, possesses a fundamental worth and dignity which are not lost as long as he or she is alive. Contrary to the view of some, human worth and dignity do not depend on acquiring and retaining some particular level of intellectual ability or capacity for choice or for communication. (Keown and Gormally 1999, 4–5)

Accordingly, Keown and Gormally argue that the only true objective criterion by which to decide the appropriateness of medical treatment for mentally incapacitated patients is by reference to the 'fundamental worth and dignity' that attaches to every individual by virtue of his or her being human.

While they do not set out a specific concept of autonomy, it is possible to identify the relationship they envisage between autonomy and their central idea of fundamental worth and dignity. An example of this can be seen in their discussion of advance directives. They argue that:

> [Another] way in which the error of denying worth to certain human lives is exhibited is in the judgement that the value of a life depends wholly on the value a person gives to his or her life through their choices, and that the loss of the capacity to choose means that the only value in continued existence depends on the value they had chosen to attach to it when competent. (Keown and Gormally 1999, 5)

In their view, the 'fundamental source of worth and value in a person's life' is not autonomy because people have 'an ineradicable value prior and subsequent to the possibility of exercising autonomy'. Thus, the choices individuals make regarding how they wish, or do not wish, to be treated do not necessarily demand our moral respect. To do so, such choices must conform to certain objective criteria, the most basic of which is 'the fundamental dignity both of the chooser and of others'. One of Keown and Gormally's main criticisms of the Paper relates to what they see as the acceptance of advance directives that would breach this fundamental dignity by allowing individuals to refuse medical treatment in a specific set of future circumstances where they believe their lives would no longer have value.

It is clear from their reference to the course of action doctors ought to take where patients 'persistently and suicidally [refuse] life-preserving treatment or care' that Keown and Gormally also intend their argument to apply to those patients who have been assessed as possessing the mental capacity to make decisions. In such a situation, the doctor would 'satisfy the prohibition of assisting suicide by, for example, discharging from their care [such] competent patients'. They do, however, acknowledge that there are circumstances in which the exercise of patient autonomy can be upheld because it does not offend the fundamental worth and dignity of human beings:

> It can be reasonable [to refuse life-prolonging treatment] on the grounds that it offers too little benefit for the burdens it involves, or because, whatever the benefits, the attendant

burdens, either of physical pain, or psychological stress, or social dislocation, or economic hardship make the treatment intolerable. (Keown and Gormally 1999, 7)

Thus, if refusals of life-prolonging treatment are based upon such exceptions and couched in the appropriate language – the language of benefits and burdens, and of intolerability – they are capable of attaining validity and, as a result, will not offend the fundamental worth and dignity that Keown and Gormally argue constitute the essential (moral) nature of human beings. It is only where such refusals are grounded in a patient's belief that his or her life is no longer worth living because it is devoid of value that their choice will be incompatible with fundamental worth and dignity and, hence, should fail to be respected.

Given the importance of the notion of fundamental worth and dignity to their argument and, specifically, to the manner in which it sets the limits of the validity of autonomy in circumstances where the existence of human life is at stake, it will be useful to delve slightly deeper into what they mean by the former notion. Specifically, it is necessary, in the first instance, to ask the following question: Exactly where, or in what, does this notion reside? While the authors do not provide a clear answer to this question, it is possible to acquire some understanding of what they may mean by consulting an earlier article written by John Keown, in which he critically discusses the judgments of the various courts involved in the case of *Airedale NHS Trust v. Bland* (1993) (Keown 1997).

What Keown, in this earlier article, calls 'intrinsic dignity', is closely bound up with the Judaeo-Christian tradition's principle of the sanctity of life:

> That tradition's doctrine of the sanctity of life holds that human life is created in the image of God and is, therefore, possessed of an intrinsic dignity which entitles it to protection from unjust attack. With or without that theological underpinning, the doctrine grounds the principle that one ought never intentionally to kill an innocent human being. (Keown 1997, 482–3; reference omitted)

He goes on to argue that the inherent nature of dignity arises as a result of the 'radical capacities, such as for understanding and rational choice, inherent in human nature … All human beings possess the capacities inherent in their nature even though, because of infancy, disability or senility, they may not yet, not now, or no longer have the ability to exercise them' (Keown 1997, 483; reference omitted). This idea of intrinsic dignity is maintained in the work of Keown and Gormally, something that can be seen from their discussion of the foundation of human rights: '[H]uman rights are enjoyed in virtue of our common humanity, not the possession of some arbitrarily stipulated human ability at some arbitrarily stipulated level' (Keown and Gormally 1999, 5). It therefore seems to be our 'common humanity', including the capacities for understanding and rational choice (even though these may be incapable of being exercised), that give rise to respect for this intrinsic or fundamental worth and dignity in their work. Autonomy, they reiterate, plays a subservient role to those wider, more fundamental principles, and '[its] invocation … should not be allowed to trump more basic considerations' (Keown and Gormally 1999, 7).

Before reflecting on their argument, it will be useful to outline very briefly the method by which Keown and Gormally translate the nature of their broad thesis into the world of medicine and patients. In other words: How does the notion of fundamental worth and dignity manifest itself in medical discourse? In their view, this occurs through the application of the 'best interests' test:

> In the area of healthcare, the concept of 'best interests' should be understood to include the standard objectives of healthcare practice: the restoration and maintenance of health, or of whatever degree of well-functioning can be achieved; the prolongation of life; and the control of symptoms when cure cannot be achieved. (Keown and Gormally 1999, 7–8)

In order to arrive at this definition, they adopt Lord Brandon's formulation of the 'best interests' test set out in *Re F (mental patient: sterilisation)* (1990) which equates 'best interests' with the preservation of life or an enhancement, or prevention of deterioration, in a patient's physical or mental health.[14] If, for the moment, one puts aside the reasons Keown and Gormally offer for legitimately withholding or withdrawing life-prolonging medical treatment, it is clear that the sole focus of their 'best interests' test is health. 'Health', of course, is an imprecise and contested concept. Nevertheless, from their definition, they equate health with physical improvement and the extension not of any particular type or form of life (or, more accurately, lifestyle), but of biological or somatic existence *per se*. This conception of the 'best interests' test is further emphasized by their refusal to accept as legitimate, reasons that go to an individual's conclusion on the usefulness of medical treatment for the quality of his or her life (in the sense of that life being worthwhile or not). Rather, reasons must solely be couched in the language of the benefits and burdens of the proposed medical treatment itself. In their view, the extent to which autonomy is to be viewed as a good in the medical context is dependent on its equation with this idea of best interests. As they say: 'The value of individual autonomy lies in serving the best interests of the individual, not *vice-versa*' (Keown and Gormally 1999, 7).

Reflections on Keown and Gormally's argument

One of the striking features of Keown and Gormally's argument is its close similarity to two aspects of Kant's moral philosophy. Firstly, there is the identification of some indelible value at the core of human nature. Their notion of fundamental worth and dignity is comparable to Kant's intrinsic worth that is to be found embedded in human beings. Secondly, there is the close relationship between those notions of fundamental value and autonomy. For both, autonomy does not equate to the satisfaction of individuals' desires and passions. Rather, it is intimately bound up with questions of morality and obligation. Thus, before individuals' choices or actions can be deemed to be ethical, there is an onus upon them to ensure that their decisions are in accordance with certain *a priori* fundamental notions and values. For Keown and Gormally, then, the meaning of autonomy is, as in Kant's theory, intimately

---

14 It should be noted that the 'best interests' test has undergone significant development in recent years. For a discussion of this, see, for example, Mason and Laurie 2006, 363–8. This development includes the creation of a statutory checklist of factors to be taken into account when determining what is in a mentally incapacitated patient's best interests. See the Mental Capacity Act 2005, Part I.

associated with, and dependent upon, a specific vision of morality – one tied to what they believe are the immanent characteristics of human beings. Autonomy involves action which respects the moral principle of the worth and dignity of human life, a principle determined not by individuals, but by some objective, perhaps religious, entity. As it is not bound up with the capacity to make, and the conditions necessary for, autonomous choices (which may include immoral decisions), it is therefore dissimilar to Beauchamp and Childress's understanding of autonomy.

Of course, an important consequence of the similarity of Keown and Gormally's argument to Kant's ethical theory is that it is susceptible to the same type of critique undertaken in relation to Kant's work earlier in this chapter. In particular, one can detect a similar confidence in identifying the moral principle (fundamental worth and dignity) that forms the central point around which decisions regarding the commencement and withdrawal of medical treatment must be justified, and the types of acceptable conduct or reasoning (the burdens they speak of) that may be given for refusing life-sustaining medical treatment (that is, that would not flout their foundational moral principle). It is worth discussing this point briefly.

It has already been seen how Keown and Gormally's fundamental *a priori* moral principle (fundamental worth and dignity) is accompanied by various assumptions. One such assumption is that the principle prevents individuals refusing life-sustaining medical treatment on the basis that they believe their lives are no longer worth living. But why should this necessarily follow? Simply because Keown and Gormally choose to base their medical ethics on the sanctity of life doctrine and to interpret 'fundamental worth and dignity' in a certain way? Two points might be made here. Firstly, it would seem that the justification – 'my life is no longer worth living' – for refusing the offer of life-sustaining medical treatment would be a perfectly understandable one in the circumstance where, say, a patient is suffering from a chronic illness that has become life-threatening. Why should patients in such a circumstance need to invent what in their eyes are artificial reasons for their refusals before these can be deemed to be legitimate? Is one of the dangers of requiring patients to couch their justifications for refusal in Keown and Gormally's preferred language and reasoning not that it may fail to reflect the reality of why some patients refuse life-sustaining medical treatment? Secondly, why should the fact that 'every human being … possesses a fundamental worth and dignity' mean that that 'worth' and 'dignity' be interpreted as preventing patients from refusing such treatment on the basis that their lives are no longer worth living? Could it not be argued that dignity, for instance, might be served by allowing such a refusal – a refusal based on that particular reason? In other words, there is a question here about the interpretation of different notions or concepts, and who possesses this interpretative power. Why, as a patient refusing life-prolonging treatment because, on the basis of dignity, I no longer think my life is valuable, should my understanding of what dignity demands be any less meaningful than that of Keown and Gormally?

Another important assumption is that only the types of reasons they suggest for refusing life-sustaining medical treatment (and the language in which these are couched) should be considered as being of sufficient weight to comply with their principle of fundamental worth and dignity.[15] Should the refusal not be in the form of a 'burden' which renders the treatment 'intolerable', it will offend that principle and, consequently, should fail to be respected. Moreover, in order to be effective, those burdens, which include physical pain, psychological stress, social dislocation and economic hardship, must be associated with the medical treatment. In other words, Keown and Gormally stipulate that the refusal of life-sustaining medical treatment cannot be justified by reference to the burdens of life more generally. But, again, it would seem artificial to try strictly to divorce the burdens of medical treatment from those of life generally. Indeed, their examples of economic hardship and social dislocation would seem to point to the fact that patients' judgments about the quality of their lives (including whether they are worth living after surgery), as much as those concerning the physical pain accompanying operations, for example, can determine whether or not they accept medical treatment. The question of medical treatment does not necessarily create such burdens; it may, rather, simply have the effect of bringing to the surface pre-existing anxieties and difficulties (themselves the result, for example, of one's social, financial or emotional position) that, while dormant, affect the daily quality of life of the individual concerned.

Finally, and still related to this question of the acceptable reasons for refusing life-prolonging medical treatment, Keown and Gormally's work fails to shed any light on who will decide what types of burdens are legitimate for the purpose of refusing such treatment. In other words, there is no discussion of who will decide which reasons (or burdens) are good enough to render autonomy compatible with their moral principle of fundamental worth and dignity. How might their desired framework operate in practice? What institutional features might have a bearing on how it functions? What about questions of power? Once again, one encounters the obstacles inherent in ethical frameworks or theories which prevent a fuller understanding of autonomy. The concern with right and wrong, and with identifying foundational moral principles, that drives Keown and Gormally's work is of limited use to any attempt to grasp how autonomy exists within specific institutional settings or social practices. Nonetheless, and like the reflections of the other authors discussed in this chapter, their work offers some important insights into autonomy. These insights will form part of the concluding reflections on this chapter.

Conclusion

What emerges from the discussion of autonomy in this chapter? One observation that can be made is that it is clear that autonomy does not necessarily mean that individuals can act in whatever manner they wish. It is not, therefore, automatically equivalent to a naked 'right to choose'. Rather, in each of the cases analysed its meaning is inextricably linked to a broader view of what constitutes morality. Whether it is Kant's 'categorical imperative', Beauchamp and Childress's 'common morality', or Keown and Gormally's 'fundamental worth and dignity', it is imperative

---

15 For critical commentary on this aspect of Keown's argument (and his work generally), see Price 2001. Price's article was, in part, a response to Keown's arguments in Keown 2000. Keown has recently responded to Price's critique in Keown 2006.

to understand their respective ideas of autonomy as inseparable from, indeed largely dependent on, their distinctive visions of the overarching structure of morality or the good. It is the goals of their ethical theories that tend to dictate their understandings of the nature of autonomy. Two important insights can be derived from this realization – both of which will assist in understanding the relationship between autonomy and the common law in the medical law sphere. The first is that the meaning of the ethical value of autonomy varies in tandem with the circumstances within which, and the purposes for which, it is deployed. In other words, the context of autonomy must be taken seriously if we are to understand it properly. This type of methodology will be utilized in the following chapter. The second insight is that, perhaps counter-intuitively (at least in the medical law field), autonomy can impose obligations on individuals (or patients), as well as affording them rights. Indeed, it can make the presence of a 'right to choose' or a 'right to self-determination', for example, dependent upon the need to demonstrate that one has satisfied various obligations. This can be seen, for instance, in relation to Keown and Gormally's work. The link between autonomy and obligation that has arisen from the analysis in this chapter is, as we shall see in the following one, crucial to an understanding of how autonomy exists within the common law.

There are, however, limits to the usefulness of the arguments about autonomy discussed in this chapter for a fuller appreciation of the role of autonomy in medical law. So, for example, while those theories valuably direct one to the general importance of context in trying to understand autonomy, they fail to enlighten with regard to how different institutional practices and requirements affect how autonomy operates and is understood in concrete circumstances. More specifically, the question of power – such as the power to define the meanings inherent in their notions of autonomy (who, for example, is O'Neill's 'incapable' or 'uncommitted' adult) and the power relations between different professions and professionals – is not something those theories can offer any purchase on. This is not meant to be a criticism of those authors for failing to rectify identifiable lacunae in their theories. Rather, one of the objectives of this chapter has simply been to note the explanatory limitations of ethics and ethical theory for an appreciation of how autonomy 'lives' within medical law. It is with the benefits and limitations of the works discussed in this chapter in mind that the focus now turns to an analysis of the relationship between autonomy and the courts in the area of medical law.

Medical Law and Conceptions of Autonomy

Introduction

The overarching objective of this chapter is to analyse the relationship between autonomy and the common law in the medical law sphere.[1] The argument advanced is essentially twofold. First, it is suggested that rather than the presence of a single idea of autonomy within the common law in this area, there exist, in fact, two conceptions – usefully described, adopting Onora O'Neill's terminology, as 'individual' and 'principled' autonomy (O'Neill 2002). The assumption that only one concept of autonomy, namely the individual type, is present in medical law owes much to the focus on patients' rights within this field. However, a close analysis of the cases demonstrates the existence of principled autonomy too – that is, a notion of autonomy inextricably bound up with ideas of obligation and responsibility. Given this, it will be argued that aspects of the various ethical theories discussed in the previous chapter are relevant to an understanding of how autonomy operates in medical law cases.

The second component of the argument is that it is impossible to understand fully why the individual and principled varieties of autonomy exist within the common law without also taking account of the role of some of the institutional or structural features of the law. In other words, in order to comprehend why different conceptions of autonomy exist within the common law in this sphere, we need to complement our knowledge of the work of moral philosophers and ethicists with an appreciation of some of the non-ethical factors that drive the manner in which the courts exercise their jurisdiction in medical law cases. Moreover, it is possible to note how the types of autonomy to be found in the courts in this area reflect the notions of choice and responsibility identified in Chapter 2 as being central themes of contemporary transformations in the social and political constitution of Western societies.

As well as shedding light on the relationship between autonomy and the common law in this area, the focus on non-ethical factors as a means of understanding how an ethical value exists within the common law is also intended to illustrate the potential explanatory power of an alternative methodological approach to the

---

1   It should be noted that this analysis focuses predominantly on a specific area of medical law, namely those cases where patients refuse to consent to medical treatment that is necessary to keep them alive. Hereinafter, those cases will be referred to as 'refusal cases'. Additionally, however, reference will be made to cases involving questions about the disclosure to patients of risks inherent in medical procedures.

study of medical law – that is, one which takes account of the role, and impact, of institutional or structural aspects of the law. This approach will also be deployed in Part III of the book.

Autonomy, Mental Capacity and Medical Law

Autonomy and rights in medical law

Autonomy in medical law has traditionally been bound up with controlling access to one's body, and what can be done to it. Mason and Laurie, for instance, have noted that:

> [T]he central position in medical law of the principle of respect for the patient's autonomy determines that the individual patient has the ultimate right to control his or her body and what is done with or to it. Primarily, that control is exercised through the concept of consent to, and its correlate, refusal of, treatment. (Mason and Laurie 2006, 511)

Thus, autonomy here is linked to bodily integrity and the opportunity for individuals to decide when it is appropriate to allow health care professionals to have access to their bodies. It is as a representation of the ethical value underlying consent to, and refusal of, medical treatment that autonomy initially emerged in medical law. Probably the most famous statement regarding the importance of consent in medical law is the following by Cardozo J: 'Every human being of adult years and sound mind has a right to determine what shall be done with his own body; and a surgeon who performs an operation without his patient's consent commits an assault, for which he is liable in damages' (*Schloendorff v. Society of New York Hospital* 1914, 126). As well as being an enunciation of patient sovereignty, what is interesting about this statement is its reference to 'a right to determine'. Very early on in medical law, we detect a close relationship between consent (and refusal), autonomy and rights. As well as being described as a right of the patient,[2] autonomy has tended to be interchangeable in medical law with the right to self-determination. This merging of autonomy and rights can be seen in a number of judicial opinions, only two examples of which need briefly be referred to here.

The first illustration can be found in Lord Scarman's opinion in *Sidaway v. Board of Governors of the Bethlem Royal Hospital and the Maudsley Hospital and Others* (1985) (hereinafter '*Sidaway*').[3] The case concerned a woman – Mrs Sidaway – who had undergone an operation to relieve persistent pain in her neck, right shoulder and arms. The operation, even if performed properly, carried two inherent risks – the first being of damage to the spinal column; the second of damage

---

2   See, for example, Lord Steyn in *Chester v. Afshar* (2004, 596): 'Her right of autonomy and dignity can and ought to be vindicated by a narrow and modest departure from traditional causation principles.'

3   It should be noted that, prior to Lord Scarman's opinion, there had already been statements in the common law about the importance of protecting the personal liberty of those of full age and capacity. See, for example, the judgment of Lord Reid in *S v. S, W v. Official Solicitor (or W)* (1972).

to the nerve roots. When she became severely disabled as a result of the operation, Mrs Sidaway sued in negligence, alleging that the surgeon had failed to disclose to her the aforementioned risks.

Unlike the other law lords hearing the plaintiff's appeal, Lord Scarman thought that, in order to establish whether there had been a breach of the surgeon's duty of care to his patient, one could not simply refer to 'the current state of responsible and competent professional opinion and practice at the time' (*Sidaway* 1985, 483). Rather, what was of crucial importance was 'the court's view as to whether the doctor in advising his patient, gave the consideration which the law requires him to give to the right of the patient to make up her own mind in the light of the relevant information whether or not she will accept the treatment which he proposes' (*Sidaway* 1985, 483). This 'right', which Lord Scarman also described as the 'right of self-determination', was 'a basic human right protected by the common law'.[4] In his view, its existence derived from the fact that the ambit of the doctor's duty of care was such that any non-medical concerns the patient may have fell within it. In other words, the doctor must acknowledge, and take account of, the fact that there may be '[non-medical] circumstances, objectives, and values' that affect the decisions individuals make about medical treatment. He concluded that there ought to be 'a legal duty [for a doctor] to warn a patient of the [material] risks inherent in the treatment proposed' (*Sidaway* 1985, 491).

The second example can be found in the following statement by Lord Donaldson in *Re T (Adult: Refusal of Medical Treatment)* (1992) (hereinafter '*Re T*'):

> The patient's interest consists of his right to self-determination – his right to live his own life how he wishes, even if it will damage his health or lead to his premature death. Society's interest is in upholding the concept that all human life is sacred and that it should be preserved if at all possible. It is well established that in the ultimate the right of the individual is paramount. (*Re T* 1992, 661)

What we see here, and in Lord Scarman's opinion, is a reiteration of some of the familiar aspects of what is commonly understood by autonomy – self-determination; living one's own life in accordance with one's values – but in the form of rights. In other words, it is a *right* to self-determination; a *right* to live your own life as you see fit; a *right* to, or of, autonomy. One important consequence of this linking of autonomy with rights is that autonomy has, to a large degree, become synonymous in medical law with the generic idea of patients' rights itself, such that the term 'patient autonomy' is often just another way of referring to 'patients' rights'. This, however, is not only relevant at the level of the enunciation, and protection, of specific rights – such as the right to consent to, or refuse, medical treatment. Rather, given the ideological role of the discourse of 'patients' rights' within medical law – in that, as we saw in Chapter 1, it functions as a tool by which to stress the importance of

---

4   This was no throwaway comment by Lord Scarman. In the course of his Hamlyn lectures ten years earlier, he had argued for a change in the common law through the adoption of a Bill of Rights. See Scarman 1974 and the subsequent symposium on his lectures – arranged by the Centre for Studies in Social Policy – in Scarman 1975. He developed this theme further in the seventh Lord Fletcher Lecture in 1985, arguing for the incorporation of the provisions of the European Convention on Human Rights into British law – see Scarman 1987.

both the position of the patient and the correlative need to curb what is perceived as excessive medical power – the association of autonomy with rights means that autonomy, too, comes, in part, to perform such a task. In particular, it is argued that autonomy can be seen to have been deployed by the courts as a means of meeting specific structural requirements within the common law. A recent example will illustrate this point.

In *Chester v. Afshar* (2004) the House of Lords was concerned with a case which, on its facts, was very similar to *Sidaway* (1985). Miss Chester had undergone an operation to relieve severe back pain and, while she had consented to the operation, she had not been informed by Mr Afshar – the consultant neurosurgeon who performed the operation – of the 1–2 percent risk of nerve damage inherent in the operation. This risk materialized, leaving Miss Chester partially paralysed. She subsequently sued Mr Afshar, claiming that, as his negligence had caused her injury, she was entitled to recover damages. Finding for Miss Chester, the majority of the law lords (Lords Bingham and Hoffmann dissenting) ruled that, in order to vindicate the right (the right of the patient to make an informed choice as to whether to be operated on) underlying the legal duty of a doctor to warn his or her patient about risks of injury inherent in operations in the particular circumstances of this case, the normal legal principles of causation had to be modified on policy grounds. The law lords' discussion of the causation principles is not relevant here. What is interesting, though, is the emphasis placed in the law lords' opinions on the rights and autonomy of patients. Of course, as one would expect, the references to these are largely related to the context of the case – what Lord Steyn calls the issue of 'informed consent'. Nonetheless, in some of the opinions one can detect the use of rights and autonomy in the service of broader – structural – objectives, including the need to demonstrate that the courts have, and are, responding both to transformations in the wider world and to the contemporary expectations of the public; and the concern to make it clear to members of the medical profession that the excessive judicial deference traditionally shown to them, and their standards of practice, has been consigned to the historical dustbin (in this regard, see The Right Honourable The Lord Woolf 2001). Thus, quoting some of Ronald Dworkin's work on autonomy (Dworkin 1994), Lord Steyn, for example, stresses the importance of informed consent, and the fact that: 'In modern law medical paternalism no longer rules and a patient has a prima facie right to be informed by a surgeon of a small, but well established, risk of serious injury as a result of surgery' (*Chester v. Afshar* 2004, 594). Concluding that Miss Chester's 'right of autonomy and dignity' should be respected by finding in her favour, Lord Steyn says that 'the decision announced by the House today reflects the reasonable expectations of the public in contemporary society' (*Chester v. Afshar* 2004, 597). Similarly, Lord Walker, highlighting Lord Scarman's description of the patient's right to self-determination in *Sidaway* (1985) as a basic human right, notes that since that case was decided, 'the importance of personal autonomy has been more and more widely recognised' (*Chester v. Afshar* 2004, 613). In this case, then, autonomy is used, at least partly, as an ideological tool – deployed as a means by which judges can justify the courts' contemporary relevance in resolving disputes arising in the course of medical practice. It becomes a way of recognizing, and responding to, the sociological shift from medicalization to legalization identified in Chapter 2. In the following statement, Lord Woolf captures part of the underlying conditions responsible for the type of deployment of autonomy and rights seen in *Chester v. Afshar* (2004), amongst other cases:

> Like it or not, we have moved from a society which was primarily concerned with the *duty* individuals owed to society to one which is concerned primarily with the *rights* of the individual. You may find this difficult to accept, but judges do move with the times, even if more slowly than some would like. The move to a rights-based society has fundamentally changed the behaviour of the courts. (The Right Honourable The Lord Woolf 2001, 3; emphasis in original)

As Lord Donaldson's statement above confirms, this stress on autonomy and rights is not confined to cases of informed consent.[5] Perhaps most explicitly, and controversially, it can be seen in Munby J's judgment in the case of *R. (Burke) v. General Medical Council* (2004). As this case will be discussed in detail in the context of the relationship between medical law and human rights in Chapter 5, little will be said of it here. It does, however, provide a novel example in medical law of the application of autonomy and rights. This is because these were relied on by Munby J to justify his ruling that a competent patient's decision that he or she requires to be provided with artificial nutrition and hydration is, in principle, determinative that the treatment is in the best interests of that patient. In other words, such a patient could effectively demand the administration of this treatment even where the doctor was of the opinion that this would be contrary to the patient's clinical needs.[6] While interesting, this use of autonomy and rights in a positive sense – that is, as justifications for upholding patients' demands for access to health care resources – will not be discussed here.[7] Rather, it is with another type of case in which autonomy and rights have played a central role that the remainder of this chapter will largely be concerned. The nature of such a case, of which *Re T* is exemplary, involves the refusal by a patient of medical treatment that is necessary to prolong that patient's life ('refusal cases'). It will be argued that what is valuable about studying refusal cases are the insights they can provide into how autonomy exists within the common law in the medical law sphere – that is, they allow us to uncover the less ideological and purportedly patient-friendly aspects surrounding this notion and to understand how autonomy within medical law relates to other legal institutional features and exigencies. In other words, we must think of autonomy as inextricably linked to the social practice or institution – the common law – within which it exists.

---

5   One might also cite the following cases as examples: *Airedale NHS Trust v. Bland* (1993); *Re C (Adult: Refusal of Medical Treatment)* (1994); *Re MB (An Adult: Medical Treatment)* (1997); and *Re B (Adult: Refusal of Medical Treatment)* (2002).

6   The Court of Appeal allowed the General Medical Council's appeal and set aside Munby J's declarations. Munby J's desire to create a culture of patients' rights to demand medical treatment can also be detected in *R. (Watts) v. Bedford Primary Care Trust and Another* (2003).

7   For a useful analysis of this emerging aspect of medical law, see Montgomery 2006, especially 193–9.

The discovery of those insights is some way down the line. Let us begin, in the first instance, by returning to Lord Donaldson's judgment in *Re T*.

Having set up refusal cases as involving a clash, or conflict, between the sanctity of life doctrine[8] and patient autonomy, or the right to self-determination (with the right of the individual being 'paramount'), Lord Donaldson continues his theme of patient sovereignty in the following statement:

> An adult patient ... who suffers from no mental incapacity has an absolute right to choose whether to consent to medical treatment, to refuse it or to choose one rather than another of the treatments being offered ... This right of choice is not limited to decisions which others might regard as sensible. It exists notwithstanding that the reasons for making the choice are rational, irrational, unknown or even non-existent. (*Re T* 1992, 652–3)[9]

The 'absolute' nature of the right to choose, and the fact that its existence in no way depends on what might be called the reasonableness of patients' decisions, purport to indicate the presence in law of unfettered patient choice. But the existence of this right to choose is dependent on the patient suffering from 'no mental incapacity'. In other words, the right only attaches to those patients who have been declared as possessing the requisite mental competence to make decisions about medical treatment. It is possible to note the presence of a two-stage procedure here: first, does the patient have the necessary mental capacity to make the decision?; if so, then he or she possesses the absolute right to choose. Given the obvious significance of a finding of mental capacity, it will be useful to consider just what it means and entails in medical law.

The importance of mental capacity in medical law

Kennedy and Grubb point out that legal capacity in medical law – or legal 'competence', as it is also called – is not based on status or age. In other words, its presence does not depend on strict criteria. Rather: 'Capacity is a question of fact in every case and requires that the patient is able to understand what is involved in the decision to be taken' (Kennedy and Grubb 2004, 160). Legal capacity is therefore measured by assessing individuals' minds to ascertain whether they have the ability to understand a number of factors, including the nature and purpose of the medical procedure, information about the medical treatment, and the possible effects or consequences of accepting or refusing that treatment. The specific legal test for determining mental capacity was laid down by Butler-Sloss LJ in *Re MB* (1997). She stipulated that: 'A person lacks capacity if some impairment or disturbance of mental functioning renders the person unable to make a decision whether to consent

---

8   Fisher has described this doctrine as dictating that 'human lives are of such intrinsic value that no choice intentionally to bring about the death of an innocent person can be right' (Fisher 1995, 317; references omitted).

9   Lord Donaldson's comment in relation to 'reasons' had first been noted by Lord Templeman in *Sidaway* 1985, at 904: 'If the doctor making a balanced judgment advises the patient to submit to the operation, the patient is entitled to reject that advice for reasons which are rational, or irrational, or for no reason.'

to or to refuse treatment' (*Re MB* 1997, 553). The factors to be taken into account when trying to establish such an ability are: whether the individual can comprehend and retain information material to the decision (particularly information regarding the probable consequences of accepting, or refusing, the relevant treatment); and, whether the patient can use that information and weigh it in the balance as part of the process of arriving at the decision.[10] Assuming those factors are met, then the individual will be declared to have mental capacity and, in keeping with Lord Donaldson's judgment, will have an absolute right to choose to make whatever decision he or she likes without fear of further scrutiny or assessment.

Kennedy and Grubb note that, strictly speaking, the law is not concerned with the nature of the patient's decision when determining mental capacity – whether, for example, it is ethical or reasonable or commonsensical – or with the reasoning process. Nor does the law demand, for example, that a patient fully appreciate what the consequences of his or her decision about medical treatment will be. In other words, broader social and ethical considerations would seem to have little, or no, part to play in the process by which law determines mental capacity or competency. Consequently, it would not be incorrect to describe the legal procedure for establishing mental capacity as aspiring to be neutral. Moreover, it would seem to involve the need to engage assessors with technical expertise – an interpretation that, as we shall see, is confirmed by the law's traditional deference to medical professionals (especially psychiatrists and psychologists) as those best qualified to undertake the procedure of determining mental capacity. Their expert assessments are thought to render the 'truest' and most objective readings of an individual's mental functioning.

Given this characterization of the legal test of mental capacity as a technical process, it is unsurprising to note that much of the commentary on this topic has been concerned with ruminating on the various options available that might act as tests for mental capacity, and which of these ought to be considered best suited to that purpose.[11] Moreover, there has been a tendency, probably due to the manner in which the courts themselves operate, to separate questions of mental capacity from the notion of autonomy. While respect for autonomy is characterized as the goal, the objective, the end-point in certain medical law cases, mental capacity is viewed as the process of arriving at that ultimate goal. Even more critical analyses, which offer important insights into the role of legal tests for mental capacity in medical law, set up autonomy and mental capacity as a two-stage procedure (see, for example, Harrington 1996). In the following section this division between autonomy and mental capacity will be analysed and questioned by reference to two cases involving refusals of life-prolonging medical treatment.

---

10 The original legal test for mental capacity was laid down by Thorpe LJ in *Re C (Adult: Refusal of Medical Treatment)* (1994). In addition to the factors above, this test required that the individual believe the treatment information. It should be noted that the legal test for mental capacity set out in *Re MB* (1997) is essentially reproduced in sections 2 and 3 of the Mental Capacity Act 2005. At the time of writing, this statute is not yet in force.

11 Indicative of this type of analysis is Gunn 1994.

Questioning the Division Between Autonomy and Mental Capacity in Medical Law

Why bother questioning the division the judiciary makes between autonomy and mental capacity in refusal cases? The simple answer is that, while judges say they are not interested in the nature of the decisions some patients make to refuse life-prolonging medical treatment and the reasons they give for such decisions (what will, here, be called the 'right to choose' or 'autonomy' stage[12]), they are very much concerned with these. And, importantly, this concern is expressed, albeit quietly and implicitly, in the judgments themselves and through the technical legal test for mental capacity. In refusal cases, the courts cannot help but be interested in the nature of patients' decisions because this strikes at the root of law's function here – that is, the regulation of the continued existence of human life. However much judges may deny the fact, they are intimately involved in making decisions about life and death. In order, though, to try to avoid questioning patients' decisions overtly in such cases, on the basis, for example, that they are ethically misplaced or irrational, the courts attempt to maintain a neutral and non-interventionist stance by stressing that the purpose of legal tests for mental capacity is merely to establish whether patients are able to make such decisions for themselves. As we shall see, this attempt is in vain and not only conceals the fact that law is intimately bound up with regulating the continued existence of human life, but that autonomy and mental capacity are inextricably linked in the manner in which the law performs this regulatory function. Those points will now be illustrated by reference to both a recent case – *Re B (an adult: refusal of medical treatment)* (2002) (hereinafter '*Re B*') – and parts of Lord Donaldson's judgment in *Re T* (1992).

Mental capacity and the nature of decisions

According to Butler-Sloss P, who delivered the judgment of the Court of Appeal in *Re B*, this case concerned 'the tragic story of an able and talented woman of 43 who has suffered a devastating illness which has caused her to become tetraplegic and whose expressed wish is not to be kept artificially alive by the use of a ventilator' (*Re B* 2002, 452). In 1999 Ms B suffered a haemorrhage of the spinal column in her neck. Hospitalized for five weeks while her condition was stabilized, she was informed that a malformation of the blood vessels in her spinal cord had caused a cavernoma which, if the slight possibility of a further bleed were to materialize, would result in severe disability. Surgical intervention carried a similar risk. She executed a 'living will' (or advance directive) in which she provided that, should she later be unable to give instructions, she wished for treatment to be withdrawn if she was suffering from a life-threatening condition, permanent mental impairment or permanent unconsciousness.[13]

---

12 The 'autonomy' stage represents those aspects – such as the nature of the patient's decision, the patient's values and his or her idiosyncrasies – that the courts say are beyond scrutiny or investigation.

13 For a recent discussion of advance directives, see Maclean 2006.

Having recovered sufficiently to return to work, Ms B's condition subsequently deteriorated and she was re-admitted to hospital in early 2001 where she was diagnosed as having suffered an intramedullary cervical spine cavernoma. She became tetraplegic as a result of this, suffering complete paralysis from the neck down. On her transfer to the hospital's intensive care unit, she encountered respiratory difficulties and was put on a ventilator. When she informed the medical staff of the existence of her living will, and the fact that she did not wish to be ventilated, she was told that the will's terms were not detailed enough to authorize the withdrawal of ventilation. Further neurological surgery to remove the cavernous haematoma was successful to the extent that it allowed her to move her head and speak, but thereafter she made several requests for ventilation to be withdrawn, and, as a result, various assessments were made of her mental capacity to decide to refuse the treatment. Although it was decided that she did have this capacity, and the hospital treated her as such, the clinicians were not prepared to withdraw the ventilator. In addition to seeking a declaration that she had mental capacity to refuse treatment, her court application sought a ruling to the effect that her continued artificial ventilation amounted to an unlawful trespass to her person. Let us now turn to the reasons why this case demonstrates that the division between autonomy and mental capacity in this area of medical law is insupportable.

In *Re B* the legal distinction between autonomy and mental capacity was, once again, put forward as being central to the management of the dispute before the court. From the outset, Butler-Sloss P was careful to stress that this was a case about ascertaining the presence or absence of an individual's mental capacity to make decisions about medical treatment. This, she said, was not to be confused with the nature of the patient's decision, however grave the consequences of Ms B's refusal of treatment would be. The patient's decision may 'reflect a difference in values rather than an absence of competence' (*Re B* 2002, 450). In other words, doctors, and presumably the courts, ought not to consider, and judge, the views, beliefs and values of a patient when determining whether he or she has mental capacity.

The first difficulty with this legal distinction arises even before beginning to analyse the elements of the test for mental capacity set out by Butler-Sloss P herself in *Re MB* (1997). The problem here is this: How is it possible to determine a patient's mental capacity without being concerned with the nature of what he or she decides? The general point is captured by Ian Kennedy:

> When devising tests for incapacity, are we talking about the patient or are we talking about a decision taken by the patient? The answer must be that we are concerned with both. We are concerned to establish that the patient meets certain criteria and one of the ways in which we seek to determine this is by examining the decision reached by the patient. The two, the patient and the decision, are inextricably intertwined. The trouble is that the moment we admit this, that the content of a patient's decision is relevant in the determination of capacity, we face the problem of autonomy simply being overwhelmed by paternalism ... It is its desire to avoid this (inevitable) conflation of decision and decision-maker that led the Court of Appeal [in *Re MB* 1997] to want to be seen to nail its colours to the mast of patient autonomy. (Kennedy 1997, 321)

Two points arise from this passage. The first is that, while Kennedy sees the patient's decision as one possible means by which to determine the presence or absence of mental capacity, it is suggested here that it is the nature of such a decision that results in the very need to question, and assess, his or her mental capacity to make decisions. Why would tests for mental capacity be required if the nature of one's decisions was beyond investigation? If Ms B had agreed with the medical staff to continue with ventilation, presumably there would have been no need to question, or assess, her mental capacity because the nature of her decision – to maintain human life – would have conformed with the traditional values of medicine overwhelmingly upheld by those working in the health care professions. So, in fact, contrary to what Butler-Sloss P, and a whole line of judicial authority, argues, the first pre-requisite for the establishment of tests for mental capacity is a consideration of the nature of patients' decisions.

Indeed, this conflation of the nature of decisions and the assessment of mental capacity can be seen in the following statement by Butler-Sloss P in her judgment in *Re B* (2002):

> I shall … have to consider in some detail her ability to make decisions and in particular *the fundamental decision whether to require the removal of the artificial ventilation keeping her alive*. It is important to underline that I am not asked directly to decide whether Ms B lives or dies but whether she, herself, is legally competent to make that decision. (*Re B* 2002, 454–5; emphasis added)

The question to be asked, then, is this: Is this woman legally competent to decide whether she lives or dies? In other words, the assessment of her mental capacity is to be measured against the 'fundamental' nature of the decision to be made – that between life and death. But the point is, surely, that the decision has already been made; Ms B has already chosen how she wishes to proceed. She clearly, then, has the ability to make such a decision. What the law is interested in, however, is something completely different – that is, does she have the legal ability to decide as she has. This ability has nothing to do with actually making a decision. If it had, there would have been little need to seek the intervention of the courts. Rather, legal ability is inextricably linked to the context of the case – that is, one involving the continued existence of human life. If Ms B is to trump the state's interest in upholding the sanctity of life doctrine, her mind must be probed for the purpose of establishing whether she has the ability, for example, to understand information and weigh it in the balance when arriving at her decision.

The second point concerns Kennedy's argument that, once it is realized that the nature of a patient's decision is relevant to the determination of mental capacity, we are confronted with the problem that autonomy is displaced by paternalism. It is suggested here, though, that this conflation of the nature of decisions with the assessment of mental capacity points not to the casting aside of autonomy; rather, it is consistent with a certain notion of autonomy, albeit one that some commentators in the medical law field, and the judiciary itself, would not feel comfortable recognizing. This autonomy is of the principled, rather than of the individual, variety. As we saw in the previous chapter, it is bound up with obligations and responsibilities, rather than with rights. The fact that the courts are concerned with the nature of patients' decisions – something that Butler-Sloss P argued had to be protected from investigation because it involved the values and beliefs of individuals – is merely the first example of the existence of principled autonomy in refusal cases. As we will see shortly, the trumping of human life by death demands more of the patient – she is obliged to explain herself and to reach certain unspecified standards of demeanour and attitude before her decision will be respected. Before identifying other instances of the presence of principled autonomy, let us simply reiterate at this stage that the legal distinction courts attempt to draw between the nature of patients' decisions and their mental capacity to make such decisions does not stand up to scrutiny; indeed, their conflation appears on the face of judicial opinions themselves.

Accounting for reasons

The second difficulty with the legal distinction between autonomy and mental capacity can be seen by returning to Lord Donaldson's statement above in *Re T*. He stresses that those adult patients who are deemed not to lack mental capacity may choose freely whether to consent to, or refuse, medical treatment that has been offered to them. There is no need for them to prove to others that their decisions are reasonable; indeed, there is no requirement to offer reasons for their decisions. But this 'right of choice' and, specifically, the reference to irrationality and the non-existence of reasons,[14] sits uneasily with that part of the legal test for determining mental capacity that refers to patients being able to use the treatment information and weigh it in the balance when arriving at their decisions.

As Kennedy points out, the problem revolves around the question of why, if patients need give no reasons for their decisions, they must demonstrate that they have taken account of anything when making those decisions (Kennedy 1997, 321). In other words, there is no need to give reasons for one's decision about medical treatment, but it is necessary, for the purposes of displaying mental competence, to show that you have performed a reasoning process in arriving at that decision. The important point is that this aspect of the test for mental capacity involves deciding or choosing, and the method of arriving at that decision or choice. The legal procedure as it currently stands would seem to read something like this: (a) the patient's decision (effectively a refusal of medical treatment); (b) assessment of mental capacity, including taking account of whether the patient can use the treatment information and weigh it in the balance in arriving at a decision; (c) finding of no mental incapacity; (d) the individual has a right to choose or to make a decision for whatever, or no, reason at all. Lord Donaldson's frequently cited words about individuals having the right mentioned in (d) would appear to be superfluous given that patients' decisions must, in the first instance, conform to a certain procedure, one of the purposes of which is to assess how patients make decisions – how they use information, balance

---

14 It is illuminating, however, to note a comment made by Lord Donaldson in another 'competency' case decided only one month before *Re T* (1992): 'I personally consider that religious or other beliefs which bar any medical treatment or treatment of particular kinds are irrational ...' See *Re W (A Minor) (Medical Treatment: Court's Jurisdiction)* (1992, 635).

it, and so on. If this is so, then what interests those assessing mental capacity is the whole decision-making, or reasoning, process, including the various factors (presumably incorporating such things as patients' values and beliefs – that is, features that are bound up with patient autonomy, and, from the courts' point of view, are beyond consideration) against which the treatment information is weighed. The procedure of assessment cannot conveniently omit consideration of those wider aspects – aspects that often lie at the root of the nature of patients' decisions. Patients are therefore under an obligation to demonstrate that their decision-making complies with a certain procedure. Their initial decisions to refuse medical treatment signal the beginning of a process of scrutiny which may legitimately involve assessment of the types of values and beliefs that Butler-Sloss P in *Re B* (2002) said were beyond the scope of investigation and evaluation. Again, it is suggested that it is possible to detect the existence of a notion of principled autonomy here – that is, one which is bound up with obligation rather than rights. The ideological equation of autonomy with the unfettered right to choose does not resonate with the more obligatory aspects inherent in the legal test for mental capacity.

Summary

It is suggested that the law seeks to set up a division between the nature of patients' decisions (more broadly speaking, autonomy) and tests for mental capacity in a way that maps directly onto a cleavage between patients' values (something the courts seek not to become involved in scrutinizing) and their ability to make decisions about whether to accept or refuse medical treatment (something which, because it is characterized as a technical undertaking falling within the expertise of certain professionals, is deemed to be legally justiciable). To push this one stage further, this split is implicitly intended by the courts to map onto a division between an overt involvement in, on the one hand, ethical questions of life and death (something falling outside of the province, or jurisdiction, of the courts) and, on the other, resolving questions about the continuation or withdrawal of medical treatment which happen to impinge on the issue of the continued existence of human life (something judges feel perfectly competent to rule on). Insofar as autonomy is concerned, these divisions allow the courts to continue to present autonomy as synonymous with the atomistic rights-bearing individual, free to make his or her choices unencumbered by the threat of intrusion or scrutiny. As such, and as we saw earlier, this shores up the ideological aspect of autonomy that exists within the common law in this area. As Harrington has noted in relation to refusal cases:

> Where refusals are overridden ... the violation of principle is clear yet autonomy must continue to be seen as the norm. It must remain the cornerstone of medical practice and judicial regulation of it, even while the law provides the exceptions and supplementary strategies which enable it to be overcome or set aside ... [T]he liberal conception of patients as autonomous, self-determining rights holders has been accepted as the paradigm in treatment refusal cases. (Harrington 1996, 363)

Whilst valuable, this analysis continues to view the relationship between autonomy and tests for mental capacity as a binary one. The foregoing analysis in this section, however, seeks to question the legal division between autonomy and mental capacity in the context of refusal cases. It has been argued that the law's determination to place the nature of patients' decisions, and the reasons given for these, beyond scrutiny is undermined, first, by the manner in which judges themselves set up the relationship between assessments of mental capacity and the fundamental nature of decisions (that is, they appear to concede that they are concerned with the nature of patients' decisions – here, those about life and death); and, secondly, by the content of the test for mental capacity that the courts employ for the purpose of assessing whether patients are competent to make such decisions. Moreover, it was suggested that this conflation of autonomy with mental capacity might be consistent with the presence of another notion of autonomy – O'Neill's 'principled autonomy' (O'Neill 2002) – within refusal cases. In other words, while the standard, ideological notion of autonomy within medical law may be revealed as being a sham in these refusal cases from time to time, this does not mean that autonomy in all its manifestations ceases to exist in such cases. Rather, principled autonomy can be detected in the manner in which courts deploy the test for mental capacity in refusal cases. In order to develop this argument further, the next two sections will consider some of the factors that might point to the existence of principled autonomy in refusal cases. In the first instance, at least, *Re B* provides a useful source of examples.

Explanation

As the assessment of mental capacity and a concern for the nature of patients' decisions merge in medical law, so, contrary to what the law stipulates, individuals must explain the reasons for their decisions.[15] It is insufficient for patients simply to say that they have used the treatment information provided to them and weighed it in the balance when arriving at their decisions. Rather, in order that the court can judge their overall ability to make decisions for themselves, they must demonstrate how they have used and weighed that information. *Re B* provides a useful example of the obligation upon patients to explain the reasons for their decisions. The case contains numerous instances of this, only a couple of which will be presented here.

Firstly, in response to questions about why she did not want the one-way weaning programme,[16] Ms B explained:

---

15 We see here (and in what follows) the expression in law of the results of a more general transformation within medicine in the early part of the twentieth century. David Armstrong has described this as follows: 'The medical gaze shifted from body to mind [during the 1920s]' (Armstrong 1983, 26). Moreover: 'The mind was represented to the gaze in words ... The patient had to speak, to confess, to reveal; illness was transformed from what was visible to what was heard' (Armstrong 1983, 25).

16 The purpose of this programme is gradually to reduce the number of breaths supplied by the ventilator, thereby allowing the patient's body to become accustomed to breathing without assistance again. If difficulty in breathing occurs, the patient is not given artificial ventilation again, but, rather, is only sedated.

[The one-way weaning programme] does not include pain control and would last for several weeks ... I have refused this option because this would be a slow and painful death and my view of this is not disputed by the doctors. I would also feel robbed of a certain amount of dignity ... My wish is to be sedated. I would expect it to be a quick and painless death and less distressing for my loved ones. Negative weaning [one-way weaning] would mean watching me die over a series of weeks, the thought of this is painful for me to accept. (*Re B* 2002, 460)

Secondly, in her written evidence she explained how she had grappled with her Christian beliefs when deciding to refuse ventilation:

It has been a very difficult process to rationalise what I am doing in the context of my faith but I feel there is no alternative, as I do not have any realistic hope of recovery. I have come to believe that people die and become disabled and God does not always intervene. It has also been difficult for me to contemplate leaving the people I love behind. (*Re B* 2002, 462)

Finally, asked whether the reason for her refusal of ventilation was because she wished to die or because she did not wish to remain alive in her present condition, she replied that it was the latter: 'Given the range of choices, I would want to recover and have my life back, or significant enough recovery to have a better quality of life. I am not convinced by the evidence that that is going to happen, and I find the idea of living like this intolerable ...' (*Re B* 2002, 461).

What is clear from these examples is that it is not sufficient to reply to an offer of medical treatment with a simple 'No thank you', especially when that treatment is needed to sustain human life. This point can also be seen in Marinos Diamantides's discussion of an American case – *State of Tennessee v. Northern* (1978) (see Diamantides 2000, 62–5). In that case, Ms Northern – an older woman who refused life-saving surgery in the form of amputation of a gangrenous foot without offering any reasons for her decision – was declared by the court to lack the mental capacity to refuse the treatment. One of the difficulties with Ms Northern's refusal was her failure to communicate, or to explain herself. As Diamantides suggests, if she wished her decision to be respected, she could not remain silent:

Ms Northern had ... declined the opportunity to pass a subjective judgement on her afflictions, and failed to give any reasons why non-treatment would be better than treatment. Ms Northern had expressed her suffering silently, passively, without subsuming it under any considerations and calculations of treatment benefits versus benefits of no treatment ... [T]he court ... appears to have made the right to refuse treatment subject to an existential requirement: the patient must take a pro-active attitude towards his or her suffering. They must speak 'of it' .... (Diamantides 2000, 64)

This need for patients to explain themselves suggests that the courts are unable to perform their role in refusal cases adequately without such explanations. But it would seem that the provision of explanations for refusals of medical treatment not only allows courts to judge those explanations; it also offers up the opportunity to judge the individuals themselves. Ms Northern's failure to advance any reasons for her refusal obviously did not create a favourable impression of her in the minds of the judges hearing her case. The patient who expresses her suffering 'silently' and 'passively' offers no material that would allow courts to form a positive impression of her character or personality. Discussing the importance of the question – 'Who are you?' – in the modern criminal tribunal, Michel Foucault makes a valuable observation that is relevant in the current context. Having quoted an 'exchange' from a French criminal court case in 1975 in which the accused remained silent in response to questions from the presiding judge designed to make the accused explain himself, Foucault continues:

> Much more is expected of him. Beyond admission, there must be confession, self-examination, explanation of oneself, revelation of what one is. The penal machine can no longer function simply with a law, a violation, and a responsible party – it needs something else, supplementary material. The magistrates and the jurors, the lawyers too, and the department of the public prosecutor cannot really play their roles unless they are provided with another type of discourse, the one given by the accused about himself, or the one he makes possible for others, through his confessions, memories, intimate disclosures, and so on ... They really ought to speak a little about themselves, if they want to be judged. (Foucault 2000a, 177)

Similarly, we might say that if patients are to have their refusals of life-prolonging medical treatment respected, they must do more than simply refuse to give their consent. Not only must they explain their reasons for refusing; they must do so in such a way that they reveal something about their characters. Only then can the courts truly judge their mental capacity to refuse treatment and perform their role of regulating the continued existence of human life. In the following section, we will see how this aspect of refusal cases has played out in both refusal and non-refusal cases in the field of medical law. For the moment, two final points regarding explanation need to be made.

Firstly, not only is the law interested in the nature of patients' decisions; it also requires explanations of the reasons for those decisions – explanations that, in Ms B's case, necessarily involved discussion of her suffering, her values and her beliefs. If the second leg of the legal test for mental capacity – that patients must demonstrate that they can use or weigh treatment information when arriving at their decisions – was designed so that patients would confine their explanations to the level of technical risk and benefit, then this was not possible for Ms B. Given the nature of the decision she was making – that is, one concerning the continued existence of human life – her explanation necessarily overflowed from the level of the technical into the realm of values and beliefs. Indeed, perhaps the idea of 'overflow' is incorrect, suggesting as it does a qualitative difference between the technical and, for want of a better word, the ethical. This is because, for Ms B, to talk about ventilators and one-way weaning programmes (and their risks and benefits) was precisely to talk about death, values and beliefs; for her, to divorce the two was just not possible. The significance of this is that these aspects of her explanation become open to judicial reflection and judgment, despite the care taken by Butler-Sloss P to stress that they are not legitimate objects of scrutiny for the purpose of determining mental capacity.

Secondly, the need to explain one's reasons for refusing life-sustaining medical treatment as part of the procedure of determining mental capacity tends to confirm the suggestion made earlier that Lord Donaldson's statement about the patient's right to choose without providing any reasons for such choices looks decidedly rhetorical. The reasons for refusing have already been provided, and analysed, at the 'mental capacity' stage of the process.

Identity, Responsibility and Medical Law

Re B

The requirement of Ms B to explain the nature of her decision led to an assessment of how well, in the judge's opinion, she had spoken of it. More specifically, what Ms B had said, and how she had approached the scenario generally, facilitated an evaluation of her identity and abilities – factors that played a crucial role in the judge's decision as to whether she possessed mental capacity.[17] This is illustrated in the following comments by Butler-Sloss P:

> Her wishes were clear and well-expressed. She had clearly done a considerable amount of investigation and was extremely well-informed about her condition. She has retained *a sense of humour* and, despite her feelings of frustration and irritation which she expressed in her oral evidence, a considerable degree of *insight* into the problems caused to the hospital clinicians and nursing staff by her decision not to remain on artificial ventilation. She is, in my judgment, an exceptionally *impressive witness*. Subject to the crucial evidence of the consultant psychiatrists, she appears to me to demonstrate a very high standard of mental competence, *intelligence* and *ability*. (*Re B* 2002, 462; emphasis added)

Who is this woman? What has the court learned about her identity from the explanation of her decision and from the manner in which she has conducted herself? From Butler-Sloss P's summary, it is clear that Ms B is not only considered to be articulate, but also knowledgeable about her condition, capable of responding to her situation with humour, and appreciative of the problems her decision to refuse ventilation has caused to those caring for her. This latter aspect seemed particularly important to the judge. It was something that needed to be present and spoken of in sufficiently lucid terms. Its negative connotation – that a patient might simply criticize members of the health care professions for keeping her attached to a ventilator when she did not want this, without any appreciation for the difficulties her decision had caused them – had to be sufficiently compensated for by her general attitude and demeanour, something that she clearly managed to achieve given the court's description of her as possessing insight, intelligence and ability. There was, we might say, an obligation, or responsibility, upon Ms B to acknowledge the difficult ethical dilemma which her decision had created for the hospital staff.[18]

---

17 For a discussion of the emerging focus on patients' personalities and identities in medicine – as opposed simply to their bodies – see Armstrong 1983 (Chapters 11 and 12) and Armstrong 2002 (Chapter 7).

18 We can see this respect for the hospital staff's dilemma in part of Ms B's evidence: 'I fully accept the doctor's right to say, "I personally will not do it" [withdraw ventilation], and

The overall impression given was that, as this 'able and talented' woman had met certain unspecified standards, or norms, of identity and behaviour, she could be assessed as having sufficient mental capacity to refuse medical treatment. The traits she displayed, one might argue, rendered her deserving of having her wishes respected.[19] In this regard, it is interesting to note the types of traits upon which emphasis was placed in *Re B*. Articulateness, knowledgeability, humour, insight – to reach certain standards of these is often difficult for healthy people, far less those who are suffering illness and contemplating death. Indeed, what we become aware of here is the need for Ms B to refuse to become subjected by that which subjects her – in other words, illness. In her attempt to have her decision respected, she must succeed in retaining, and demonstrating, some semblance of a healthy life or, more accurately, some of the characteristics that are associated with the lives of the healthy.

It is suggested that what can be seen here is the production in law of the responsible patient. On the one hand, this patient is someone who realizes the difficulties and problems her decision causes to others (in *Re B*, the health care professionals) who have their own professional and personal ethical obligations.[20] On the other hand, this type of patient is someone who is self-responsible; that is, there is a tacit obligation upon the patient to demonstrate a high degree of self-control, together with the kind of attributes associated with this – she must maintain the traits of the stereotypical healthy citizen (insight, clear communication, conviction, confidence, a sense of humour, an expression of the importance of dignity, amongst other things) and suppress those characteristics that one might associate with the suffering patient (anger, refusal to co-operate, silence or inability to express oneself coherently, for example). Only this type of patient – the responsible one – has the chance of being deemed to be mentally competent in refusal cases.

One final point concerning the relationship between, on the one hand, questions of identity and behaviour, and on the other, tests for mental capacity should be noted. This regards the assessors of mental capacity. Where the courts become involved, the determination of mental capacity is, ultimately, a matter for the presiding judge(s). Their conclusions, however, are heavily influenced by those they privilege with the task of assessing mental capacity – namely, medical professionals. In particular, it is the psychiatrist and the psychologist who are considered best qualified to undertake this procedure. Importantly, though, while the nature of the test for mental capacity is held out by the courts as being technical, the priority given to such experts does not

---

I respect that position, but I was angered at the arrogance and complete refusal to allow me access to someone that would' (*Re B* 2002, 461).

19 It is possible to detect the importance of the role played by identity and demeanour in another refusal case – *Re C (Adult: Refusal of Medical Treatment)* (1994). In that case, a prisoner refused medical treatment for the gangrene which had developed in one of his feet. Ruling that C had the mental capacity to refuse amputation, Thorpe J remarked of the patient: '[T]here was no sign of inappropriate emotional expression. His rejection of amputation seemed to result from sincerely held conviction. He had a certain dignity of manner that I respect' (*Re C (Adult: Refusal of Medical Treatment)* 1994, 823).

20 As Brazier wrote recently: 'Responsibility for one's choice demands consideration of how those choices will affect others' (Brazier 2006, 401).

mean that patients' identities and biographies, for example, are beyond consideration and scrutiny in establishing whether mental capacity exists. Once again, *Re B* provides a useful illustration of these points.

It was not merely the Court's assessment of Ms B that mattered. Given, as Butler-Sloss P said, that refusal cases required 'the highest degree of scrutiny', the evidence of the two consultant psychiatrists called to testify was 'crucial'. While there was much emphasis placed on the need to respect the values individuals often express through their decisions about medical treatment, and to reiterate that questions of mental capacity were to be distinguished from the nature of individuals' decisions, the significance attached to the evidence of psychiatrists in ascertaining the presence or absence of mental capacity confirms the depth and range of possible factors the law considers may validly impinge on the state of an individual's mind. Here, for instance, questions were raised regarding the possibility of psychological regression, the patient's childhood experiences, and whether she suffered from mental illness. And, while those temporary factors were not sufficiently present in this case to render Ms B mentally incompetent to refuse medical treatment, their broader significance lies in their validity to the legal process, and, consequently, the importance of the expert to this process.

Butler-Sloss P's stress on the distinction between assessing people's mental capacity and the way in which they choose their own ends was, in part, intended to define the proper scope of the medical expert's role in refusal cases. The legitimate authority of the expert was to be confined to the apparently technical matter of assessing the individual's mind with a view to ruling on mental capacity. However, it is clear that the psychiatrist and psychologist are not only involved in assessing the extent to which individuals can understand and retain treatment information and weigh it in arriving at a decision; they are also concerned to investigate the possible causes of why individuals decide as they do. What produces someone that chooses death over life (that is, someone who makes a decision of that nature)? Is there something in this person's past, an incident or experience for instance, that might explain such a decision? Does some factor exist that may suggest the patient is 'not thinking straight' and, thus, does not really intend to refuse the life-prolonging medical treatment? But to ask such questions with the purpose of establishing the presence or absence of mental capacity is to find oneself in the role of examining lives, the courses they have taken, the influences that have shaped them, the decisions that have affected them. In other words, the investigation of such factors has, as its objective, the identification of any events in the past that may explain why the individual chooses as she does. The patient's life – in all its complexity – potentially becomes subject to an examination that seeks to identify causal explanations for making treatment decisions one way rather than another. Indeed, this complexity, and the possibility of interpreting a person's life in numerous ways, assists the medical professional insofar as it offers up a malleable object for study. Past events or personality traits can be interpreted in various ways, with at least the possibility that minor occurrences come to play a more central role in assessing the level of a patient's mental capacity.

Pregnancy and medical treatment

Questions of identity and responsibility have also arisen in the medical law sphere in relation to the treatment of pregnant women. These questions have been especially evident in the area of abortion law and in cases where women refuse to consent to delivery of children by way of Caesarean section. As a substantial amount of literature already exists on both topics (written mainly by medical law academics adopting a feminist legal perspective), the treatment of them here will be very brief.[21] The objective is simply to draw out the presence of questions of identity and responsibility in those areas.

In her analysis of the Abortion Act 1967 (hereinafter 'the Act'), Sheldon argues that, rather than promoting the rights and freedoms of women seeking abortions, this Act created a certain type of power over them. Drawing on Michel Foucault's work on subjectivity, she argues that this is a productive power – that is, the Act produces, or conjures up, an image of the woman wishing to abort as 'a peripheral subject, distinguishable from "normal" women, characterised by certain qualities and inadequacies ... the Abortion Act is predicated upon certain ideas of maternity as the female norm, female irresponsibility and emotional instability and implicit assumptions about appropriate female sexual morality' (Sheldon 1997, 47). In other words, the woman seeking abortion fails to meet assumed expectations of the role a pregnant woman should play. Her identity is legally defined by her lack of responsibility and morally aberrant nature. This, Sheldon argues, is merely enhanced by the power the Act assigns to members of the medical profession to decide which women are to be granted access to abortion services.

During the 1990s, the courts heard a series of cases concerning women who had refused consent for their babies to be delivered by way of Caesarean section. In almost all of the cases, the discussion revolved around whether the woman had the mental capacity to refuse this delivery procedure.[22] What follows are two brief examples of how those cases may be interpreted as involving questions of identity and, especially, responsibility.

In *Norfolk and Norwich Healthcare (NHS) Trust v. W* (1997) (hereinafter '*Norfolk*'), Miss W arrived at hospital in a state of arrested labour. The consultant obstetrician sought authority to proceed with a forceps delivery and, if required, to perform a Caesarean section. Accepting the consultant psychiatrist's opinion that Miss W was incapable of weighing up the considerations involved in arriving at her decision to refuse, Johnson J held that she lacked the mental capacity to make a decision about the proposed treatment. The judge authorized the treatment on the basis that it would be in the best interests of Miss W. Of particular relevance to this ruling were the following factors: 1) Miss W had had to make the decision to

---

21 Interested readers may, in the first instance, wish to consult Sheldon and Thompson 1998a; Bridgeman and Millns 1998; Sheldon 1997; and, Scott 2000 and 2002.

22 Only in the first case of its kind – *Re S (Adult: Refusal of Medical Treatment)* (1992) – was the question of mental capacity not considered. Instead, the presiding judge authorized an emergency Caesarean section on the basis that the operation was in the vital interests of the mother and the unborn child. For critical commentary on this case, see Thomson 1994.

refuse treatment 'at a time of acute emotional stress and physical pain in the ordinary course of labour made even more difficult for her because of her own particular mental history [a history of psychiatric treatment]' (*Norfolk* 1997, 272); 2) Should there be no Caesarean section, the probable death of the foetus within Miss W would create a risk of physical damage to her, and may even result in her death; 3) The termination of the pregnancy 'would avoid her feeling any feeling of guilt in the future were she, by her refusal of consent, to cause the death of the foetus' (*Norfolk* 1997, 272). Reasons 2) and 3) point to the sort of responsible pregnant woman the Court envisages as the norm in such cases. She is the self-responsible type, seeking to avoid physical damage to herself (or even death) and the guilt of having caused her baby's death. However, while stressing that his focus was upon Miss W's interests, as opposed to those of the foetus, Johnson J also points to the responsibility that Miss W (and presumably pregnant women generally) has to ensure the production of human life: '[T]he reality was that the foetus was a fully formed child, capable of normal life if only it could be delivered from the mother' (*Norfolk* 1997, 273).

In *Re MB (An Adult: Medical Treatment)* (1997), the Court of Appeal was presented with a slightly different scenario. There, Miss MB had, in fact, consented to delivery by Caesarean section, but owing to a fear of needles, refused to consent either to blood samples being taken or to undergo anaesthesia by way of injection. Holding that the patient temporarily lacked the mental capacity to make a decision about anaesthesia, the Court ruled that it was lawful to administer the anaesthetic (thus allowing the Caesarean section to be performed) as it was in her best interests for the child to be born alive and healthy. The consultant psychiatrist – Dr F – gave evidence that Miss MB lacked the capacity 'to see very far beyond the immediate situation'. He described her as 'a naïve, not very bright, frightened young woman' and stated that it was highly probable that she would suffer significant long-term damage should the operation not be performed and the child was born handicapped or died. Conversely, he felt the non-consensual imposition of the injection would not result in any permanent damage to Miss MB.

Again, piercing the façade of the use of mental capacity to force medical treatment on Miss MB, what the consultant psychiatrist and the Court seem to be saying here is that the patient is temporarily unable to appreciate what is good for her. Her fear of needles has obstructed her demonstrated ability to act responsibly (she consented to the Caesarean section), both in so far as her own health, and that of her child, is concerned.

As in Sheldon's analysis of abortion law, it is possible to detect in the two foregoing examples a concern by the courts to produce an image of the responsible pregnant woman – one who not only must consider the consequences for herself of refusing a Caesarean section, but, perhaps more important, also needs to prioritize the welfare of her baby. As in *Re B*, yet again we encounter the courts' use of the legal test for mental capacity as a purportedly uncontroversial mechanism through which to establish, silently and implicitly, the desired norms of patient behaviour and identity against which the real pregnant women whose cases come before the courts are measured.

Non-refusal cases

The importance of the identity and attributes of patients within medical law is not confined to refusal cases. It can also be found in other branches of the subject, particularly those cases where patients allege that medical professionals have failed to inform them adequately about the risks involved in specific medical treatment procedures.[23] This can be illustrated by returning to Lord Scarman's judgment in *Sidaway* (1985).[24] While the stress he places on the patient's right to self-determination is widely referred to, what is less well appreciated is the fact that he envisaged certain limitations applying to the exercise of this right. One way in which the right of patients to decide for themselves could be restricted lay in the idea of a 'therapeutic privilege'.[25]

Lord Scarman says that this idea, in law, dates from the American case of *Canterbury v. Spence* (1972), and goes on to outline its purpose as follows: '[It] enables a doctor to withhold from his patient information as to risk if it can be shown that a reasonable medical assessment of the patient would have indicated to the doctor that disclosure would have posed a serious threat of psychological detriment to the patient' (*Sidaway* 1985, 493). The House of Lords in *Sidaway* assumed that Mr Falconer (the neurosurgeon who advised Mrs Sidaway to undergo the operation, and subsequently performed it) had omitted to warn her of the risk of injury to the spinal cord. One of the reasons she failed to succeed in her action was that Mr Falconer could no longer provide evidence of his assessment of the character of his patient (or, as Lord Diplock put it: 'We know nothing of the emotional idiosyncrasies of the plaintiff ... even in ordinary health let alone under the stress of ill-health and the prospects of waiting for surgical treatment at the hands of Mr Falconer' [*Sidaway* 1985, 496]) because he (Mr Falconer) was now dead. In other words, the House of Lords could not declare that he had failed in his duty to warn his patient of the risk because there was a possibility that, had he thought Mrs Sidaway too fragile to cope with the information, he would have been justified in not disclosing the risk. This possibility prevented a finding of negligence. What should be noted, however, is that an assessment of her character or personality was integral to the medical decision as to how to proceed:

> [T]he medical evidence also emphasised that in reaching a decision whether or not to warn his patient a competent and careful surgeon would attach especial importance to his assessment of the character and emotional condition of his patient, it being accepted that a doctor acting in the best interests of his patients would be concerned lest a warning might

---

23 For a discussion of how courts construct doctors' and patients' identities in medical negligence cases, see Sheldon 1998.

24 This focus upon patients' identities in this type of case had already received judicial endorsement in *Chatterton v. Gerson* [1981]: 'In what he says [regarding warnings of any real risks in the medical treatment] any good doctor has to take into account the personality of the patient, the likelihood of the misfortune, and what in the way of warning is for the particular patient's welfare' (*Chatterton v. Gerson* 1981, 266, per Bristow J).

25 Further discussion of the therapeutic privilege can be found in Harrington 1996, at 355.

frighten the patient into refusing an operation which in his view was the best treatment in the circumstances. (*Sidaway* 1985, 489, per Lord Scarman)

Since *Sidaway*, the therapeutic privilege has continued to find favour with the judiciary.[26] What is interesting, though, is that, even with the courts' growing concern to emphasize the importance of autonomy and patients' rights to self-determination, there has been no diminution in the assessment of the characters and personalities of those who claim to have been negligently treated by members of the medical profession. Rather, what has changed is the fact that, rather than simply leaving it to doctors to determine what type of treatment information different patients can withstand, it is the courts too that are now involved in making assessments of patients' personalities. The following passage by Rougier J in a case before the High Court is an indication of this trend:

My reasons for coming to this view [that the patient would have declined to undergo the operation had she known of the various risks of medical intervention and non-intervention] are as follows:

1. Mrs McAllister's own personality. I readily concede that my knowledge of this factor can in no sense be described as profound since my acquaintance with her is limited to listening to her for approximately an hour in the witness box. However, that was sufficient, in my judgment, to demonstrate that she was a sensible and independent minded woman, not given to flights of fancy or panic, and one who could be expected to make a rational judgment on a matter such as this. Additionally, her history after this disaster befell her shows a woman of no little determination and courage. After one fit of wholly understandable depression of the blackest kind which caused her to try to put an end to her life, she has buckled down to making the best of what is left ... I do not think that Mrs McAllister's fear of death would be chimerical or irrationally greater than normal. (*McCallister v. Lewisham and North Southwark Health Authority and Others* 1994, 353)

Again, the same sorts of questions arise: What type of person was this woman? Could she think for herself? Could she be considered able to make rational judgments? What was the nature of her 'fear of death' and how did it compare to what the law thought was the norm in this regard? There was an implicit obligation upon Mrs McCallister to conform to a particular, but unspecified, identity.

Medical Law and Conceptions of Autonomy

In this, the final section of the chapter, the foregoing analysis will be placed within a wider explanatory framework. This framework is premised on a distinctive methodological approach to autonomy within medical law. Drawing on work by Nicola Lacey in the field of criminal law, it will be argued that, in order to understand the relationship between medical law and autonomy more fully, it is useful to analyse autonomy as an interpretive concept (Lacey 2001). This entails that, rather than trying to explain how autonomy exists in medical law by relying solely on *a priori*

---

26 The most recent affirmation of this privilege can be found in Lord Steyn's opinion (para. 16) in *Chester v. Afshar* (2004).

concepts of autonomy developed within moral philosophy or bioethics or medical ethics, for instance, it is, in addition, necessary to study the ways in which autonomy is deployed within the common law in this area. The benefit of such an approach resides in its ability to uncover the impact that institutional exigencies and features have on which concepts of autonomy exist within the common law at any particular time.

From the analysis undertaken in this chapter, it is suggested that two conceptions of autonomy exist simultaneously within medical law – conceptions that may conveniently be described by adopting O'Neill's terms of 'individual' and 'principled' autonomy. It will be recalled that what O'Neill meant by individual autonomy was either independence from something or, at the least, a capacity for independent decision-making or action. This notion of autonomy is posited as a feature of individuals, rather than as being bound up with what might loosely be called moral or ethical conduct. Assuming individuals demonstrate that they have the capacity to make independent decisions, they are free to make whatever decision they wish. This gives rise to the kind of atomistic, independent, rights-bearing individual that has largely defined the development of academic medical law since its inception. In this chapter we have seen how individual autonomy also dominates the thinking of members of the judiciary. Indeed, patient autonomy has so closely been identified with patients' rights that the two have become virtually indistinguishable.

But why has individual autonomy been so prominent in the courts? One obvious reason would be the need to ensure that patients' voices are heard and respected. We all value being able to make our own decisions, and individual autonomy is thought to be a useful mechanism by which to recognize this. The presence of this concept of autonomy in the courts can, however, also be attributed to more structural, or institutional, exigencies. Thus, as we saw earlier, the promotion of individual autonomy allows the judiciary to present the law as a social institution that assists in the process of redressing the traditional imbalance of power between doctor and patient. In doing so, judges seek, as Lord Woolf argues, to reflect broader transformations in modern social life, and thereby, to maintain the relevance and usefulness of the common law in contemporary society. If the erosion of trust in professionals, and in those professing expertise generally, is an identifiable characteristic of our times, not only do the courts in the medical law field reflect (and, by so doing, reinforce) this trend by stressing that it is patients, and not paternalistic doctors, who now have priority, but, in doing so, they also, somewhat paradoxically, prevent any dissipation of trust and confidence in the usefulness of the institution of law and its practitioners. The concept of individual autonomy offers a way for the courts to claim to meet the expectations of individuals today – their desire for choice, self-determination and the exercise of rights. Putting it slightly differently, it could be said that the assertion of this type of autonomy allows the courts in medical law cases to reflect, and reinforce, the mode of governmentality – legalization – that, as we saw in Chapter 2, constitutes part of the sociological backdrop to the emergence, and development, of medical law.

As well as this, a commitment to individual autonomy helps the courts to assert their role in this relatively new area of litigation. That is, this idea of autonomy can be used by judges as a means of developing a distinct identity to the common law's increasing involvement in this sphere. As such, and similar to the use of autonomy and patients' rights by some academic medical lawyers, individual autonomy is an important and visible way in which the courts exercise and organize their jurisdiction in this field.

The courts' promotion of individual autonomy seeks to serve a further structural need – that is, to stress the objective role of the courts. This is connected to the question of mental capacity. As one possible meaning of individual autonomy is a capacity for independent decision-making or action, clearly the establishment of tests for determining this capacity becomes crucial. The precise nature of the legal test for mental capacity is set out earlier in this chapter. But beyond the specific components of this test, its broader function is to facilitate the presentation of the courts' involvement in refusal cases as neutral, objective and, therefore, uncontroversial. The determination of mental capacity is held out as a technical procedure, distinguishable from the nature of patients' decisions and the moral attributes of patients. As Lacey puts it when discussing the emergence of the idea of criminal responsibility based on capacity in the nineteenth and twentieth centuries: '[T]he criminal process was in search of a conception of criminal responsibility which could be explicated in legal, technical terms, and hence legitimated as a form of specialist knowledge underpinning an impersonal mode of judgment' (Lacey 2001, 267–8). Individual autonomy therefore has the dual benefit of allowing the courts, on the one hand, to present patients' rights as the guiding principle in refusal (and other) cases, and, on the other, to characterize its role in the procedure by which those rights come about – the legal test for mental capacity – as purely technical and, therefore, neutral. As such, the impression given is that the courts have no intention to, and do not, judge patients, or fail to acknowledge their independence, or interfere with their decisions; assuming they have mental capacity, the courts are merely concerned to uphold patients' rights.

Despite its clear presence in medical law, the concept of individual autonomy does, in fact, play an ideological role in this area. Its function is to promote a certain image of the patient and of the courts themselves – one which, after the type of analysis conducted in this chapter, might be thought to bear only the slightest of resemblances to reality. This reality, it is argued, is much more in line with the existence within medical law of O'Neill's concept of principled autonomy, and it is to a discussion of this that we now turn.

As set out in the previous chapter, for O'Neill, principled autonomy is that type of autonomy which resonates most closely with Kant's concept and his moral philosophy generally. Principled autonomy, it will be recalled, is bound up with constraint, obligation and responsibility. Individuals act autonomously and, therefore, ethically only if they act on the basis of 'principles of obligation'. Autonomous action in the principled, or Kantian, sense is inconsistent with arguments promoting individuals' rights to choose how to act for any, or no, reason at all. It has been shown in this chapter how patients, especially those refusing life-sustaining medical treatment, are obliged by the courts to do various things – for instance, they must explain the reasons for their decisions, demonstrate that they have taken account of others' situations and interests when making their choices, and reach certain unspecified standards relating to demeanour and personality (traits that are synonymous with what might be called the 'morally' responsible patient). This latter factor – unspecified standards – illustrates the presence in medical law of Kant's and, by extension, O'Neill's confidence in their own ability to identify the sound ethical principles and obligations that must be met for there to be autonomous action. In a case like *Re B*, there is an indication of the type of conduct and personality traits that need to be met before a finding of mental capacity will be made. But the standards of humour, intelligence and ability, for example, are very much in the eye of the beholder – that is, the court. Indeed, the general idea of the morally responsible patient, the production of which, it is argued, the process of ascertaining mental capacity in refusal cases is dedicated, is an unclear one – dependent on whether the particular patient's approach and performance in court happens to coincide with the views and visions of members of the judiciary.

What it is possible to see here is the replication in medical law of a concept of autonomy – principled autonomy – that has its foundations in moral philosophy. But, whilst true, we should not assume that this fully explains the presence of principled autonomy in this area of the common law. Rather, and in keeping with the foregoing analysis of individual autonomy, we must also consider the possible structural reasons why principled autonomy is to be found in the types of cases discussed in this chapter. In other words, in methodological terms, just because medical law is traditionally presented in the academic literature as being intimately related to questions of ethics, should not mean that explanations of the role of autonomy in medical law need be confined to the ethics-law axis. What other types of factors, then, might contribute to the existence of principled autonomy in medical law?

One such factor relates to what Montgomery, referring to the medical law field, has called 'inter-professional politics' (Montgomery 2006, 207). The foundations of this 'politics' can be traced to the traditional deference shown by the judiciary to the medical profession's own standards of practice. Those standards would, effectively, be determinative of the legal obligations owed by doctors to their patients.[27] As indicated in the discussion of individual autonomy above, there has been an effort by members of the judiciary to present this as an outmoded form of judicial practice and, simultaneously, to assert the importance of patients' rights. What is clear from the analysis in this chapter, however, is the continued reliance by the courts on the medical profession in pursuing this increased focus on the position of patients and their rights. Somewhat paradoxically, the historical respect shown to doctors by the judiciary is retained in refusal cases as part of the wider effort to reduce the power of the medical profession *vis-à-vis* the patient. This works in the following way. As we have seen, the involvement of psychologists and psychiatrists in the legal procedure for establishing patients' mental capacities is intended to be consistent with the movement towards a discourse of patients' rights and individual autonomy. This is because those medical professionals are portrayed as experts in a procedure which is held out as being technical and objective, rather than evaluative and judgmental.[28] The split constructed within the courts between the nature of patients' decisions

27 The classic example is *Bolam v. Friern Hospital Management Committee* (1957).

28 It should be noted that the legal test for mental capacity in medical law originated from a member of the medical profession – a Dr Eastman. In *Re C (Adult: Refusal of Medical*

(something which cannot be questioned) and tests for mental capacity (which, because they are designed to assess understanding and use of treatment information, are supposed to be neutral) is meant to subvert the possibility of medical paternalism by confining the medical professional's role (like that of the judiciary itself) to that of judging the state of the patient's mind, while allowing the courts to assert the importance of individual autonomy.

In reality, however, this reliance of the courts on psychologists and psychiatrists is consistent with the existence of – indeed helps produce – principled autonomy. This is because, as we saw earlier, those medical professionals consider a range of factors when trying to establish if patients have mental capacity. Importantly, they have the power to construct patients' identities in such a way as to influence not only the courts' impressions of patients, but, potentially, the very types of factors looked to by courts as constitutive of mental capacity. In other words, the supposedly technical inquiry into whether a patient can use and weigh treatment information in the balance can, as we have seen, involve investigations into the patient's biography; judgments about how well the patient expresses herself under questioning; assessments as to whether her decision displays a responsible disposition; evaluations about her character and the extent to which this conforms to, or differs from, an unspecified norm.[29] As Butler-Sloss P said in *Re B*, the evidence of psychologists and psychiatrists is 'crucial' in refusal cases. But it is crucial in its ability, amongst other things, to construct images of the responsible patient in particular cases and to determine the approximation of different patients to those images. This evaluative role, which it is the purpose of the legal test for mental capacity to preclude, can be seen to subsist through the category of capacity itself. It is, therefore, the wider aspects of the psychologist's and psychiatrist's roles, and the respect shown by the courts to those medical professionals, that contribute to the existence of the concept of principled autonomy in refusal cases.

Another reason for the presence of principled autonomy in refusal cases relates to the nature of the cases themselves. At root, refusal cases concern the question of the continued existence of human life – they are, literally, matters of life and death. The courts therefore become directly involved in regulating the existence of human life. Given the gravity of the specific issue, and the medical profession's objective of sustaining human life, decisions by patients to refuse medical treatment that will result in their deaths must be investigated in great detail. Individual autonomy – with its stark focus on rights to the exclusion of obligations and responsibilities – offers too cumbersome a conception of autonomy to allow for the type of subtle investigation of patients' decisions (and patients themselves) required in refusal cases. Similarly, and as we have seen, blind faith in medical paternalism is no longer considered acceptable by the judiciary. Principled autonomy, on the other

---

Treatment) (1994), Thorpe J adopted Dr Eastman's procedure for determining the mental capacity of patients.

29 As Nikolas Rose says: 'Psychological agents and techniques are involved in assessment and diagnosis of problems of individual conduct in institutional sites such as hospitals, schools, prisons, factories and in the army' (Rose 1985, 1). We might add the courts to this list of 'institutional sites'.

hand, offers the possibility of stressing the importance of patients being able to decide for themselves, while simultaneously allowing for an investigation into the extent to which they have met various indeterminate standards of obligation and responsibility. Principled autonomy is therefore a useful tool by which the courts can negotiate the delicate task of regulating the continued existence of human life. It creates the necessary flexibility that allows judges to manage, and weigh, the various interests involved in refusal cases – including, as we saw in *Re B*, those of the patient and the ethics of medical professionals. In other words, principled autonomy serves a structural need of the common law – it helps it to perform its growing task of regulating the continued existence of human life.

Finally, just as the ideological use of individual autonomy in medical law reflects elements of the wider shift in governmentality from medicalization to legalization (that is, the displacement of values such as dependency and solidarity by notions of individual choice and self-determination – 'the right to choose' has become a staple feature of judicial discourse in this area), so the presence of principled autonomy within this field is, albeit loosely, indicative of the movement (also outlined in Chapter 2) towards the responsibilization of individuals both within the sphere of health care and in late modern Western societies generally. Principled autonomy essentially captures the idea of responsible choice and the examples referred to in this chapter reflect this phenomenon. Admittedly, they do not map directly onto Rose and Miller's idea of governance 'at a distance' which we encountered in Chapter 2. That is, the refusal cases are not concerned with persuading individuals to exercise their choice in accordance with broader political ideas of what is normal or healthy. Nonetheless, cases such as *Re B* illustrate the same underlying concern with producing certain types or images of individuals (in our case, patients) – those who are deemed to have exercised their choices responsibly because their actions conform to unspecified, but desired, norms of conduct and behaviour. Moreover, like the mechanisms used by political actors to influence individuals' choices, the processes (especially the legal test for mental capacity) for establishing whether patients conform to those norms are subtle in nature and virtually conceal the imperceptible forms of control and power that, in reality, define them.

Conclusion

It was suggested in Chapter 1 that a concern for the position of patients and, specifically, the need for their empowerment, is one of the ways in which some academic lawyers claim legal jurisdiction over issues arising in the domain of medical practice. Rights discourse is the primary mechanism through which the law is meant to redress the imbalance of power perceived to exist within the doctor–patient relationship. Autonomy is advanced as the ethical foundation of patients' rights. From the discussion in this chapter, it is clear that such arguments have found favour with the judiciary in a number of different cases within the medical law field. But the use of autonomy to support the right to self-determination is of limited use in explaining how the courts have, in practice, dealt with refusal (and other types of) cases. The reason for this is that the use of 'autonomy' in medical law is predominantly intended to represent O'Neill's individual autonomy. In other words, it equates solely to patients' rights and individuals who can demonstrate capacity to make their decisions free from any outside interference or vigilance. But it is suggested that this is only true – and therefore the concept of individual autonomy as an explanatory tool only useful – at the level of rhetoric or ideology. To grasp what actually occurs in practice in such cases demands that we consider whether, in fact, different conceptions of autonomy are at play within medical law. The concept of principled autonomy captures more fully this reality – a reality that displays the common law's less romantic, more complicated engagement with the patient in this area of the law. It has the ability to explain the subtle mechanisms deployed by the courts to ensure that patients' choices, and patients themselves, are responsible. It helps us to comprehend how surveillance and obligation, as much as rights, characterize the means by which the common law negotiates the empowerment of patients.

It has also been argued that the presence of individual and principled autonomy within such cases cannot be accounted for merely by the expression in law of philosophical reflections on autonomy within the fields of moral philosophy, bioethics and medical ethics. Rather, in addition, the existence within medical law of both those types of autonomy can also be explained by identifying the particular structural, or institutional, exigencies and problems existing within the common law in this area at any one time. The use of such a methodology renders it possible to understand how, and why, different conceptions of autonomy are deployed within the common law. Finally, it was suggested that the concepts of autonomy that currently exist within medical law can be seen to reflect, at least partially, the types of broader sociological shifts outlined in Chapter 2. In other words, the relationship between autonomy and the common law in this field constitutes a microcosm of wider sociological transformations.

All of the foregoing directs us to the potential benefits to be gained from a particular methodological approach to autonomy, and perhaps other ethical values and principles, within the medical law field. What defines this approach is the priority it assigns to social practices. In other words, in order to grasp the relationship between autonomy and medical law, it is necessary to analyse, and understand, the manner in which the common law works in particular sets of cases – what its function is; how it performs this function; what tests, for instance, it uses; what its relationship is to other actors; how, if at all, it relates to more general shifts in contemporary society. In attempting to understand how autonomy lives within the common law in the medical law sphere, it is argued that this type of methodology is a necessary complement to the more traditional approach of focusing on ethics and moral philosophy. More broadly, it contributes to our understanding of how a central plank of the case for increased legal jurisdiction within this area of the common law – that is, the need to empower patients – is managed in practice.

PART III

Chapter 5

Human Rights and the Power of Medical Law

Introductions

Part III

In this, the final, part of the book, our attention turns to the second feature identified in Chapter 1 as being central to some academics' claims to legal jurisdiction over medical matters – that is, that the ethical issues arising within medical practice should be determined outside of the medical profession. Moreover, it will be recalled that those claims included the argument that law is the most suitable institution within society to determine the nature of the ethical principles to be applied to the various moral controversies occurring in the field of medical practice. The overriding purpose of the next two chapters is to test the degree to which such claims stand up in the face of evidence from what are commonly assumed, at least within the medical law field, to be several important cases. More specifically, the choice has been made to focus on two types of cases – those involving human rights claims, and those where the question of moral conflict defines the nature of the case. The reason for electing to concentrate on such cases is that, if any cases present the opportunity for the courts to become actively engaged in analyses of ethical issues, determinations of the nature of ethical principles, and applications of those principles to resolve ethical controversies, then those involving questions of human rights and moral conflict are surely high on the list of potential candidates.

In order to determine whether or not judges have adopted a proactive role in those types of cases, the analysis will centre on the workings and practices of the common law. Thereafter, the discussion will turn to consider what some of the consequences of the operation of those institutional features might be – not only for the aspirational type of argument within the academic medical law literature that constitutes the focus of the analysis in this part of the book, but also for the nature of the ethical issues themselves and for claims that the courts have the ability to play a wider role in helping to redress the democratic deficit that, as we saw in Chapter 2, Beck argues lies at the heart of developments in medicine and biomedical science today. Thus, in this part we will again be engaged in analysing how the judiciary asserts the courts' developing jurisdiction, or power, over ethical issues and controversies arising in medical practice and from developments in biomedical science.

Human rights and the power of medical law

It has been suggested that:

> Perhaps the most massive recent penetration of extra-medical considerations into medical ethics has been the acknowledgement, partly under political compulsion, that the distribution of medical care in our society must be rationalized to a greater extent in terms of 'health rights' which citizens hold simply by virtue of membership in society. Here, medicine is adapting its ethical system to moral considerations of a predominantly political and legal character ... In terms of medical ethics, this change must be adjudged a great victory. One concomitant of this victory – in certain respects a cost and in others a benefit – will be the further projection of medical responsibilities into the realm of public discourse. When massive social planning for new systems of health care is undertaken, medical advice takes on a new importance in public affairs. The fiduciary responsibilities of the medical profession then come to include the task of providing expert leadership for the public's deliberation on health policy. (Parsons et al. 1999, 144; reference omitted)

Parsons et al.'s description of medicine's role in the delivery of health care in American society is interesting because it suggests that, rather than having the effect of restricting the functions of a profession, the presence of a rights discourse may widen and deepen them in influential ways. Thus, medicine's adjustment to a discourse ('health rights') characterized largely by its legal and political nature forms the basis for its claim to a broader – one might say political – function. No longer are members of the medical profession merely concerned with tackling disease; additionally, the presence of a rights discourse affords them a privileged public position in the debate about health generally, and the delivery of health care in particular.

This observation that a profession's accommodation of a rights discourse can have the effect of extending its reach provides a useful working hypothesis for thinking through the relationship between human rights and the common law generally, and human rights and the role of the courts in medical law cases specifically. Altering Parsons et al.'s terms slightly, it can be asked whether the legal positivization of human rights (by way of the Human Rights Act 1998 [hereinafter 'HRA']) is resulting in the courts adapting to 'moral considerations of a predominantly political character' in the field of medical law. To put it differently, given the nature of human rights – that is, that they represent fundamental human values whose precise meaning in specific circumstances is often the source of conflict and disagreement, and that, amongst other things, they are deployed to criticize actions of the state (including oppressive laws) – one can ask if the judiciary is altering its practices to recognize and accommodate those features of human rights.

The institutionalization – or positivization – of human rights in law certainly has potential consequences for traditional understandings of the role of courts. Specifically, it is capable of extending the judicial function (traditionally associated with upholding the rule of law) so as to incorporate contentious political and ethical tasks.[1] For some, this amounts to the creation of an unjustifiable judicial power to 'resolve' controversial issues that are the subject of legitimate and profound

---

1   For a useful discussion of this, see Campbell 2006, Chapter 5.

disagreement within societies (that is, they are properly political questions) by determining which of those fundamental human rights are most significant and what they should mean in particular contexts. For others, this widening of the judicial role is a cause for double celebration. Firstly, it signals the dawn of an era in which the courts can truly set about doing some justice by defending individuals against the might of the state; secondly, it means that judges can now openly, and rightly, perform the function – the determination, and recognition, of human rights – that lies at the heart of others' criticism.

The argument advanced in this chapter is that, at least insofar as medical law is concerned, the legal positivization of human rights has tended not to result in the courts adapting to moral considerations of a predominantly political character. In other words, the judiciary has largely refrained from using the passing of the HRA as a vehicle to become actively involved in debating the ins and outs of the ethically contentious issues that have been the subject of human rights claims in the medical law sphere; nor has it adapted its practices to contain the critical and agonistic features of human rights described above. Rather, in emphasizing the importance of applying traditional techniques of legal reasoning, the courts have sought to avoid such a role and have, instead, presented the exercise of judicial power as conservative and objective. The assertion of such a power, however, masks its controversial effects at the moral and political levels, not the least of which is to deny what many consider to be the essential characteristics of human rights. Moreover, because this legal power appears objective and neutral, and therefore uncontroversial, the structural apparatus of the common law is never really thought to be deserving of critical attention in the academic medical law literature. With academic energy diverted elsewhere – to the ethics of the specific issue and/or which human rights ought to have been upheld in the instant case, for example – the danger is that the controversial effects of the operation of this structural apparatus will remain hidden from view. It will be argued here that, if we are to understand the relationship between medical law and human rights more fully, we must pay more attention to the role, and implications, of those structural features of the common law.

The discussion in this chapter is arranged around two focal points. Firstly, drawing on critical work on rights and human rights in legal and political theory, the general relationship between the legal positivization of human rights and the common law will be discussed. This wider inquiry is essential if a fuller understanding of the relationship between human rights and medical law is to be gained. Secondly, through a consideration of a few prominent legal cases, this critical literature will be used as a platform from which to assess the judiciary's reception of human rights in the medical law sphere to date.

Debating the Legal Institutionalization of (Human) Rights

Politics and the legal positivization of rights

In his book, *Sword and Scales*, Martin Loughlin sets out some fundamental features of the historical relationship between law and politics (Loughlin 2000). He traces how constitutionalism, and the meaning and role of rights, have evolved over time. Beginning with John Locke's argument that individuals possess certain inalienable natural rights, Loughlin charts the political importance of the idea of rights from the American Declaration of Independence 1776 and the French Declaration of the Rights of Man and Citizen 1789, to the present day. The current instantiation of rights discourse, he argues, has resulted from 'a fundamental shift in our perception of the nature of political order' (Loughlin 2000, 202).[2] The state no longer exists for a limited number of 'negative' purposes; rather, it has also become subject to the demands of individuals who make claims upon it to take positive action to fulfil their rights.

Loughlin emphasizes the political nature of rights claims. By 'political' he does not simply mean that the state must arrive at a conclusion as to which rights will be privileged. Rather, it also conveys the fact that a feature of rights claims is their contestability. The very terminology of such claims results in issues becoming polarized, meaning that the ensuing conflicts are highly charged and difficult to resolve. This notion of the political as conflict differs from what Loughlin, referring to T.H. Marshall's work on citizenship, describes as 'political rights'. The latter, incorporating such rights as the right to vote, are to be viewed simply as the mid-point of the development of rights discourse from the abstract natural rights of the eighteenth century to the 'practical' social rights (welfare, health and education, for example) of today. For Loughlin, though, what is significant is that social rights, for example, are political in the sense that, as well as placing positive obligations upon the state, they are matters for debate and argument – they engender fundamental conflicts over, and disagreements about, the ways in which we are to live.[3]

In his view, the law does not remain immune to the effects of these transformations in the nature of rights. With individuals now able to use codified charters of rights to justify their rights claims, the law, rather than the political sphere, becomes the preferred location for the advancement of such claims. Moreover, this 'institutionalisation of rights in legal systems' produces a shift in the function of law:

> Rights which previously received their recognition through legislation, now find their source in a rational claim to the inherent dignity and worth of the human person. And when these assume the status of 'fundamental human rights', they become the criterion against which the legality of legislation may be measured. The rule of law is no longer treated as a set of techniques through which an independent judiciary can keep government within the bounds of the rules of law. The rights conception insists that the judiciary ensure that the moral and political rights which citizens possess ... are accurately identified and fully and fairly enforced. The rights conception blurs the distinction between moral/political and legal discourse and converts the rule of law from a political ideal into a foundational juridical principle. (Loughlin 2000, 212–13)

---

2   For further discussion of the relationship between rights, politics and law, see Loughlin 2004, Chapter 7.

3   More recently, Loughlin has described what he calls 'the first order of the political' in the following terms: 'Politics is rooted in human conflict arising from the struggle to realize our varying ideals of the good life' (Loughlin 2004, 52).

Law, therefore, begins to assume a role (the identification and application of 'principles of right conduct') that, hitherto, was a strictly political one. This 'politicization of law' – as Loughlin calls it – results in the intensity of political debate being channelled through the more calming features of the law. Indeed, it means that politics must be conducted within a legal framework that is based on 'a set of foundational [or higher order] principles'. The extent of political debate and action is, therefore, set by law. A major consequence of this is that, 'the political critique of law can no longer come mainly from the outside; the moralization of law means that political critique must also come from within' (Loughlin 2004, 128).

As Loughlin notes, the legal positivization of rights places a significant degree of power in the hands of unelected judges to determine political and moral conflicts (which do not admit of any objective resolution) on the basis of their judgments as to which basic values are more deserving of being upheld. This process, he says, is 'intrinsically political' (Loughlin 2004, 129).

The next section will consider a specific instance of Loughlin's general argument. To do so, reference will be made to some related material presented by Tom Campbell (Campbell 1999 and 2006).

Diminishing the critical potential of human rights

Like Loughlin, Campbell's focus is the positivization – or, as he calls it, the 'legal institutionalization' – of rights (specifically human rights) and the potential consequences of this for democracy and our idea of politics. The main danger he envisages is the transfer of discussion and debate about the content and form of human rights from the forum of 'representative politics' to the courts, with an unelected judiciary acquiring the power to determine the precise meaning of abstract human rights in particular cases before them. While there is consensus on the basic principles underlying human rights, the substantial and legitimate disagreement concerning what such rights mean, and demand, in practice, suggests that the case for the removal of their determination from the sphere of democratic debate is insupportable.

Adopting a legal philosophy perspective, Campbell discusses two possible ways in which the legal positivization of human rights might be understood. On the one hand, this could be seen as an attempt to create clear and specific rules within which governments must operate. In other words, it would provide an identifiable mechanism through which the courts could determine the legality of acts of government and, thereby, perform their traditional 'rule of law' function.[4] On the other hand, given the nature of the interests that human rights claims seek to protect (fundamental values), and the need for a framework that would allow the judiciary to reflect upon questions of ethical principle, the narrow character of the traditional 'rule of law' function would be insufficient. Instead, what would be required is a less structured framework, which would be more concerned with general ethical principles and 'moral deliberation'. Campbell argues that this latter observation points to a much more discretionary role for the judiciary, with its members devoting more of their

---

4   On the rule of law, see Campbell 2006, 91–5.

time to identifying what they consider to be the moral values upon which human rights provisions were founded, and intended to protect.

Three main criticisms of this specific growth in judicial power can be identified from Campbell's work. Firstly:

> Such a system of moral supervision is defensible, however, only to the extent that there is accessible knowledge of objective universal values available to courts. It may be seen as an achievement of the human rights movement that there is a widespread belief that such knowledge is indeed available. However ... this neo-natural law philosophy with its high confidence in the accessibility of human rights to human reason and the capacity of judges to reach an objective assessment of the content and priority of such rights far outstrips any available epistemological foundations which would justify taking such issues outside the domain of political disagreement. (Campbell 1999, 10)

The 'epistemological foundations' he refers to are bound up with questions regarding the content and form of human rights. He notes that these factors, despite, or perhaps because of, their contestability, are often conveniently ignored in arguments that merely concern themselves with the most appropriate forum within which the objectives that human rights claims are assumed to secure can be upheld. But it is just those objectives that form the subject of often profound disagreement. To proceed as if there existed some overwhelming consensus on the nature of human rights, and what these demand in practice, is falsely to present the form of their institutionalization as the only legitimate issue over which debate is required.

Secondly, if one accepts the argument that human rights are best positivized, these important abstract and theoretical questions naturally come to take their place in the form of legal principles and rules which are applied to practical problems coming before the courts. The content of human rights therefore becomes subject to what Campbell calls the 'familiar methods of legal reasoning'. The problem is this:

> [A]s we institutionalize human rights, they become just another set of rules and principles and just another set of human organizations which embody just another set of negotiated and enforced compromises between the dominant values of the time. *Positivizing human rights undermines the power of the concept to provide a source of morally imperious critiques of ordinary laws and legal systems.* (Campbell 1999, 14–15; emphasis added)

In other words, the previously strong identification of human rights discourse with the critique of law is weakened as human rights increasingly become part of the law. The insertion of human rights within the boundaries of law removes that feature of externality which was previously a pre-requisite for the use of such rights as critical weapons. As Loughlin notes, the consequence is that any critique must largely emanate from within the law itself. This, of course, matters greatly as there will be many occasions when judges interpret specific human rights in ways we do not agree with, but are impotent to criticize using an 'external' human rights discourse because we have entrusted the judiciary with the power to manage questions of human rights.

Finally, while Campbell's critique is predominantly directed at those constitutions (such as that of the United States) that empower the judiciary to invalidate legislation which is declared to be incompatible with certain fundamental rights, he is equally suspicious of less democratically erosive measures, such as the HRA (see Campbell 2006, 101–2). These 'compromise solutions', as he calls them, do not necessarily reduce the power of judges[5] and can, indeed, contribute to the process by which the 'responsibility for the pursuit of rights [is taken away] from the democratic process' (Campbell 2006, 101).

Summary

Loughlin and Campbell inject some much-needed scepticism into the otherwise celebratory mood that often accompanies the legal positivization of rights and human rights. They both agree that this development has significant consequences for law, politics, and the critical potential of human rights. Two points should be noted here.

Firstly, human rights can be thought to be contestable in a dual sense. On the one hand, they reflect basic interests and values whose precise meaning in concrete circumstances is properly the subject of conflict and disagreement. On the other hand, they traditionally represent the language of dissent in the face of state oppression. They are deployed as a means of contesting what are considered to be unfair exercises of state authority, including oppressive laws.

Secondly, the legal positivization of human rights has the effect of diluting, or even smothering, their contestable character. For both Loughlin and Campbell, this occurs as part of the politicization of law. For them, this politicization entails the transfer of power to members of the judiciary to make decisions about controversial moral issues (for example) based on apparently objective determinations of the content of specific human rights – a content that is, in fact, capable of many, conflicting, interpretations. It is this discretion that judges have been handed to identify the precise nature of individuals' moral and political rights that both authors describe as 'political' and signal out as the real danger of the legal positivization of human rights. It might be said, then, that this politicization of law is, simultaneously, a *depoliticization* as it diminishes the contestable character of human rights in the following ways: on the one hand, the possibility of the legitimate conflict and disagreement over the specific meaning of human rights being played out in the courtroom is severely diminished, and perhaps even removed; on the other hand, it dilutes the ability to deploy human

---

5   This can be illustrated by reference to the HRA in the UK. While that Act does not permit judges to invalidate legislation passed by Parliament, a judicial declaration that a statute, or a part of it, is incompatible with a provision of the European Convention on Human Rights (hereinafter 'the ECHR') is likely to result in remedial action being taken by the government of the day. See, for example, the declaration of incompatibility by the judicial committee of the House of Lords in *A. v. Secretary of State for the Home Department* (2005), and the Government's response (the repeal of Part 4 of the Anti-Terrorism, Crime and Security Act 2001, and its replacement with a system of 'control orders' under the Prevention of Terrorism Act 2005. Some of these 'orders' have themselves subsequently been declared incompatible with Article 5 of the ECHR – see *Secretary of State for the Home Department v. JJ and others* (2006)). The conclusion to be drawn is that judges exercise a significant degree of power even under 'compromise solutions'.

rights discourse as a means of performing one of its traditional functions – that is, to criticize the content of particular laws and legal systems.

By way of an analysis of three recent cases, the following section will attempt to illustrate how Loughlin's and Campbell's analyses of the legal positivization of human rights are directly relevant to an understanding of the nascent relationship between medical law and human rights. It will be argued, however, that the courts' determinations of the specific meaning of human rights in the cases to be discussed are inextricably linked to the judges' perceptions of the proper role and requirements of the common law. In other words, in order to comprehend how the deflationary effect of legal positivization on the critical potential of human rights in the medical law sphere occurs, it is necessary to focus on the *relation* between judges' interpretations of human rights and other, institutional, exigencies. Confronted with the task of assessing the compatibility of both statutes and common law rules with human rights provisions, the judiciary has overwhelmingly sought to delimit the 'political' nature of their new function by deploying traditional techniques of legal reasoning – for example, a concern to respect legal precedent – to resolve cases, and by stressing the need for a restrained judicial role. The resulting impression given is of an exercise of power that is measured, objective and conservative. This is important as it tends to obscure both the central role that such techniques play in 'human rights' cases and just how controversial the effects flowing from their operation are. Without further ado, then, let us turn to a discussion of the cases.

Medical Law and Human Rights

R. (on the application of Pretty) v. Director of Public Prosecutions *(2002)*[6]

Dianne Pretty suffered from motor neurone disease, described by Lord Bingham as 'a progressive degenerative illness from which [Mrs Pretty] has no hope of recovery' (Pretty 2002, 5). The illness causes muscular weakness in several parts of the body – the arms, the legs and the muscles used for breathing and controlling speaking and swallowing – leading eventually to respiratory failure and pneumonia. In Mrs Pretty's case, the disease had advanced to a stage where, although mentally alert, she could not physically arrange to take her own life. The only way in which she could end her life was with the assistance of another person. To this end, she had asked her husband to help her. The obstacle confronting them was s.2(1) of the Suicide Act 1961 (hereinafter 'the 1961 Act') which provides that: 'A person who aids, abets,

---

6   Hereinafter '*Pretty*'. Strictly speaking, this would not be classified as a 'medical law' case. Nonetheless, given its relevance to the issue of physician assisted suicide and the discussion which it has elicited within the academic medical law community, the case merits inclusion here. For a useful overview of, and commentary on, this case, see Freeman 2002. It should be noted that in November 2005 Lord Joffe introduced the Assisted Dying for the Terminally Ill Bill into the House of Lords. This would allow mentally competent adults suffering unbearably as a result of a terminal illness to request medical assistance to die. In May 2006 The House of Lords voted to delay the Bill's second reading for six months, thus reducing its chances of making progress through Parliament.

counsels or procures the suicide of another, or an attempt by another to commit suicide, shall be liable on conviction on indictment to imprisonment for a term not exceeding fourteen years.' And although s.2(4) of the 1961 Act permits the Director of Public Prosecutions (hereinafter 'the DPP') to refuse to consent to prosecute the person assisting suicide, the DPP gave no such undertaking in Mrs Pretty's case. Mrs Pretty applied to the Queen's Bench Divisional Court seeking judicial review of the DPP's refusal to provide such an assurance. The Court did not find in her favour. She then unsuccessfully appealed to the House of Lords, which decided that the DPP was under no obligation to make the undertaking sought by Mrs Pretty. It also ruled that s.2(1) of the 1961 Act was not incompatible with the human rights provisions of the ECHR relied on by Mrs Pretty.[7] It is the law lords' deliberations on this latter aspect of the case that is of interest here.

When a human rights claim is brought to court, the role of the judiciary under the HRA is to decide whether the legislation, or the acts of a public authority, being challenged, is compatible with the article(s) of the ECHR upon which the claim is based. In *Pretty* the question was whether s.2(1) of the 1961 Act was compatible with Articles 2 and 8 of the ECHR.[8]

Article 2(1) of the ECHR states: 'Everyone's right to life shall be protected by law. No one shall be deprived of his life intentionally save in the execution of a sentence of a court following his conviction of a crime for which this penalty is provided by law.' In Lord Bingham's opinion, this provision was solely about the protection of the sanctity of life. Contrary to Mrs Pretty's argument, it had nothing to do with a right to self-determination regarding the existence of human life – that is, a right to choose how to live that incorporated a right to determine how and when one's life would end. Article 2(1), it was said, had nothing to do with death whatsoever. The 'right to life' could in no way be interpreted as including a right to die – it could only be interpreted as the protection of human life from outside attack. The other law lords agreed with Lord Hope's comment that: '[T]he protection of human life is [the] sole object [of Article 2]' (*Pretty* 2002, 36). This meant that individuals had a right to have the state preserve their lives, not a right to have the state permit them to extinguish their lives as part of a right to choose how to live. Given that the objective of s.2(1) of the 1961 Act was the protection of human life, it could not be declared to be incompatible with Article 2 of the ECHR. The ECtHR agreed.

If Article 2 had nothing to do with rights to self-determination, perhaps Article 8 offered better prospects for success. This Article states that:

1. Everyone has the right to respect for his private life and family life, his home and his correspondence.

---

7   Thereafter, Mrs Pretty applied to the European Court of Human Rights (hereinafter 'the ECtHR') which ruled that there had been no violations of any of the Convention rights upon which she had relied. See *Pretty v. United Kingdom* (2002).

8   Mrs Pretty also relied on other Articles of the ECHR (Articles 3, 9 and 14). For the purposes of the present discussion, however, the analysis will be confined to the law lords' reflections on Articles 2 and 8.

2. There shall be no interference by a public authority with the exercise of this right except such as is in accordance with the law and is necessary in a democratic society in the interests of national security, public safety or the economic well-being of the country, for the prevention of disorder or crime, for the protection of health or morals, or for the protection of the rights and freedoms of others.

The House of Lords and the ECtHR differed in their responses to the question of whether Mrs Pretty's rights under Article 8 were engaged.

While none of the law lords found Article 8 to be engaged, there was a slight difference of approach in their reasoning. In coming to this conclusion, Lords Bingham and Steyn accepted the argument of the Secretary of State for the Home Department that, while Article 8 is intended to protect the manner in which an individual chooses to conduct his or her life, it does not provide a right to choose when or how to die. Consequently, Mrs Pretty's attempt to utilize Article 8 encountered the same difficulty that confronted her when trying to rely on Article 2. In other words, if Article 8 was interpreted in the way she suggested, this would destroy what was considered to be its very essence – that is, its protection of choice in respect of *life* and *living*, and not in relation to death.

Lord Hope adopted a different approach. Like the other law lords, he said that the right to respect for a person's private life contained in Article 8 concerned the way in which individuals choose to live their lives. However, in contrast to Lords Bingham and Steyn, he reasoned that the manner in which a person decides to pass the closing moments of his or her life forms part of the individual's 'private life'. Rather than couching Mrs Pretty's claim in the language of a right to die, Lord Hope argued that decisions made about the end of one's life formed 'part of the act of living'. He went on: 'In that sense, her private life is engaged even where in the face of a terminal illness she seeks to choose death rather than life' (*Pretty* 2002, 39). Ultimately, however, Lord Hope decided that Article 8 was not, in fact, engaged because: '[I]t is an entirely different thing to imply into these words ["respect for a person's private life"] a positive obligation to give effect to her wish to end her own life by means of an assisted suicide. I think that to do so would be to stretch the meaning of the words too far' (*Pretty* 2002, 39).

The ECtHR, on the other hand, decided that Article 8 was engaged in Mrs Pretty's case. Agreeing with Lord Hope's opinion that the choices an individual makes about the end of his or her life form part of the act of living (and, thus, part of the individual's 'private life' under Article 8), the ECtHR ruled that, because the 1961 Act prevented Mrs Pretty from choosing to take steps 'to avoid what she considers will be an undignified and distressing end to her life', it would not rule out the possibility that this amounted to an interference with her right to respect for private life under Article 8. Effectively, then, the ECtHR decided that Article 8 was engaged.

If, in the opinion of the ECtHR, Article 8 was engaged, then why was there found to have been no violation of this? In order to come to this conclusion, it had to be demonstrated that the interference with Mrs Pretty's right to respect for private life was necessary in a democratic society.[9] In finding that this provision had been met, the ECtHR stressed the underlying justification for the prohibition of assisted suicide in the 1961 Act – namely, the protection of the lives of others who may be weaker and more vulnerable than Mrs Pretty, and who may be unable to express whether, and if so how, they wished to end their lives. In the first instance, it was for States to measure the risk and likelihood of abuse should the law on assisted suicide be relaxed. As the possibility of abuse in this context was real,[10] States were afforded a greater margin of appreciation. Consequently, as the blanket ban on assisted suicide in the 1961 Act was proportionate to the legitimate aims of the legislation (the maintenance of human life through protection of the weak and vulnerable), Article 8 had not been violated.

What does the manner in which the House of Lords approached Dianne Pretty's case reveal about the emerging relationship between the common law and human rights? First, it suggests that the positivization of human rights in law will not necessarily result in a more interventionist role for the courts. This much is clear from the following comment by Lord Bingham:

> The committee [the appellate committee of the House of Lords] is not a legislative body. Nor is it entitled or fitted to act as a moral or ethical arbiter ... The task of the committee is not to weigh or evaluate or reflect [the different] beliefs and views [about whether people should be allowed to seek assistance in taking their lives] or give effect to its own but to ascertain and apply the law of the land as it is now understood to be. (*Pretty* 2002, 5–6)

This latter, and 'proper', judicial task can be seen more clearly in the committee's approach to the question of the relationship between the provisions of the 1961 Act and Articles 2 and 8 of the ECHR. Thus, the interpretation of Article 2 proceeds on the basis of logic (an article which talks of a right to life cannot, by implication, relate to anything concerning death, including a right to die) and not from the perspective of whether the right to life *should* include a right to die. Similarly, Lord Bingham's and Lord Steyn's approach to Article 8 was based on a literal interpretation of the first paragraph. In relation to Article 8(2), the committee's concern was with identifying the objective underlying the passing of the 1961 Act, rather than advancing its own view of whether, today, the prohibition on assisted suicide is 'necessary in a democratic society'. This move to dissociate itself from any direct involvement in managing a sensitive ethical issue which might, for example, involve asserting the significance of ethical principles not recognized in the 1961 Act (such as the freedom and dignity of the individual), is at odds with the sort of proactive judicial role advocated by some academic medical lawyers who see this field as inextricably linked to human rights (see Kennedy 1988a and McLean 1999). Rather, the evident

---

9 Article 8(2), ECHR. Of course, as the House of Lords decided that Article 8 was not engaged, resolution of this point was not required and, hence, not critical to the outcome of the appeal. Nonetheless, the law lords – particularly Lord Bingham – set out what their stance would have been had it been necessary to decide whether Article 8 had been violated. Their conclusions on Article 8(2) were endorsed by the ECtHR.

10 As Montgomery points out, the ECtHR accepted this argument without any evidence being submitted to demonstrate that such a risk did, in fact, exist (see Montgomery 2006, 208).

judicial power arising from the passing of the HRA was, in this case, constructed in such a way as to reassure litigants and the public that it would not be exercised controversially. The emphasis placed on the traditional judicial function of statutory interpretation, and the logical analysis of the relevant ECHR Articles, signifies the assertion of a measured, conservative and neutral judicial power in the wake of the legal positivization of human rights. The message is that judges must show restraint after the passing of the HRA.

Of course, and this is the second observation arising from *Pretty*, the construction of judicial power in this manner does not mean that the law lords fail to determine the specific nature of the human rights relied on by Mrs Pretty; they clearly do define what those rights mean in the context of the case. But two points need to be stressed here. The first is captured in the following observation by Campbell: 'The core point … is that, while we can agree on general human rights principles, such as the dignity of human existence, the basic equality of all human beings and the wickedness of inflicting unnecessary human suffering, we disagree what these fundamental principles require in practice' (Campbell 2006, 98). Thus, the presence of such abstract principles does not necessarily mean that, in practice, they will be protected in the manner in which we might hope and expect. This point is especially relevant to work in the area of academic medical law, where, as we saw in Chapter 1, arguments about the need to involve law are often justified on the basis of its ability to ensure that fundamental principles and values – such as justice and dignity – are respected and upheld. Campbell, however, urges us to focus on what meanings such abstract principles receive in practice. We cannot simply assume that, because law has the ability to respect such fundamental principles and values, it will in fact do so. *Pretty*, itself, is an excellent example of it *not* doing so (we need only consider the value of human dignity). Thus, the workings of the common law can result in outcomes that are not only controversial, but undermine the claims some academic medical lawyers make for the involvement of law in this area.

The third point concerns the relation between those judicial determinations/ definitions of the nature of the specific human rights provisions and the need to ensure that judicial power is presented in the manner described. Again, the law lords' interpretation of one of the relevant Articles (Article 2) is illustrative. By ruling that the right to life in Article 2 is 'merely' protective of human life, and does not involve a right to choose how to live (itself including a right to choose how to die), the law lords clearly determine what meaning 'the right to life' will have in the current context. But their logical, deductive, method of arriving at this determination also contributes to the presentation of a conservative and apparently uncontroversial judicial power. Whilst it is impossible to go so far as to say that the judicial definition of the meaning of Article 2 is a direct product of the need to assert this neutral judicial power, it is suggested that the two are related, and that this relation is important in trying to understand the form that the legal positivization of human rights have taken in the common law.

The final observation arising from the case is that the law lords' approach suppresses the contestable features of human rights outlined earlier. Thus, on the one hand, the law lords' specific determinations of the meanings of the abstract rights in Articles 2 and 8 of the ECHR in the particular context of this case are not the only possible interpretations. Many, for instance, would no doubt argue that a 'right to life' is capable of including a right to choose how to live. Similarly, there would be those who contest the finding that the legal restriction on assisted suicide is 'necessary in a democratic society'. The crucial point here, though, is that these interpretative disagreements are not played out in the courtroom; instead, the law lords simply give effect to their own ideas of what the human rights in question mean – ideas that are enforced without the possibility of being contested. And where conflict over the meaning of an Article does surface (such as was the case with Article 8), it is simply one *between the law lords themselves*, rather than one reflecting the variety of possible interpretations that might legitimately exist.

On the other hand, the ability to deploy the language of human rights to criticize the content of the particular law (the 1961 Act) is weakened. As Loughlin argues, the institutionalization of human rights in law robs such rights of the quality of externality – a quality upon which their critical potential depended. Rather than equipping Mrs Pretty with the tools to undertake her true objective – that of criticizing an oppressive law that not only denied her any shred of dignity by preventing relief from the suffering so cruelly, and randomly, inflicted upon her by the onset of disease, but also threatened to imprison her husband for up to 14 years, should he have been convicted of assisting in relieving her of said suffering – human rights merely offer her legal counsel the opportunity to advance interpretations of Articles of the ECHR with which the law lords may or may not agree. Institutionalizing human rights in law means that their management (how they are defined and how they can be used, for example), at least partly, becomes dependent on internal institutional features, such as techniques of common law reasoning and the judicial perception of the proper role of the courts.[11] On the evidence of *Pretty*, then, the language of human rights after their positivization is, in the words of Campbell, unlikely 'to provide a source of morally imperious critiques of ordinary laws and legal systems'.[12]

It should be noted, however, that it is not just the critique of the oppressive content of specific laws that is rendered more difficult as a result of the legal positivization of human rights. Equally, it is less likely that the mechanisms responsible for the above effects – such as the need to deploy traditional techniques of legal reasoning – will be identified and subjected to analysis. The assertion of conservative judicial power that those mechanisms facilitate tends to mean that the role these play in

---

11 Or, as Douzinas puts it, their legal positivization has meant that human rights have become the 'bedfellows of positivism' (Douzinas 2000, 243).

12 It might be objected that this is precisely the type of case, and judicial approach, that both Loughlin and Campbell would have little problem with. This is because the judiciary is merely interpreting a statute that has been passed after debate in a democratic institution (Parliament). However, if, as Loughlin argues, the legal positivization of fundamental rights means that individuals increasingly seek to claim their rights through the courts, there is little perceived need to use human rights discourse to challenge oppressive laws through democratic channels. As Campbell points out: '[A]ll of these compromise devices [such as the HRA] ... suffer from the consequence that they are either ineffective or *they take responsibility for the pursuit of rights away from the democratic process*, something whose debilitating effects are the greater as we increase the range and scope of what counts as a human right' (Campbell 2006, 101–2; reference omitted; emphasis added).

the production of the types of controversial effects just outlined is masked from view. Somewhat ironically, their very ordinariness and unexceptionality render them crucial, but unlikely, objects of critical inquiry.

NHS Trust 'A' v. M; NHS Trust 'B' v. H *(2001)*

This relationship between the institutional features of the common law and the judicial reception of the positivization of human rights after the passing of the HRA is evident in other cases too. It should be noted that the cases discussed in this subsection – those involving patients in a permanent vegetative state (hereinafter 'PVS') – differ from *Pretty* in a few respects. Firstly, they involve no human rights challenge by an individual. Secondly, given their subject matter, they directly involve the question of the role of medicine and medical practice (that is, they can properly be called 'medical law' cases). Finally, rather than a statute, it is the common law's own rules and principles that are the subject of assessment for compatibility with the Articles of the ECHR. Notwithstanding those differences, it will be argued that the PVS cases discussed here afford similar insights into the legal positivization of human rights as those provided by *Pretty*.

Mrs M and Mrs H were both declared to be in a PVS. The hospital trusts responsible for their care wished to discontinue the artificial nutrition and hydration (hereinafter 'ANH') keeping them alive and, to this end, applied to the Family Division of the High Court seeking declarations that their proposed actions would be lawful. The women's families and the hospitals' staff supported the applications, which were not opposed by the Official Solicitor appointed to represent M and H. The diagnoses of PVS had been unanimous and the President of the Family Division – Dame Elizabeth Butler-Sloss – commented that there was a very strong case for granting the declarations, assuming the proposed actions were lawful.

The main question posed by the President was this: Would withdrawal of ANH contravene Article 2 of the ECHR (the 'right to life')?[13] An answer to this demanded consideration of two further, separate questions. First, would the cessation of ANH constitute an 'intentional deprivation of life' (Article 2(1))? In answering this negatively, the President relied on the distinction made in the common law between acts and omissions. She ruled that, while the intention of the withdrawal of ANH was to bring about death, this could not amount to a deprivation as it was an omission to provide medical treatment, and not a deliberate act (which, she argued, the word 'deprivation' implied here):

> A responsible decision by a medical team not to provide treatment at the initial stage [and also to withdraw treatment already begun because it was no longer deemed to be in the patient's best interests] could not amount to intentional deprivation of life by the state. Such a decision based on clinical judgment is an omission to act. The death of the patient is the result of the illness or injury from which he suffered and that cannot be described as a deprivation. (*NHS Trust 'A' v. M; NHS Trust 'B' v. H* 2001, 809)

---

13 Article 3 (the prohibition on torture and inhuman or degrading treatment) was found to have no relevance to PVS cases.

The second question was this: Do the specific circumstances of the case mean that a positive obligation is imposed on the state to provide life prolonging treatment to the patients? Noting that the positive obligation to safeguard life in Article 2 was not an absolute one, the President ruled that this obligation had been discharged in the present case because a responsible clinical decision had been made to withdraw the treatment. Provided this decision was based on a judgment that continued treatment would not be in the patients' best interests, and was in line with a respectable body of medical opinion, the positive obligation on the state had been discharged. In other words, while a positive obligation to safeguard life exists in Article 2, whether or not it has been discharged in cases of PVS depends on those doctors' opinions as to whether prolonged treatment would, or would not, be in the best interests of their patients.

Having answered those two questions, the President concluded that, as it was in the best interests of Mrs M and Mrs H to discontinue ANH, the hospital trusts' proposed course of action was lawful.

The President's management of the legal positivization of human rights in those PVS cases offers a number of insights. One relates to a point that Alasdair Maclean has made about 'human rights' cases in the medical law field generally. He has noted how those cases have been an exercise in judicial efforts to fit the provisions contained in the Articles of the ECHR to existing common law principles, and not, as ought to be the case, vice versa:

> With the HRA 1998 coming into force the courts must examine established common law principles that should, where necessary, be redefined to ensure compatibility with the Convention rights. This allows the courts a unique opportunity to improve the consistency and coherence of the common law without being unduly fettered by precedent. I have argued throughout that, while the outcome may be justifiable under the HRA 1998, Dame Butler-Sloss P [in *NHS Trust 'A' v. M; NHS Trust 'B' v. H*] interpreted the rights in that Act to ensure they were compatible with the common law rather than by adapting the common law to concord with those rights. (Maclean 2001, 793)

We might briefly note two instances of this in the President's judgment. Firstly, having interpreted Article 2 to mean that there is a positive, but not necessarily absolute, obligation to safeguard life, she states, 'This approach is entirely in accord with the principles laid down in *Bland*'s case ...' (*NHS Trust 'A' v. M; NHS Trust 'B' v. H* 2001, 811). Secondly, her interpretation of 'intentional deprivation of life' in Article 2 is made in such a way as to ensure compatibility with the common law. Thus, because the lawfulness of withdrawal of ANH in the common law relies on that discontinuance being viewed as an omission, and not as a deliberate act, 'deprivation' in Article 2 must only refer to the latter. Otherwise, the right to life would be incompatible with the common law rule. The common law distinction between acts and omissions is therefore one of the measures by which the 'right to life' in Article 2 is accorded meaning in the specific circumstances.

Alasdair Maclean argues that the cautious approach of the courts to interpreting human rights provisions in medical law cases stems from 'judicial concern regarding resource allocation and clinical integrity and a desire to avoid a flood of dubious claims ...' (Maclean 2001, 793). While all these are plausible explanations, it is suggested that the explanation for the Court's approach in the instant case resides at a deeper level. As in *Pretty*, what needs to be analysed here is the relation between the judicial interpretation of human rights provisions and institutional factors. This is especially so given that the rules and principles being scrutinized are those constructed by the judiciary – in other words, the common law. The Court is effectively being asked to assess the judiciary's own work.

The manner in which the President interprets Article 2 suggests a determination to ensure that the existing common law principles in this area (worked out, not without some difficulty, in *Airedale NHS Trust v. Bland* [1993]) are not tampered with at any cost. Thus, not only are those principles declared to be 'ECHR compliant', they are also presented as possessing authority because they constitute 'an important part of international jurisprudence on this subject [the withdrawal and withholding of ANH from patients in a PVS]. The existing practice in the United Kingdom is accordingly compatible with the values of democratic societies' (*NHS Trust 'A' v. M; NHS Trust 'B' v. H*, 2001, 812). Moreover, the President takes the opportunity to point out that the fact that the High Court reviews medical decisions about best interests in PVS cases means UK law has in place a more rigorous test than that set by the ECtHR. Cumulatively, the impression given is that, as the common law principles enunciated in *Bland* provide for something that the legal systems of other 'democratic societies' around the world also permit (withdrawal of ANH in PVS cases), these principles must be both sound and compatible with human rights provisions. The need to determine the compatibility of the common law rules with the relevant provisions of the ECHR is simply treated by the President as an opportunity to affirm this.

Again, as in *Pretty*, we can detect a conservative power at work here. Not only does the manner in which human rights are deployed in the instant case conserve the validity of the common law's current rules and principles in this area, it also contributes to the sense that, at least in medical law cases, the judiciary has no intention of using its powers under the HRA in controversial or political ways. Once more, however, this assertion of conservative power obscures the contentious consequences that flow from its exercise. So, for example, despite the fact that any reasonable person would understand the removal of medical treatment to be an act, rather than an omission, the President's decision (upon which the interpretation of 'intentional deprivation' in Article 2 depends) that it is the latter passes without any contest or disagreement. 'Deprivation' means 'a deliberate act', and that is the end of the matter. Similarly, this deployment of human rights as a means of defending current common law rules and principles severely diminishes the ability of individuals to use the discourse of human rights as a means of criticizing both the specific content of the law[14] and the fact that the legal institutionalization of human rights in law has taken the form that it has – that is, that it has been used as a way of justifying the existence of common law rules and principles that, while controversial, are made to appear quite the opposite.

---

14 Although note Munby J's judgment in *R. (Burke) v. General Medical Council* (2004) – discussed in the next subsection.

R. (Burke) v. General Medical Council *(2004 and 2005) (hereinafter* 'Burke'*)*

It is perhaps fitting to end this section with a discussion of a case in which two contrasting conceptions of the judiciary's function after the legal positivization of human rights can be seen. On the one hand, the opportunity to consider human rights provisions results in the pursuit of a more proactive judicial approach to cases within the medical law field. This style of judging – apparent in Munby J's judgment in the High Court – is much closer to the vision of those academic medical lawyers who characterize medical law as a subset of human rights law. The need to stress patients' rights and, thereby, to limit medical power; the willingness to use the law as a forum for discussing and determining controversial ethical issues; the use of human rights discourse to stress fundamental moral values and principles, such as human dignity – all appear in abundance in Munby J's 225-paragraph judgment.[15] On the other hand, the Master of the Rolls – Lord Phillips – counsels against such a sweeping and interventionist judicial role.[16] In his view, the passing of the HRA ought to be treated by the courts as an opportunity to re-emphasize the need for a conservative judicial role in medical law cases. It will be suggested here that it is in this reassertion of a limited judicial function that the significance of the case lies, rather than in Munby J's voluminous discussion of human rights jurisprudence and his attempt to carve out a more prominent role for patients.

Mr Burke suffers from spino-cerebellar ataxia – a degenerative illness that will eventually result in him having to receive ANH if he is to remain alive. He sought clarification from the High Court of the circumstances in which ANH may lawfully be withdrawn. He did so because he claimed that the General Medical Council's (hereinafter 'the GMC') guidance in respect of withholding and withdrawing life prolonging medical treatments (hereinafter 'the Guidance') was incompatible with his human rights under Articles 2, 3, 8 and 14 of the ECHR. To put it bluntly, Mr Burke wanted the Court to recognize that he had a right to insist, by way of an advance directive, that ANH be continued so long as he remained conscious.

Munby J upheld Mr Burke's challenge to the Guidance by ruling that its legal content was incompatible with his human rights under Articles 3 and 8 of the ECHR.[17] In particular, Munby J noted four specific criticisms of the Guidance. Firstly, it stressed the right of competent patients to refuse medical treatment, rather than their right to require treatment. Secondly, the fact that it was the duty of doctors, who were unable or unwilling to comply with their patients' wishes, to continue to provide treatment until they found another doctor who would do so, was not made sufficiently clear. Thirdly, the Guidance failed sufficiently to acknowledge the heavy presumption in favour of life prolonging treatment and to recognize that the touchstone of best interests was intolerability. This meant that, if life prolonging

---

15 *R. (Burke) v. General Medical Council* (2004). For a useful discussion of Munby J's use of human rights discourse in this, and a number of medical law cases, and its potential consequences for the courts' relationship with doctors, see Montgomery 2006, 204–6.

16 *R. (Burke) v. General Medical Council* (2005).

17 Relying on the judgment of the President of the Family Division in *NHS Trust 'A' v. M; NHS Trust 'B' v. H* (2001), Munby J ruled that Article 2 was not engaged in Mr Burke's case.

treatment was of some benefit, it ought to be provided unless the patient's life, if so prolonged, would be intolerable from the patient's point of view. Finally, it failed to spell out that there was a legal requirement to secure prior judicial sanction for the withdrawal of ANH in certain circumstances.

Relying on the ruling of the ECtHR in *Pretty*, Munby J stated that Article 8 incorporated a right to self-determination, which included both how one chose to pass the closing days and moments of one's life and how one managed one's death. Article 8 also ensured a right to dignity, including the preservation of mental stability, and the physical and psychological integrity of individuals. To withdraw ANH against Mr Burke's wishes, and before he lapsed into a coma, would, in principle, therefore breach Article 8. Although not entirely clear from Munby J's judgment, presumably it was the fact that the Guidance failed sufficiently to recognize that it was the patient's view of what was intolerable that mattered in determining whether discontinuing treatment would be in his best interests that rendered it incompatible with Article 8. Article 3, too, incorporated a right to dignity – specifically, a right to die with dignity – which included a right to be protected from treatment, or a lack of treatment, which would result in dying in avoidably distressing circumstances. Assuming he wished to have ANH continue, its removal prior to Mr Burke lapsing into a coma would, in principle, breach Article 3, as it would expose him to acute mental and physical suffering. Drawing the strands of his reflections on Articles 3 and 8 together, Munby J concluded:

> If the patient is competent (or, although incompetent, has made an advance directive which is both valid and relevant to the treatment in question) his decision to require the provision of ANH which he believes is necessary to protect him from what he sees as acute mental and physical suffering is likewise in principle determinative. There are two separate reasons why this is so. The first is based on the competent patient's rights under Article 8. The second is based on his rights, whether competent or incompetent, under Article 3. (*R. (Burke) v. General Medical Council* 2004, 1184)

On appeal, the GMC succeeded in having all of Munby J's declarations set aside.[18] Amongst other things, the Court of Appeal held that patients had no right to insist on receiving a particular medical treatment. They could not demand that a doctor administer a treatment which he or she considered to be adverse to the patient's clinical needs. Moreover, the idea of 'best interests' was not synonymous with the patient's wishes. Rather, the meaning of this concept depended on the specific context in which it was used. What is truly notable about Lord Phillips' judgment, however, is both the virtual absence of consideration of the human rights dimensions of Mr Burke's claims and the broader reflections it contains on the proper function of the courts in medical law cases. It is with these aspects that the following discussion is concerned.

In Lord Phillips' opinion, there were two principal errors inherent in Munby J's approach to Mr Burke's judicial review proceedings. The first regarded the High Court judge's failure to confine his analysis to answering Mr Burke's specific

---

18 See *R. (Burke) v. General Medical Council* (2005). The ECtHR upheld the Court of Appeal's decision. See *Burke v. UK* (App. No. 19807/06).

concern. This concern was that a competent patient, who had clearly expressed his wish to have life prolonging medical treatment continued, may have those wishes overridden by a doctor who deliberately removed ANH. Rather than focusing solely on this, Munby J had also considered the human rights implications of removing such treatment from Mr Burke when, on the one hand, he was no longer competent (but still sentient), and, on the other, he finally lapsed into a coma. This sweeping approach was strongly criticized by Lord Phillips. It was imperative, he said, that the judiciary avoid succumbing to the temptation to speculate on purely hypothetical circumstances that may or may not arise at some point in the future. For his part, if one concentrated on a competent patient like Mr Burke, it was difficult to follow Munby J's reasoning that, while such a deliberate removal of ANH would infringe Articles 3 and 8 of the ECHR, it would not also violate Article 2. He thought such a removal would clearly infringe Article 2. This is basically the extent of Lord Phillips' discussion of the ECHR. Indeed, in saying the fact that Articles 2, 3 and 8 may be engaged in Mr Burke's specific circumstances does not 'advance the argument or alter the common law', he plays down their importance and relevance.

The second error, while related to the first, was much more fundamental in that it contravened a central tenet of judicial reasoning. Munby J had incorrectly used Mr Burke's case as a vehicle to, in Lord Phillips' words, 'set out to write a text book or practice manual'. The liberty had been taken to engage in a wide-ranging discussion of central issues within the field of medical law and ethics, issues which bore no relation to the factual circumstances of Mr Burke's case. Munby J's judgment had, he said, been interpreted as a reflection on the right of patients to require medical treatment generally, and not simply treatment intended to sustain human life. Essentially, it might be interpreted as offering a broad critique of what has traditionally been viewed as the power imbalance at the heart of the doctor–patient relationship. In other words, it is a thinly veiled attempt to empower patients.[19]

Moreover, Munby J effectively deployed the discourse of human rights in an effort to secure a central role for members of the judiciary at the heart of debates about controversial ethical issues arising from medical practice. This implicit claim to exercise judicial jurisdiction over such issues more proactively drew a stinging riposte from Lord Phillips. In counselling against such a role, he cited the following words from Lord Bridge's judgment in *Gillick v. West Norfolk and Wisbech Area Health Authority* (1986):

> In cases where any proposition of law implicit in a departmental advisory document is interwoven with questions of social and ethical controversy, the court should, in my opinion, exercise its jurisdiction with the utmost restraint, confine itself to deciding whether the proposition of law is erroneous and avoid either expressing ex cathedra opinions in areas of social and ethical controversy in which it has no claim to speak with authority or proffering answers to hypothetical questions of law which do not strictly arise for decision. (*Gillick v. West Norfolk and Wisbech Area Health Authority* 1986, 227)[20]

---

19 It is interesting to note the following comment from Mr Burke on the Guidance: 'I am concerned that too much power is placed in the hands of the medical profession.'

20 Cited in *R. (Burke) v. General Medical Council* (2005), at 181, per Lord Phillips.

The clear implication was that Munby J had failed to display such 'restraint'. In Lord Phillips' opinion, he had transgressed the boundary of legitimate judicial reasoning, a reasoning which stipulates that the only occasion on which judges should address ethical issues is where resolution of the specific dispute before the court compels them to do so.

It is suggested that this aspect of Lord Phillips' judgment represents an unequivocal statement of the proper nature of the judicial role in medical law cases after the passing of the HRA. The emphasis placed on restraint, the avoidance of judicial engagement in discussing controversial ethical issues (unless absolutely necessary), and the requirement to focus solely on whether provisions of the Guidance are lawful (that is, on making determinations of legality), resonates with the judicial approaches witnessed in the cases discussed above. If there was a 'public' aspect to the case, it could be thought to lie in a reassurance to the public that the legal positivization of human rights would not be used as a vehicle for judges to become involved in discussing various ethical issues.[21] And while the Court of Appeal found little need to engage in the sort of extensive interpretation of human rights provisions undertaken by Munby J, it is clear from what Lord Phillips says that any such interpretative judicial function would need to be performed narrowly and directed only to the particular issue(s) at hand.

Two points should be noted here. The first is the same observation that was made above in relation to *Pretty* – that is, that Lord Phillips' characterization of the judicial role is entirely at odds with the type of aspirational view of the law advanced by some academic medical lawyers, and which we encountered in Chapter 1. The degree of criticism levelled against Munby J's judgment in the Court of Appeal confirms the reluctance of the appellate courts to become involved in debating grand ethical issues arising from medical practice. The Court of Appeal's decision in *Burke* is one of the most powerful examples yet of how much at odds the claims made by some academic medical lawyers to the benefits to be derived from developing legal jurisdiction over the various ethical issues in the field of medicine are with the judiciary's own perception of the nature of this jurisdiction – a jurisdiction that, as Lord Bridge says in *Gillick*, must be exercised with 'the utmost restraint' and must be directed to establishing whether the proposition of law at the centre of the case is, or is not, 'erroneous'.

The second point flows from the first. Thus, simply because the nature of judicial power is asserted as being minimal and conservative, does not mean that it ceases to exist. It simply means that its expression is to be found somewhere other than in the overt discussion and determination of contentious ethical issues. In *Burke* we can see this power operating through the stress placed on the need for a case-by-case approach and the deployment of standard techniques of legal reasoning with the objective of determining questions of legality. Moreover, and as in *NHS Trust 'A' v. M; NHS Trust 'B' v. H*, Mr Burke's reliance on human rights as the source of his challenge is effectively transformed by the Court of Appeal into a defence of current

---

21 Mr Francis QC, acting for the Official Solicitor, had submitted to the Court of Appeal that, by bringing the case, Mr Burke had undertaken a 'public service' by allowing wider issues of general public importance to be considered in court.

common law principles and rules. His human rights claims are all but excluded from Lord Phillips' judgment and, instead, it is the existing common law that is applied to ascertain the lawfulness of the Guidance.[22]

As aspects of the Court of Appeal's approach in *Burke* are similar to those found in *Pretty* and *NHS Trust 'A' v. M; NHS Trust 'B' v. H*, Lord Phillips' judgment is susceptible to the same types of criticisms levelled against those cases above. Thus, the assertion of a conservative judicial power masks the fact that the judiciary, through, for example, its defence of existing common law rules and principles, is engaged in negotiating and determining the values that ought to be upheld in cases involving withdrawal of ANH. Furthermore, the deflationary consequences of Lord Phillips' reception of the legal positivization of human rights in this case (resulting in the reduction of their contestable character, in the sense outlined earlier), while more difficult to detect as a result of the manner in which judicial power is asserted (that is, conservatively), are no less real for that. As in *Pretty*, the critical potential of human rights discourse is all but snuffed out in the Court of Appeal, and the reasons for this are intimately related to the operation of institutional factors within the common law.

Conclusion

At the beginning of this chapter it was suggested that one might apply Parsons et al.'s general thesis to law in order to ask whether the legal positivization of human rights is forcing the courts to adapt to moral considerations of a predominantly political character. The answer is: it is not, although the judiciary's reception of this positivization *is* having a significant impact at the moral and political levels. The cases discussed in this chapter illustrate that the legitimate disagreement over the meaning of particular human rights provisions in specific contexts is not currently played out in the courtroom. Equally important, the institutionalization of human rights has the consequence that the meanings ascribed to those provisions by judges cannot be contested. Judicial interpretations are final. Nor have the decisions of the appellate courts done anything to suggest that individuals will be able to use those rights in such cases as a means by which to criticize the oppressiveness of particular laws. Rather, the judiciary's approach to date may be thought to contribute to a process of depoliticization as its decisions tend to erode the contestable, political character of human rights. All this does not mean that the courts do not have a powerful role to play; on the contrary, and as Campbell and Loughlin point out, they do, in fact, determine what meaning human rights provisions are to have in specific circumstances – determinations that have tangible effects on the lives of individuals. It is just that the disagreement surrounding such meanings does not surface in the process.

It has been argued that those consequences are the product of how the legal positivization of human rights after the passing of the HRA has been received

---

22 It is noteworthy that, of the seven cases referred to in the course of Lord Phillips' judgment, six are domestic common law cases.

by the judiciary in the cases referred to. It has responded to this development by emphasizing, on the one hand, the importance of applying traditional techniques of legal reasoning – such as respect for legal precedent and the literal interpretation of statutes – to resolve cases, and, on the other, the scope of the courts' legitimate function when dealing with controversial ethical issues. The stress placed upon those institutional features has allowed the judiciary to present its power as conservative and objective, something which helps mask the role of such a power in the production of controversial effects.

How might we couch this state of affairs in jurisdictional terms? First, it can be said that the second mechanism by which some academics' claim the need for law to develop jurisdiction over problems and disputes arising in medicine – that is, that the ethical issues arising from medical practice should be determined externally to medicine and that law is the most appropriate institution within society to undertake this task – is at odds with the evidence available from the human rights cases discussed above. Indeed, the more proactive judicial approach called for in the literature has been roundly dismissed by the appellate courts. The judiciary talks of exercising its undeniably expanding jurisdiction in the era of human rights (the passing of the HRA will inevitably result in more human rights claims in the area of medical law) with 'the utmost restraint', not with abandon. It is concerned 'to ascertain and apply the law of the land as it is now understood to be', not 'to act as a moral or ethical arbiter'. But this should not compel us to throw up our hands and argue that, in future, everything would be much better if judges only grasped the opportunity presented by the legal positivization of human rights to become more proactive in dealing with such ethically controversial disputes by openly identifying, and applying, the values they consider are more deserving of being upheld. As Loughlin says, such a procedure would be 'intrinsically political'. Rather, what is being suggested here, and this might be viewed as the second jurisdictional point, is quite simply that there needs to be more analysis of the ways in which the courts in 'human rights' cases in this area actually exercise their jurisdiction, and, importantly, what the effects or implications that flow from this are. We need, in other words, to understand how traditional techniques of legal reasoning, mundane though they may appear to be, are implicated in the production of the types of controversial consequences and effects identified in this chapter.

Chapter 6

Moral Conflict, Debate and Medical Law

Introduction

It was suggested in the previous chapter that one of the consequences of the legal positivization of human rights in the medical law field has been the erosion of the fundamental disagreement and conflict that characterize human rights discourse. Given that conflict pervades the types of issues medical law is concerned with, it will be discussed in more detail in this chapter. Drawing on work in legal theory, and through the use of two case examples – one of which concerns developments in biomedical science – this chapter seeks to demonstrate not merely how and why conflict is suppressed and excluded in the courts, but also why this matters. Moreover, given that developments in medicine and biomedical science often proceed without any democratic debate regarding the ethical acceptability of those advances, it will be useful to ask whether the increasing involvement of the courts in managing controversial ethical issues arising from such developments is likely to have any positive impact on redressing this democratic deficit.

Once again, the overriding objective here is to try to understand how the judiciary exercises the courts' expanding jurisdiction over ethically contentious issues arising from advances in medicine and biomedical science. Building on the analysis in the previous chapter, it will be observed that judges are often unwilling to become actively involved in discussing the ethical aspects of the cases before them. Rather, they have responded to this new type of litigation by adhering to traditional techniques of legal reasoning, such as a respect for legal precedent and the underlying purpose of judicial review. The operation of these institutional exigencies, as they are called here, has a number of significant effects, one of which is to undermine the claim some academic medical lawyers make that the courts are places where the controversial ethical issues in this area can be addressed and the community's values declared.

Given this latter point, it will be helpful to set the following discussion against some recent writing in academic medical law that supports a more proactive approach by the courts to its management of cases involving contentious ethical questions. This work is Robert Lee and Derek Morgan's reflections on the role played by law in what they call 'regulating the risk society'. It is to their argument that we turn first.

Morgan and Lee – Law, Risk and Biomedical Diplomacy

In a recent article, Robert Lee and Derek Morgan set out an interesting and novel approach to the problems raised by what they perceive to be the incessant march of biomedical science and its technologies (Lee and Morgan 2001).[1] Taking their cue from Ulrich Beck's work on risk, they seek to think through the role of law in regulating developments in biomedicine and its associated technologies (see Beck 1992). Before discussing this aspect of their work, it is worth briefly setting out their view of the relationship between biomedical science, risk society and regulation.

It was stressed in Chapter 2 that the significance of the shift from medicine to biomedical science cannot be overstated. Given that its existence is relayed to us through the media on a daily basis, rarely do we need to look hard for evidence of this incipient transformation. The miracles of IVF technology and cloned sheep, and the awe-inspiring (depending on one's point of view) predictions for the capabilities of human genetic technology – all reflect the growing influence, and potential, of biomedical science. According to Lee and Morgan, however, there are significant problems allied to those developments. In particular, the extent to which not only specific applications of scientific knowledge, but the entire entity of biomedical science can be considered to constitute a worthwhile endeavour needs to be looked at carefully. The difficulty in trying to do so, however, is compounded by the realization that we are living in Beck's 'risk society'. Part of Beck's argument is that, due to developments in technology, human beings are today no longer at the mercy of an uninhibited nature but can, and do, control and adapt this to their desired ends. Advances in biomedical science, however, inevitably involve the production of unintended and, therefore, unforeseeable excess, some of which may have detrimental consequences for human societies generally. If it is recalled that sub-political mechanisms – such as science and technology – first, play a central role in creating those consequences and, secondly, do not exhibit democratic procedures in the process of doing so, there is a real danger that wider debate on crucial questions of public interest (the possible implications of decisions to be taken in the field of biomedical science) will not occur. Confronted with such a state of affairs, how are we to seek to regulate the applications of biomedical technology, especially in a manner that permits discussion of, and reflection on, the human values affected by, and the ethical implications of, what is proposed? Where can we go to debate what the good life ought to consist of and to assess which of the proposed applications would contravene whatever the outcome of such a debate happened to be?

In Chapter 2 we saw that Beck thought critical engagement by professionals within medicine and science and 'strong and independent media' had crucial roles to play in helping to redress the democratic deficit created by advances in those fields. It is, however, his suggestion of the need for 'strong and independent courts' that Lee and Morgan have picked up on and run with. In their view, law has a central role to play here. Specifically, it is what they call law's 'colloquial' nature – 'the ability of law to provide a forum within which such matters may be addressed' (Lee and Morgan 2001, 315) – that marks it out as especially useful as a regulatory tool in the risk society. Law is a stage upon which 'morality plays' are conducted; it is where the stories about encounters with biomedical science – whether in the context of

---

1   Their argument draws heavily on Morgan's theoretical approach in Morgan 2001. See, especially, Chapters 1–3.

conjoined twins or permanent vegetative states – can be told. The courts, especially, have acquired a prominent position in this respect in the medical law field:

> This [the colloquial response] lays a particularly heavy burden and responsibility upon legislators but perhaps especially on courts which are then called upon to examine the nature of these regulatory responses, and, it must be added, their obverse, legislative silence. This responsibility may be seen and may be keenly sought in what we have called 'stigmata' cases. These are those cases in which (and through the use and expansion of the mechanism of judicial review, increasingly) courts will be used as an arm of regulation in moral politics. *This will require that they develop and declare an explicit moral framework to their decision-making* … [A]s Lords Mustill and Browne-Wilkinson recognised in *Bland*, it is far from evident that the lexicon of law rather than the vocabulary of values will of itself be sufficient to carry their voice in this colloquy, to sustain their vote in this parliament of moral politics. (Lee and Morgan 2001, 315–16; emphasis added; reference omitted)

Thus, whether acting as a mediator among various regulatory responses emanating from the legislature – its traditional 'judicial review' function – or having to provide its own regulatory response to 'stigmata' cases,[2] Lee and Morgan insist that it will be necessary for courts to become engaged in the 'moral politics' surrounding the issues arising from developments in biomedical science. This, however, does not simply entail that members of the judiciary should declare their moral stances on the particular issues coming before them. If, as Lee and Morgan contend, ethical debate, and not politics, is emerging as the primary mode of participation today, and law, generally, has a vital function to perform in 'stimulating and contributing to ethical debate', then the courts necessarily also assist in the broader objective of establishing a democratic institutional response to the technological innovations in the risk society (Lee and Morgan's 'parliament of moral politics'). It is therefore the centrality of ethics and ethical debate that makes the need for judges to develop a clear moral framework to their decision-making so urgent. The significance of this deep role for law (including the courts) is neatly summed up in the following statement by Lee and Morgan, the first half of which is one of Sheila McLean's concluding remarks in her book *Old Law, New Medicine* (McLean 1999): "'It is not the *mechanics* of the law's response which are so important as its *content* – a content informed by concern for liberty, for the protection of the vulnerable and for the reinforcement of ideals" … Scientific citizenship requires that courts develop a moral vision and vocabulary so that we shape the moral economy of the emergent bioeconomy'[3] (Lee and Morgan 2001, 318; emphasis added; reference omitted).

---

2   Lee and Morgan's notion of 'stigmata cases' was originally articulated in Morgan and Lee 1997. As well as obliging courts to develop a moral vision, such cases are characterized by the following features: They are relatively novel and ethically controversial; they raise the balance of personal interests and public interest; they force us to focus on the goals of medical practice; and they allow us to reflect on the boundaries between, *inter alia*, the normal and the pathological.

3   Lee and Morgan use the term 'scientific citizenship' to refer to the public understanding of science *and* the scientific understanding of the public, the latter including the need for scientists to 'be able to comprehend, criticise and observe ethical or philosophical claims'.

Two questions arise from Lee and Morgan's article. Firstly, do 'stigmata' cases *require* courts to establish 'an explicit moral framework to their decision-making'? And, secondly, are there any difficulties confronting their idea of the colloquial nature of law? Responding to their arguments, Jonathan Montgomery has identified some discrepancies between these and what actually happens in the courts. He points out that: '[A] new type of case is emerging that actually *obscures such value conflicts* and in which the translation of conflict into the discourse of law *excludes moral debate rather than enables it to be addressed*. If this type is to become the norm, then, once again, more law turns out to mean less morality' (Montgomery 2006, 190; emphasis added). Whilst it does not respond entirely negatively to the first question posed above, this statement does suggest that there are likely to be problems with the idea of the colloquial nature of law. That is, whilst morality may or may not be driven out of the courts' decisions entirely, there are potential obstacles confronting Lee and Morgan's suggestion that law, and therefore the courts, can act as fora within which the ethical issues and implications arising from medicine and developments in biomedical science may be addressed.

The main difficulty here revolves around the question of the relationship between the courts and moral conflict. In the first instance, it is necessary to recognize that the types of ethical issues that arise in stigmata cases are often the subject of profound disagreement, in the sense that they spark off deep-seated moral values that are in conflict with one another. One need only think of research involving human embryos and physician-assisted suicide, to take just two examples, to illustrate the profound degree of moral conflict that exists in this area. Indeed, given the interminable debates about such issues in medical ethics, bioethics and, for that matter, medical law, it might be thought that inveterate moral conflict, rather than consensus, is *definitive* of them. By describing ethics as 'a concern with different values', and defining 'stigmata' cases as 'ethically controversial', Lee and Morgan implicitly acknowledge this. But if this is the case, if this conveys the complexity of the world and the fact that the good life is the subject of profound disagreement and conflict, and the courts are fora within which those ethical issues can be addressed, then one might expect to find those moral conflicts not only being played out in the courtroom, but being done justice to. Another reason why we might be entitled to expect this to be the case is because Lee and Morgan argue that law has an essential role to play in stimulating and contributing to ethical debate in today's risk society. If it is to undertake such a fundamental task successfully, presumably some in-depth discussion by judges of the moral conflicts inherent in the various ethical issues coming before the courts can be anticipated. Otherwise, the law might by thought to provide an inadequate template for the 'wide ethical debate' that Lee and Morgan argue is so essential to producing democratic vigilance over the practices of biomedical science. Montgomery argues, rightly it is suggested here, that evidence of this moral conflict is not to be found in the courts because value conflicts are obscured and moral debate excluded when the law becomes involved. But what are the reasons for this state of affairs? And, why should it matter that it exists?

The two questions raised above regarding Lee and Morgan's argument shall be addressed in two separate sections later in the chapter – one dealing mainly with moral conflict, the other with the question of whether the courts can be seen to contribute to debate about the ethics of advances in the area of biomedical science. By reference to two cases (one in each section), it will be demonstrated that, as Montgomery argues, value conflicts are obscured, and moral debate excluded, when the courts become involved in a certain type of case – those concerning questions about the existence of human life – that might be thought to display some characteristics of Lee and Morgan's 'stigmata' cases. First, however, and by way of establishing the theoretical basis upon which the analysis of the relationship between conflict and the courts in this chapter rests, the following section will set out some of Emilios Christodoulidis's work to be found in his book *Law and Reflexive Politics* (Christodoulidis 1998).

Law, Conflict and Politics

Christodoulidis advances a critique of legal ideology in which he claims that 'the law ... conceal[s] and ... its ideology ... mask[s] the exclusion and the compulsion of meanings' (Christodoulidis 1998, xiii). The purpose of his argument is to question those who believe that law can contain the politics of society and exhaust all that these involve. This 'containment thesis', as he calls it, is especially prevalent in the arguments of republican constitutionalists who claim that it is the law (the constitution) that allows for 'the possibility of politics and the substantiation of community'[4] (Christodoulidis 1998, 61). On this view, law is the place where we can discuss, and deliberate on, matters affecting the community. In having the ability to contain those discussions – that is, to remain true to them without distorting their meaning(s) – law acts as the mechanism through which the community comes to define itself. Citizens engage in this deliberation and '[d]uring the communicative exchange principles to guide public life are hammered out' (Christodoulidis 1998, 61). According to Christodoulidis, there are two pre-requisites for the notion of legal containment to hold true. The first is that *all* opinion will register in law; the second is that law will remain true to this opinion and not distort it in the process of its transfer into the legal realm. Republicans, he says, do, indeed, make such claims on behalf of law through recourse to arguments about its indeterminacy, for example. It is this legal openness and legal flexibility, they argue, that renders law suitable as *the* mechanism for the containment of all that is involved in politics; and it is through this politics, and hence through law, that the community manifests itself.

Christodoulidis suggests that the involvement of law has quite the opposite effect to that envisaged by republicans as it undermines 'the emancipatory potential of politics' (Christodoulidis 1998, xiii). For him, politics is about conflict and disagreement, especially over meaning(s), and his theory of reflexive politics is intended to guard against the ossification of such meaning(s). By definition, he argues, the political equates to the ongoing possibility of disrupting and revising 'the political constellation of meanings'. It is by working towards the closure of such a politics that law suppresses all that is involved in reflexive politics. The relevance

---

4   By the idea of containment, Christodoulidis does not intend to convey a sense of restriction. Rather, he means 'undistorted accommodation' of all that is involved in politics.

of Christodoulidis's argument in the current context revolves around his discussion of the relationship between conflict and law, and in particular how, for example, law operates to stifle and transform conflict into a form that it can manage. Fundamental to an understanding of his arguments in this regard is an appreciation that it is the structural characteristics of law that must form the focus of analysis.

Unlike Lee and Morgan, Christodoulidis argues that the notion of juridification is not to be thought of as an increase of law(s) or the subjection of ever-wider areas of social life to legal discipline.[5] As such, it is not to be defined in quantitative terms. Rather, juridification is the fact that the expropriation of conflict by law results in its depoliticization. In other words, all political conflict that comes to law immediately loses its political character because law precludes 'the freedom to contest the terms in which conflict is cast' (Christodoulidis 1998, 101). And because, for Christodoulidis, this freedom is what he means by the term 'political', its loss or denial results in depoliticization. It is this prevention of conflict over the 'staging' of conflict or the terms in which it is cast that amounts to what he calls expropriation and, hence, depoliticization. The questions that follow are these: Why does this occur? What is responsible for political conflict losing its political character when it enters law? Christodoulidis suggests that there are four ways in which advocates of the containment thesis misrepresent conflict. They either 'conflate', 're-enact', 'sever' or 'normalise' it. Here, only a brief outline of the nature of two of these – conflation and re-enactment – will be provided.[6]

Conflation is the name Christodoulidis gives to the collapse of the systems of law and conflict into one entity. The problem with republican constitutionalism, he argues, is this failure to keep the two systems apart. Referring to the theory of Ronald Dworkin – who views law as the proper home for argumentation and conflict in communities – Christodoulidis suggests:

> [T]he republican containment thesis extends an invitation to read conflict in the community as a conflict around positions in law. There is a political question that needs to be rescued from this imperialism: it is the question over the *staging of the conflict*. In republican theory, law is always-already the stage that will host conflict over normative understandings. (Christodoulidis 1998, 138–9; emphasis in original)

This, he argues, is the crux of the problem with republican theory. Arguing for the centrality of law as the locus of the community's debate pre-determines the form and content of such debate: 'To put it briefly, in the legal system conflict is necessarily aligned to legal co-ordinates where concepts of rights, liberties, legal notions of harm and legal analogies, legal tests and legal presumptions first make sense of it' (Christodoulidis 1998, 138–9). Law therefore forecloses conflict over the method and means of communication. The relevant conflict does not revolve around the how of the process – how are we to discuss conflict; how are we to stage it? Rather, the acceptance that law is the community's forum for debate results in questions about

---

    5   Further analysis of the idea of juridification can be found in the essays in Teubner 1987b.

    6   As severance and normalization are not as relevant for the purposes of the present argument, they will not be discussed here.

the best way in which to resolve specific conflicts. Should there be more rights for a specific group; what does the reasonable man standard have to say about certain conduct – the conflict here is not over the usefulness of law as a place where we can go to resolve our conflicts; it concerns, rather, how law should manage the particular conflicts with which it is confronted. The language and concepts in which such conflicts are cast in law are not things that can form the subject of debate within law. It is their relative appropriateness in each specific case that defines the nature of legal conflict.

A further problem here concerns distortion. The containment thesis assumes that social conflict can be transplanted into law in all its authenticity. However, what parties consider to be at stake in any conflict often differs and, thus, so does their view of that conflict. For instance, one party may think of a conflict in a certain way while the other party believes this misrepresents what is at stake. The latter party may then seek to have their belief in the distortion of the conflict upheld in law in an attempt to conceal the reality of the conflict. Should they succeed, the problem lies in the fact that law disallows questions about conflicts over the meaning of conflicts. As such, the former party has no way of contesting the (distorted) meaning ascribed to the conflict in law.

This distortion of conflict is further evidenced and reinforced by what Christodoulidis calls 're-enactment'. This notion denotes the conversion of social and political conflict into terms which the legal system can manage or recognize. More specifically, it concerns the idea that the legal system projects legal concepts, for example, into its environment in order to make sense of the conflict law sees in that environment. What this means is that the conflict is always set up on the basis of the legal system's own concepts and doctrines (such as interests and rights). The conflict that comes to resonate in law therefore depends on law's own self-reference. While Christodoulidis employs systems theory to make this point, it is his broader argument that is of interest here. This argument is that social conflict is not brought to law in all its reality. Rather, by projecting legal concepts into its environment, law re-enacts this conflict in order that it can be both discussed in legally meaningful terms and resolved legally. And yet, importantly, the legal conflict that law comes to resolve is often assumed not to be a distorted one, but the original social conflict in all its complexity. This is because, for law (that is, as a result of its projections), it appears as the natural conflict that required legal resolution all along. As Christodoulidis puts it: '*Law is innocent of its blindspot* ... It cannot see that what it takes to be "brute" conflict is always-already institutionalised conflict; it cannot see its re-enactment of conflict' (Christodoulidis 1998, 163; emphasis in original).

In summary, then, Christodoulidis's argument is that the attempt to contain all that is involved in political conflict within law results in the depoliticization of that conflict. This impoverishment of conflict occurs as a result of law's need to have a conflict that is legally manageable.

The following section will, amongst other things, seek to demonstrate the relevance of Christodoulidis's arguments about conflict and law to a well-known case within the medical law field. The main objectives of the analysis are to stress the potential difficulties confronting the replication in law of Lee and Morgan's notion of the colloquial nature of law, and to note the implications of the courts' expanding jurisdiction in this area.

Re A (Children) (2000)[7] and the Question of Conflict

It is useful to preface what follows with a few comments by one of the Court of Appeal judges in *Re A (Children)*, as these shed some light on how the judiciary interprets the nature of the courts' involvement in ethically controversial medical law cases. Thus, Ward LJ states:

> Deciding disputed matters of life and death is surely and pre-eminently a matter for a court of law to judge. That is what courts are here for. (987)

> This court is a court of law, not of morals, and our task has been to find, and our duty is then to apply the relevant principles of law to the situation before us – a situation which is quite unique. (969)

> They [cases where providing or withholding medical treatment is a matter of life and death for the incompetent patient] are always anxious decisions to make but they are invariably eventually made with the conviction that there is only one right answer and that the court has given it … The only arbiter [of the differing views of the doctors and the twins' parents] is the court. (968)

Two points should be noted here. Firstly, it is clear that decisions regarding conflicts surrounding the life and death of human beings properly fall within the jurisdiction of the courts. Indeed, the claim is a stronger one – it is that courts ought to have such a jurisdiction over and above any other institutions or means a society might offer for deciding contested matters of life and death. Secondly, the exercise of that jurisdiction occurs not through the language of morals, but by means of the discourse of law. In other words, judicial power does not manifest itself in the identification, and application, of appropriate ethical principles to the facts of the case. Rather, it displays itself in the discovery within the canon of the common law of the relevant legal principles that will be decisive in deciding the situation before the Court. Moreover, it must be stressed that there is not, of course, one moral but one legal answer. There will only be one correct result in law.

Ward LJ's reference to 'disputed matters of life and death' points to the question of conflict and it is in his opinion that one discovers how the Court responded to the fundamental conflict of values at the heart of this case. As such, it will be this opinion that will form the sole focus of discussion here. Before turning to this, however, it is necessary to state the facts. Given that these are generally well-known, a short summary, provided by Ward LJ himself, suffices:

> Jodie and Mary are conjoined twins. They each have their own brain, heart and lungs and other vital organs and they each have arms and legs. They are joined at the lower abdomen. Whilst not underplaying the surgical complexities, they can be successfully separated. But

---

7   Unless otherwise indicated, references to page numbers in brackets after quotations in this section are to the report of this case cited in the bibliography.

the operation will kill the weaker twin, Mary. That is because her lungs and heart are too deficient to oxygenate and pump blood through her body ... She is alive only because a common artery enables her sister, who is stronger, to circulate life sustaining oxygenated blood for both of them ... [I]f the operation does not take place, both will die within three to six months, or perhaps a little longer, because Jodie's heart will eventually fail. The parents cannot bring themselves to consent to the operation. The twins are equal in their eyes and they cannot agree to kill one even to save the other. The doctors are convinced they can carry out the operation so as to give Jodie a life which will be worthwhile. So the hospital sought a declaration that the operation may be lawfully carried out. Johnson J. granted it ... The parents applied to us for permission to appeal against his order [and] [w]e have given that permission. (969)

At this early stage in his judgment, Ward LJ identifies the parties – the twins' parents and the doctors – who are in conflict about how to proceed, and the nature of that conflict. The doctors wish to separate the girls; the parents cannot agree to the performance of the operation required to carry this out. The hospital staff want to save a life; the parents say they cannot choose between the lives of their daughters. On the one side, there are the doctors' professional ethics that stress the need to save human life; on the other, the beliefs and wishes of the twins' parents which are captured in the Court's transcript:

We cannot begin to accept or contemplate that one of our children should die to enable the other to survive ... Everyone has the right to life so why should we kill one of our daughters to enable the other to survive ... We have faith in God and are quite happy for God's will to decide what happens to our two young daughters. (985–6)

At its root, then, this case was brought to court because of a fundamental conflict of moral values between the hospital staff and the twins' parents. This is what constituted the 'disputed matter of life and death' that necessitated the law's intervention. What is therefore remarkable about Ward LJ's judgment is that this conflict of values is neither the main focus of attention, nor the dispute whose resolution determines the outcome of the case. Rather than discussing this conflict, and debating the moral ins and outs of the parties' respective positions, Ward LJ turns to concentrate solely on the circumstances of the twins themselves. The reason for this is the obligation of the court to identify, and apply, the relevant legal principles to what it considers to be the situation before it, and it will be useful to outline how Ward LJ carries this out.

He begins by stressing that the welfare of the child is to be the Court's paramount consideration.[8] However, the difficulty of applying that principle here is that there are two conflicting sets of interests. In other words, if the duty of the Court is to give paramountcy to Jodie's interests (by proceeding with the operation and ensuring her survival), then this would simultaneously contravene Mary's paramount interests (which would be best served by doing nothing, thereby extending her life, albeit briefly). Thus, as it is impossible to make the welfare of each twin paramount, the relevant legal principle becomes inappropriate for the purpose of deciding the case. However, Ward LJ states that this does not mean that the Court can simply refuse to

---

8   Section 1(1) of the Children Act 1989.

resolve the case. Judicial inertia, he says, would amount to 'a total abdication of the duty which is imposed on us' (1006).

After much discussion, Ward LJ duly discovers what will become the defining legal principle – the least detrimental alternative – in the judgments of Kennedy LJ and Evans LJ at the Court of Appeal stage in *Birmingham City Council v. H. (A Minor)* (1994).[9] Relying on these judgments, he comments: 'I can see no other way of dealing with [the conflict of duty] than by choosing the lesser of the two evils and so finding the least detrimental alternative. A balance has to be struck somehow and I cannot flinch from undertaking that evaluation, horrendously difficult though it is' (1006). But what was this legal principle to be applied to here? If it could not settle a conflict of interests between the twins because each twin's interests were paramount (that is, the welfare principle could not be applied), what, precisely, would it resolve?

It would be applied to a legally constructed 'physical' conflict between the twins. Ward LJ sets himself an 'analytical problem' that involves weighing, in a set of hypothetical scales, what he identifies as being the respective interests of the twins and '[doing] what is best for them' (1010). An example of this process can be seen in the manner in which the judge constructs the twins' respective, conflicting, physical attributes. Thus, in contrast to Jodie, who is portrayed as strong and having the potential to engage in life, Mary's condition means that, whatever action is taken, she is 'doomed for death'. The way in which Ward LJ summarizes the physical characteristics of the twins leaves little room for debate in establishing what the least detrimental alternative is: '[The weaker] sucks the lifeblood out of [the stronger] ... If [the stronger twin] could speak, she would surely protest, "Stop it, Mary, you're killing me". Mary would have no answer to that' (1010). Having placed several other factors in the scales, the judge arrives at his 'actual balance sheet of advantage and disadvantage', concluding: 'The best interests of the twins is to give the chance of life to the child whose actual bodily condition is capable of accepting the chance to her advantage even if that has to be at the cost of the sacrifice of the life which is so unnaturally supported' (1011). In Ward LJ's view, this was the least detrimental alternative. The Court of Appeal therefore concluded that it would be lawful to perform the operation to separate the twins, and this was duly carried out.

What might the manner in which Ward LJ proceeds to decide this case reveal about the relationship between the common law and conflict in ethically controversial medical law cases? In general terms, it demonstrates the important role that institutional features of the common law can play in determining how conflict is constructed and resolved within the courts. Two examples will illustrate this point. Firstly, while the original moral conflict between the twins' parents and the doctors is obscured during the case, Ward LJ offers his view of how parents in such a position ought to proceed:

---

9   In this case, the local authority had applied for a care order in respect of a baby. The baby's mother, however, was only 15 years old at the time, and thus a 'child' herself. Unlike the House of Lords on appeal, the Court of Appeal in that case viewed the issue of contact between mother and child as incorporating the question of the upbringing of each of them. Consequently, each child's welfare was paramount.

In my judgment, parents who are placed on the horns of such a terrible dilemma simply have to choose the lesser of their inevitable loss. If a family at the gates of a concentration camp were told they might free one of their children but if no choice were made both would die, compassionate parents with equal love for their twins would elect to save the stronger and see the weak one destined for death pass through the gates. (1009–10)

Although not forming the conflict whose resolution would determine the outcome of the case, what we effectively see here is an application of the definitive legal principle – the least detrimental alternative – to the original conflict of values that initially prompted the Court's involvement. But rather than viewing this solely as a straightforward moral condemnation of the parents' beliefs (which it clearly is), there is also a need to consider how this statement relates to, and indeed is a product of, the institutional context within which it is made. Discussing the same quotation, Scott Veitch has argued:

The two objective, universalised, values or norms – Ward LJ's and the parents' – may conflict in an incommensurable way – that is, in such a way that to make them commensurable would fundamentally misunderstand and destroy the meaning and practice of one of them – yet, and this is the key point, the legal institution cannot countenance incommensurables. Its decisionistic imperative and its social priority impel it to commensurate, and for this reason the law cannot truly countenance, cannot bear, the tragedy thrown up by the situation. It must resolve it, and this is the particular force of law. (Veitch 2006, 151)

In its raw state, therefore, this conflict of values cannot be resolved without negating the meaning of one of those values. The reality of the conflict is that the values simply stand opposed to each other. The judge's value has no common measure with that of the parents because, owing to their beliefs, choosing 'the lesser of their inevitable loss' is not an option for them. Their religious views mean that there is no alternative, far less a least detrimental one. But as Veitch notes, given that the essence of judging lies in making decisions, such a conflict cannot be left hanging. If the judges are to perform their jobs properly, it must be hammered into such a shape that it becomes resolvable. Christodoulidis would interpret this state of affairs as a re-enactment of conflict. By projecting the legal principle of the least detrimental alternative into its environment, the common law finds there not the 'brute', incommensurable conflict that is incapable of resolution, but a commensurable one that it can manage and, ultimately, resolve. In other words, the law's involvement here obscures the reality – and transforms the meaning – of the original moral conflict by converting it into a legally meaningful conflict.[10]

Secondly, this same concern with upholding established institutional practices of judicial reasoning in the face of what is a 'hard' case is more obvious in relation to the physical conflict between the twins constructed by Ward LJ. His claim to the pre-eminence of law courts resolving contested matters of life and death would be much stronger if the Court could be seen to have performed its task successfully. This task – the discovery of the relevant legal principle in the canon of the common law and its

---

10 As he comments: 'The conflict is first set up around a stake that is a stake in law' (Christodoulidis, 1998, 154).

application to a conflict with the purpose of resolving this and producing the correct legal answer – had more chance of being completed effectively if the conflict before the Court could be resolved definitively and relatively easily. The 'conflict' between the twins – made tangible by their opposing characteristics (weak/strong, capable/ not capable of engaging in life) – fitted the bill. The outcome of the application of the least detrimental alternative would be unambiguous, thereby not only justifying Ward LJ's claim for the role of the courts in disputed cases of life and death, but also reinforcing the institutional practices of the common law. The importance of respect for traditional techniques of legal reasoning forms a central aspect of Ward LJ's judgment.

If this illustrates how the institutional exigencies associated with the common law are intimately bound up with the question of moral conflict in this case, what might be thought to be the consequences of this way in which judicial power is exercised? One effect is that more general issues that may be considered to arise from the original moral conflict between the parents and the doctors are suppressed during the case. The re-enactment of this conflict into a legally resolvable one results in the absence from the judges' opinions of the debate and disagreements surrounding fundamental questions such as the following: What is the nature of parenthood?; Is this really a matter for the State?; To what extent should the State be allowed to interfere in the private lives of its citizens?; Should the State be able to ride roughshod over parents' religious beliefs? Thus, it is not merely the reality of the original conflict of values that finds no place within the common law; what could be called the broader social or political conflicts of which it is a microcosm also fail to be played out in the courtroom. Moreover, it should be stressed that, although those underlying questions, and the debate and disagreement they provoke, are suppressed, the Court still, implicitly, makes decisions about those issues. The deployment of traditional techniques of legal reasoning has the effect of allowing focus on the circumstances of the twins whilst simultaneously obfuscating the fact that decisions are being taken about those broader questions.

A second effect is the difficulty of challenging the structural apparatus of the common law that is responsible for the problems outlined in the foregoing discussion of this case. In order to understand this point, we need to return to Ward LJ's general assertion that courts of law are society's pre-eminent arbiters of contested matters of life and death. From one angle, this judicial appropriation of an increasingly important category of moral conflict within the medical law field appears unremarkable, perhaps even natural. Given its expertise in conflict resolution, the judiciary would seem to be the most obvious and legitimate professional body to claim authority to resolve this type of moral conflict. Moreover, the fact that the traditional techniques of legal reasoning are presented as operating in an objective manner tends to create the impression that courts of law can rightly be entrusted with the task of dispassionately resolving such conflicts. However, this assumption has tended to render both the question of this legal appropriation and the structural characteristics of the common law immune to criticism whenever judges resolve a conflict in a manner attracting controversy.[11] Rather than those features becoming the subject of inquiry, the source of the difficulty is invariably identified as lying elsewhere – in the misplaced ethical reasoning of the relevant judge(s), or in the wrong choice of ethical principle to be applied, for example.[12] The unquestioned assumption about the legal *appropriation* of disputes concerning life and death diverts critical attention away from the wider question of the *appropriateness* of subjecting those disputes to the practices and techniques of common law reasoning in the first place. What can be witnessed here is Christodoulidis's conflation of conflict. To assume that law is the pre-eminent arbiter of conflicts in the area of life and death means that conflict over the terms, or the staging, of those conflicts becomes impossible. In his terms, conflict here is 'expropriated' by law and, as a result, 'depoliticised'. The subsumption of the specific conflict under the structural features of law denies the freedom to contest the fundamental assumption that such a conflict should be legally privileged – that is, cast in legal terms in the first place.

Finally, there are consequences for the argument advanced by some academics that law is an institution within society where the ethical issues arising from medical practice and developments in biomedical science can be addressed. In this chapter, that feature of academic medical law has been portrayed by reference to Lee and Morgan's work and it will be through a consideration of the two questions posed earlier in respect of their arguments – do stigmata cases require courts to construct an explicit moral framework?; and, are there any difficulties confronting their notion of the colloquial nature of law? – that the possible implications of a case such as *Re A (Children)* for this general claim will be thought through.

One characteristic of Lee and Morgan's stigmata case is that it requires courts 'to develop a social, even a moral vision with which to respond to the dilemmas created by the social and cultural revolution of contemporary medicine' (Lee and Morgan 2001, 298). They argue that, although judges have so far not developed any sophisticated moral vocabulary in which to couch their judgments, Ward LJ's utilitarian approach in *Re A (Children)* supports their contention that the judiciary makes decisions in the medical law field within the parameters of an explicitly moral framework. But even if Ward LJ's judgment is interpreted in this way, as Lee and Morgan themselves acknowledge, it represents nothing more than 'an unadulterated utilitarianism'. As such, is this framework, which fails to address many other significant ethical features and moral viewpoints, to be indicative of the type of 'moral vision' that Lee and Morgan argue courts must develop if they are to 'sustain their vote in [the] parliament of moral politics'? If so, we can expect an impoverished 'vision'.

This latter point leads us on to Lee and Morgan's notion of the colloquial nature of law. Is *Re A (Children)* an example of law providing a forum within which debate

---

11 For an interesting article warning against the monopolization of conflict resolution by professionals generally, see Christie 1977. Relevant in the current context is his observation that: 'Lawyers are particularly good at stealing conflicts. They are trained for it. They are trained to prevent and solve conflicts' (Christie 1977, 4).

12 For critical analysis of this sort in relation to the Court of Appeal's ruling in *Re A (Children)*, see, for example, Harris 2001 and Michalowski 2002.

about 'what the good life consists [of], and how it is to be achieved or maintained' can take place (Lee and Morgan 2001, 315)? The analysis in this chapter suggests that it is not. If anything, Ward LJ's judgment illustrates how the involvement of the courts in ethically controversial issues can result in the curtailment of such debate. The inability of the law to represent the original moral conflict as incommensurable; the virtual dismissal of the parents' views and beliefs; the lack of discussion about the broader social and political questions raised by the case – all of these point towards the absence, rather than the presence, of the colloquial nature of law in the medical law field. If this is the case, then it would suggest that there are difficulties inherent in viewing the courts as institutions that might assist in furthering what Lee and Morgan consider to be law's central role 'in stimulating and contributing to ethical debate' in the risk society. If, as they argue, 'Ethical debate, perhaps more than politics, is becoming the paradigm form of participation' in the risk society, and such debate is missing in the courts, it is imperative that we ask whether courts have any legitimate role to play in redressing the democratic void Lee and Morgan, and by extension Beck, argue lies at the heart of the sub-politics of medicine and biomedical science (Lee and Morgan 2001, 306).

All of this is not to say that the wide ethical debate regarding the consequences of developments in contemporary medicine and biomedical science which Lee and Morgan call for is unnecessary. It does, however, suggest that, when thinking through what role the courts might play in all of this, we need, in the first instance, to analyse critically the impact that the involvement of the common law has on the possibility of democratic ethical debate in this area. With the inexorable expansion of the courts' jurisdiction in the medical law field, and the increasing tendency of the judiciary to assert the power accompanying this jurisdiction by deploying traditional techniques of legal reasoning to decide cases involving contested ethical issues, there is a danger that, like medicine and biomedical science, the courts may themselves come to constitute the type of undemocratic sub-political institution that forms the target of Lee and Morgan's, and Beck's, critique.

Medical Law and the Possibility of Moral Debate

This section continues the analysis of the relationship between the courts and moral debate in medical law cases begun in the previous one. In order to do so, the discussion will centre on a recent case heard in the Court of Appeal.[13] There are three reasons why this case acts as a useful marker against which to measure the ability of law to act as a forum where the ethical issues arising from developments in medicine and biomedical science can be addressed. Firstly, rather than concerning a dispute between private individuals[14] and members of the medical profession, the challenge in this case came from a pressure group whose existence is driven by ethical beliefs

---

13 *R. (on the application of Quintavalle) v. Human Fertilisation and Embryology Authority* (2003a) (hereinafter '*Quintavalle*').

14 Although it should be noted that it was a family's desire to make use of new human fertilization techniques that prompted the challenge by Josephine Quintavalle of the pressure group Comment on Reproductive Ethics (hereinafter 'CORE').

and arguments. Consequently, it might be thought to present an excellent opportunity for the Court to engage in moral discussion and debate. Secondly, the case offers a glimpse of the nature of the courts' involvement in regulating disputes arising from cutting edge developments in one area of biomedical science – human fertilization techniques. Finally, it is an example of the type of case that Lee and Morgan argue will become increasingly frequent in this area – that is, one in which the courts, through the means of judicial review, 'will be used as an arm of regulation in moral politics' (Lee and Morgan 2001, 316). Thus, and as in the previous section, the analysis of this case allows us to ask, on the one hand, whether the Court responded to its involvement by developing and declaring 'an explicit moral framework to [its] decision-making' and, on the other, if its approach reflects Lee and Morgan's notion of the colloquial nature of law. Before addressing these questions, it is necessary to set out the facts and the Court of Appeal's ruling.

Mr and Mrs Hashmi's immediate concern arose as a result of their fourth child – Zain – being born with a blood disorder known as beta thalassaemia major. This disorder – which results from the lack, or inadequacy, of red blood cells, and requires that affected individuals take various drugs and receive regular blood transfusions in order to remain alive – can be cured by a transplant of stem cells from another person with matching tissue. The possible sources of such tissue are either bone marrow or the blood of a newborn child's umbilical cord. It is the tissue from a sufferer's siblings that may provide the best prospects of a match (reportedly 98 percent). As none of Zain's four siblings had tissue that matched his, Mr and Mrs Hashmi sought the help of an in vitro fertilization (hereinafter 'IVF') clinic. They were told that a new procedure existed whereby a single cell from each of several embryos created from their gametes could be removed by biopsy and examined for two purposes: first, to establish whether the embryo carried the beta thalassaemia disease (this procedure being known as 'pre-implantation genetic diagnosis' [hereinafter 'PGD']); and, second, to ensure that its tissue type matched Zain's (this procedure, which involves the examination of proteins called human leukocyte antigens, being commonly known as 'tissue typing'). Only an embryo that did not carry the disease and matched Zain's tissue would be implanted in Mrs Hashmi's womb.

One of the Human Fertilisation and Embryology Authority's (hereinafter 'the HFEA') functions is to decide whether to grant licences to bodies to allow them to undertake IVF treatment. While it had authorized PGD before, a licence had never been granted to cover tissue typing as part of the IVF procedure. Nonetheless, the HFEA agreed in principle to, and in fact granted, a licence for the treatment required by Mr and Mrs Hashmi, albeit subject to various conditions. In particular, it stressed that it was only prepared to grant such a licence in circumstances where the procedure was also intended to benefit the child being born. In other words, and unlike the case of the Whitakers, where the HFEA refused to grant a licence for tissue typing to be carried out because it was not intended to benefit the future child, IVF was authorized in the Hashmis' case as it included PGD designed to ensure the absence of hereditary disease.[15] The procedure commenced, but before it had a chance to succeed, the respondent – Josephine Quintavalle – who was acting on behalf of CORE, a public interest group whose purpose is to focus and facilitate debate on ethical issues arising from human reproduction (especially assisted reproduction), challenged, by way of judicial review, the HFEA's original decision to grant a licence for the IVF procedure. At first instance, Maurice Kay J accepted her argument that the HFEA had no power to issue a licence permitting the use of tissue typing to choose between healthy embryos, granted her application, and quashed the HFEA's decision (*R. (on the application of Quintavalle) v. Human Fertilisation and Embryology Authority* 2003b). The HFEA appealed and the Court of Appeal – with Lord Phillips MR, Schiemann and Mance LJJ sitting – handed down judgment on 16 May 2003.

Given the extremely technical and dense nature of the Court's judgment, an exposition of its minutiae would add little to the discussion in this chapter. What must be noted, however, is the reason for this detail and complexity. Any doubt that may have persisted regarding the function of the Court in such a case was swiftly clarified by Mance LJ: 'The facts of this case excite great sympathy. But the issue is one of law' (*R. (on the application of Quintavalle) v. Human Fertilisation and Embryology Authority* 2003a, 276). More specifically, the overriding legal task was the construction of the Human Fertilisation and Embryology Act 1990 (hereinafter 'the 1990 Act'). Like the approach adopted by the courts in a slightly earlier case which also arose as a result of the intervention of a member of the Quintavalle family – a case that will be referred to here as *Quintavalle [2]*[16] – the judgments in the Court of Appeal represent an exercise in one of the traditional tasks undertaken by the judiciary – statutory interpretation. The application of logic, together with some assessment of the legislative history of the 1990 Act, led to the Court's conclusion that it was lawful for the HFEA to grant a licence authorizing both PGD and tissue typing. Whether tissue typing – because it sought to discriminate between 'healthy'

---

15 It should be noted that in July 2004 (that is, after *Quintavalle*) the HFEA revised its policy on pre-implantation tissue typing. Now, the HFEA does not, in principle, distinguish 'between cases in which pre-implantation tissue typing is used in combination with PGD for serious disease [the "Hashmi"-type situation] and where discovering tissue type is the sole treatment objective [the "Whitaker"-type situation]' (Human Fertilisation and Embryology Authority 2004, 5). Subject to appropriate safeguards, tissue typing should be available 'in cases in which there is a genuine need for potentially life-saving tissue and a likelihood of therapeutic benefit for an affected child' (Human Fertilisation and Embryology Authority 2004, 10).

16 *R. (on the application of Quintavalle) v. Secretary of State for Health* (2003). In this case, Bruno Quintavalle, director of the Pro-Life Alliance, applied for judicial review by way of a declaration that a human embryo created by the cell nuclear replacement technique was not an 'embryo' within the meaning of s.1(1) of the 1990 Act, and was therefore not subject to the regulation of the 1990 Act. The House of Lords held that a human embryo created by this technique did fall within the definition of 'embryo' in s.1(1) of the 1990 Act. The consequence of this was that cloning by means of this technique fell within the HFEA's regulatory powers. As nothing in the present context turns on the precise details of *Quintavalle [2]*, no more shall be said about these here.

embryos – ought to be practised, and whether there existed any ethical difference between this procedure and PGD were not questions that concerned the Court of Appeal. Having found that the HFEA alone had competence to decide on the relative ethical merits of the two procedures, and how any moral conflict should be resolved, the Court remained true to its traditional role in dispensing its function of judicial review – that of upholding the rule of law. It decided that the HFEA had not exceeded its legal powers in permitting tissue typing because the 1990 Act allowed it to do so, and not because the Court was of the view that tissue typing was ethically permissible.[17]

This adherence to the traditional function of judicial review results in the exclusion of any substantive moral debate about the ethics of tissue typing and genetic testing from the legal forum in this case. Similarly, in his discussion of *Quintavalle [2]*, Montgomery notes the stress placed by the law lords on what he calls 'issues of formal legitimacy' – that is, whether the HFEA has legitimate power to regulate cloning – rather than on examining the substantive moral debates revolving around cloning (see Montgomery 2006, 191–2). The power to discuss the ethical dimensions of cloning, genetic testing and tissue typing lies with the HFEA, and not with the courts. Summing up the approach of the House of Lords in *Quintavalle [2]*, Montgomery comments:

> This is a classic strategy of legal positivism, an approach to legal theory that seeks to argue that legal legitimacy and moral authority need to be considered separately not as an integrated activity. Where the approach holds, the stigmata of our value system will no longer appear on the bodies of our judgements. The morality will be sucked out of them. (Montgomery 2006, 192; reference omitted)[18]

This, of course, depends on what kind of value system we are referring to. As Tom Campbell points out, a number of *moral* reasons can be advanced to support the idea of the rule of law, which the process of judicial review is intended to uphold (see Campbell 2006, Chapter 5). We might legitimately ask if we would wish the

---

17 Quintavalle's appeal against the Court of Appeal's decision was dismissed by the House of Lords. See *R. (on the application of Quintavalle) v. Human Fertilisation and Embryology Authority* (2005). Like the judges in the Court of Appeal, Lord Brown identifies what the case is, and is not, about: 'Your Lordships are simply not concerned with the conditions under which tissue testing should be licensed, assuming it is licensable at all – nor even, indeed, with *whether* it should be licensed. Your Lordships' sole concern is whether the 1990 Act *allows* the [HFEA] to license tissue typing were it in its discretion to think it right to do so' (*R. (on the application of Quintavalle) v. Human Fertilisation and Embryology Authority* 2005, 567; emphasis in original).

18 It should be noted that, while Montgomery is critical of what he calls the general demoralization of medical law, and does not wish to see the morality being 'sucked out of' court judgments, he differs from Lee and Morgan in the sense that he seeks to uphold the classic legal position (to be found in *Bolam v. Friern Hospital Management Committee* 1957) where the courts view medical and moral decision-making as indistinguishable. The law's role here is not to become involved in determining ethical issues but, rather, to reflect the indistinguishableness of the medical from the moral by deferring to the professional standards of the health care professions.

courts to proceed in a manner in any way different to that visible in the *Quintavalle* cases. Why should unelected judges use judicial review proceedings in the medical law field as opportunities to engage in reflection on the ethical issues surrounding developments in biomedical science and to declare what they perceive to be the moral values that deserve to be upheld?

Montgomery's comment, however, is no doubt directed at the type of argument advanced by Lee and Morgan. It is clear from *Quintavalle* and *Quintavalle [2]* that the judges neither sought to establish an explicit moral framework to their decisions nor performed a role in keeping with the colloquial nature of law. Indeed, and once again in a case whose subject matter raised contentious ethical issues, the judiciary sought to define its function by distancing, rather than aligning, itself with a more 'ethically' interventionist role. It was, instead, a concern with upholding traditional techniques of legal reasoning that defined the judiciary's approach. Consequently, the prospects of moral debate occurring within the courts in future cases of judicial review in the medical law field seem poor.

In spite of this judicial unwillingness to become embroiled in ethical debate, it could be argued that CORE's legal action, and its reporting in the media, may, tangentially, have the effect of stimulating wider public interest in, and debate about, the ethical consequences of developments in genetic testing and human fertilization techniques. However a perusal of the law reports will fail to enlighten the interested lay member of the public who wishes to understand the moral values at stake or to appreciate the contours of the relevant ethical debates. Rather, he or she will discover the entrenchment of a law – the 1990 Act – that effectively places the power to determine the content, terms and outcomes of the ethical debates to be had regarding technological developments in human fertilization and embryology in the hands of a very small number of predominantly professional people at the HFEA.[19]

Once again, the danger of critical analyses that find fault with the courts for failing to adopt a proactive stance in relation to the ethical issues and controversies surrounding advances in the fields of medicine and biomedical science is that important questions arising from the manner in which it actually functions may be lost from view. In other words, there needs to be an appreciation of the impact that the structural features of law have on the possibility of law contributing to an improved democratic framework within which medicine and biomedical science can operate in future. This does not equate to blaming judges for applying traditional techniques of legal reasoning to resolve ethically controversial cases; as noted above, in *Quintavalle* we should expect nothing less than that the judiciary adheres to its proper function of judicial review. It does, however, suggest that if we are truly to re-ignite what Lee and Morgan call 'public debate' over 'central issues of public policy' legal academics would do well to begin by debating the usefulness of law – especially the courts – in contributing to that worthwhile objective.

---

19 In October 2006 there were 19 members of the HFEA. See <http://www.hfea.gov.uk/cps/rde/xchg/SID-3F57D79B-CE3C16C7/hfea/hs.xsl/384.html> for the list of current members (accessed 17 April 2007).

Conclusion

This chapter seeks to reinforce the general point made in this part of the book that a disparity exists between the aspirational nature of some academic writing in medical law – here, in the form of arguments that the courts should play an important role in managing, and determining, the ethical issues arising from medical practice and developments in biomedical science – and the manner in which courts function in practice.[20] At root, some academics' aspirations for how the courts should exercise their increasing jurisdiction in the medical law field fail to take sufficient account of both the manner in which judges in fact exercise this power and the actual and potential implications of this. In attempting to ascertain the causes of the various effects of the courts' involvement we would, in a reversal of McLean's argument, do well to pay more attention to the *mechanics* of the courts' exercise of this growing jurisdiction. In other words, more analysis of the role that institutional exigencies – such as the need to maintain, and deploy, traditional techniques of legal reasoning – play in medical law is required.

At a time when what might be thought to define developments in medicine and biomedicine is their contestability and tendency to produce disagreement, on the basis of the cases discussed in this chapter, the operation of the common law has the effect of masking this reality, thereby curtailing the possibility that the moral conflicts inherent in such developments may be played out, and respected, in the courts. Similarly, there would seem to be little prospect of the courts' involvement either resulting in debate over the ethical implications of such advances within the boundaries of specific cases or contributing to wider ethical debate generally. This state of affairs arises as a result of various institutional exigencies that structure the manner in which the judiciary exercises the courts' expanding jurisdiction in the medical law field. We might say that the effect of this jurisdictional expansion has been to narrow, or contract, the fundamental nature of the ethical issues produced by the practices of medicine and biomedical science. In light of Lee and Morgan's valuable highlighting of Beck's identification of the democratic deficit which exists in relation to progress in medicine and biomedical science, perhaps the most worrying implication of arguments that call for more legal jurisdiction over ethical issues is that, rather than helping to redress this deficit, the increasing involvement of the courts in this area may assist in compounding it. As a suggested starting point, we would do well to consider whether courts are in any sense fit to perform the types of roles that we have seen in this book some academics and judges urge for them in the field of medical law.

---

20 Lee and Morgan note how the courts in some 'stigmata' cases have not yet developed the explicit moral framework to their decision-making that they say is necessary in the medical law field. Rather, they argue that the judiciary has tended, unsuccessfully, to 'disguise its judgments as no more than a positivistic exercise concerned only with its own internal, self-referential logic' (Lee and Morgan 2001, 306). As in the previous chapter, the point made here is that it is precisely this 'positivistic exercise' that should be taken more seriously in the effort to understand the role of the courts in this area.

Conclusion

In Chapter 1 of his book, *An Invitation to Reflexive Sociology*, written with Pierre Bourdieu, Loïc Wacquant quotes Ludwig Wittgenstein: 'Getting hold of the difficulty *deep down* is what is hard. Because it is grasped near the surface it remains the difficulty it was. It has to be pulled out by the roots ...' (Bourdieu and Wacquant 1992, 1; emphasis in original). To a large degree, this book has been an attempt to get a hold of some of the difficulties of medical law 'deep down'. It has sought to identify, and critically reflect on, a few of the fundamental building blocks and constitutive assumptions of medical law. In order to do so, it has utilized a methodological approach that concentrates on the institutional features of law, as opposed to the ethical supportability of court rulings. This 'institutional' mode of analysis, it is suggested, has the ability to shed light on issues and problems that would otherwise remain obscured from view. Thus, it allowed us, for instance, to pierce the rhetoric of patient autonomy and self-determination and identify the various mechanisms, practices, interests and exigencies that do, in fact, determine how courts go about empowering patients. The result was the discovery of a less idealistic legal incarnation of the patient – one who is assessed, probed and examined for the purposes of determining whether or not he or she conforms to certain unspecified standards of, *inter alia*, character. Ultimately, it led us to conclude that a more realistic understanding of patient autonomy – the ethical value that, whilst prayed in aid so frequently in this area, is, ironically, very rarely taken as an object of research in itself – within the common law would be one which admitted of different conceptions ('individual' and 'principled') of this value. Such an understanding more accurately reflects the fact that, as well as rights, patients have obligations and responsibilities too.

The 'institutional' mode of analysis also facilitated a critical analysis of the claim to be found in some of the academic medical law literature that ethical issues arising in the course of medical practice and from applications of technological developments in biomedical science should be determined outside of medicine and science, and that the most appropriate site for this ought to be the law. Focusing on how judges organize and exercise their power in cases whose subject matter involves difficult, and contentious, ethical issues, it was argued that the courts are very reluctant to become embroiled in discussing such issues. Indeed, there are several examples of senior members of the judiciary explicitly declaring that this is not a legitimate role for the courts. Moreover, there is clear evidence in such cases that appellate judges deploy standard techniques of legal reasoning to resolve them. While appearing unremarkable in itself, this conservative exercise of judicial power has important consequences, whose common feature might usefully be identified as silencing. Thus, we saw, for example, how the critical potential of human rights discourse can be smothered as a result of the institutionalization of human rights within law. Similarly, we witnessed how the meaning of moral conflict can be subtly transformed, and therefore lost, by subsuming such conflict under the workings and established practices of the common law. Finally, we noted how the application of judicial review to the decision of a public body about a matter (tissue typing) raising fundamental ethical questions had the effect of suppressing discussion and debate about those questions within the courtroom. Rather, the central issue became whether the HFEA's decision had been lawful – something whose resolution did not require engagement with the ethical questions. This latter example is an excellent illustration within the medical law sphere of Mathiesen's observation (set out in Chapter 2) that the process of determining the legality of a specific decision or action has the ability to transform political (in our case, read 'moral') debate into 'an exchange of opinions concerning the apparently neutral and unpolitical issue of whether legal authority or basis "exists"' (Mathiesen 2004, 17). The battle over the fundamental moral, or political, issue at stake, with all that that entails, is lost as the dispute crosses into the legal sphere, where it is reconstructed as a legal issue or question that is amenable to resolution. As Mathiesen notes, whilst appearing as a 'neutral and unpolitical issue', the question of whether or not a decision or action is lawful is, in fact, anything but this. Of course, the court's decision has direct implications for the parties to the case. But, more than this, it produces, through a procedure that prides itself on its impartiality, the broader types of controversial consequences just outlined. To put it briefly, the precise effect of the courts' involvement here is to depoliticize, or demoralize, issues that, by their very nature, are political, or moral. This is a controversial consequence, and one that, through the procedure designed to determine what is, or is not, lawful, comes about in a subtle, almost imperceptible, way.

The effects just outlined contradict the types of visions of law's involvement in medical matters to be found in much of the academic medical law literature discussed in this book. Law was to be the saviour of patients' human rights; it was to play an active role in contributing to the 'parliament of moral politics' urgently required to oversee the rapid advances in medicine and biomedical science; it was to develop a moral framework within which to hear, and respond to, the increasing number of disputes and claims arising in this area. Crucially, however, the effects set out above have arisen precisely as a result of legal involvement in the various disputes emanating from medical practice. Those consequences flow directly from the application and operation of traditional methods of organizing and exercising power within the common law. To adopt Beck's phraseology, this is how the courts have been 'strong and independent' in the face of progress in medicine and biomedical science – not actively engaged in checking the purported moral irresponsibilities of this progress, but stressing the need to maintain the traditional function of the judiciary, which eschews such a role.

It is suggested that the existence of this disparity between the aspirations for law's role in this area and the consequences that flow from how it actually functions in practice, points to the need to develop an alternative mode of critical analysis in the medical law field. Rather than urging the courts to reform their current practices by developing a more robust moral discourse through which to respond to the issues arising in this area, what is required is a critical approach that is willing to question the assumption that the structural features of the common law should host those issues, and the conflicts inherent in them, in the first place. Without such an approach, not only does the cause of the disparity remain unidentified, additionally there is the danger that the broad agreement in the academic medical law literature that the courts have an important role to play in regulating ethical matters in this area will help to sustain, and reinforce, the institutional exigencies and features responsible for the controversial effects identified in this book – effects that, as we have seen, can be the exact opposite of those envisaged by advocates of active judicial involvement. To put it in Wittgenstein's language, because some of the difficulties of medical law are presently 'grasped near the surface', they remain the difficulties they were; in order to get hold of those difficulties 'deep down', they need 'to be pulled out by the roots' – a task, it is suggested here, that can only be achieved by the deployment of a critical methodology that focuses upon, and questions, the role, impact and usefulness of the structural features of the common law.

To conclude, there is a need to complement an analysis of the factors underlying the undeniable expansion of the courts' jurisdiction in this area (including the claims for the need to develop legal jurisdiction that can be found in the academic medical law literature discussed in this book) with a corresponding study of how that jurisdiction has been, and is being, asserted, or exercised, in practice. Or, what is essentially the same thing, it is necessary that an identification of the underlying conditions and arguments responsible for the emergence and growth in judicial power in this sphere is accompanied by an investigation into how that power is organized and deployed by the judiciary in specific cases. And, having undertaken such inquiries, we must not only be prepared to acknowledge that, in some instances, incongruities exist between how the courts are expected to act and how they do, in fact, act in practice; additionally, and more important, we need to be willing to accept that the causes of these disparities may lie in the very structure of the common law itself. Once we are ready to concede those observations, we might tentatively begin to address the question of whether the courts are the most appropriate fora through which to manage the types of issues referred to in this book. That, however, must be the subject matter of future research.

Bibliography

Cases

A. v. Secretary of State for the Home Department, [2005] 2 WLR 87.
Airedale NHS Trust v. Bland, [1993] 1 All ER 821.
Birmingham City Council v. H. (A Minor), [1994] 2 AC 212.
Bolam v. Friern Hospital Management Committee, [1957] 2 All ER 118.
Burke v. UK, (App. No. 19807/06).
Canterbury v. Spence, (1972) 464 F 2d 772.
Chatterton v. Gerson, [1981] 1 All ER 257.
Chester v. Afshar, [2004] 4 All ER 587.
Gillick v. West Norfolk and Wisbech Area Health Authority, [1986] 1 FLR 224.
McCallister v. Lewisham and North Southwark Health Authority and Others, [1994]
  5 Med LR 343.
NHS Trust 'A' v. M; NHS Trust 'B' v. H, [2001] 1 All ER 801.
Norfolk and Norwich Healthcare (NHS) Trust v. W, [1997] 1 FCR 269.
Pretty v. United Kingdom, (2002) 35 EHRR 1.
R. (Burke) v. General Medical Council, [2004] 2 FLR 1121.
R. (Burke) v. General Medical Council, [2005] 3 FCR 169.
R. (on the application of Pretty) v. Director of Public Prosecutions, [2002] 1 All ER 1.
*R. (on the application of Quintavalle) v. Human Fertilisation and Embryology
  Authority*, [2003] 3 All ER 257 (2003a).
*R. (on the application of Quintavalle) v. Human Fertilisation and Embryology
  Authority*, [2003] 2 All ER 105 (2003b).
*R. (on the application of Quintavalle) v. Human Fertilisation and Embryology
  Authority*, [2005] 2 All ER 555.
R. (on the application of Quintavalle) v. Secretary of State for Health, [2003] 2 All
  ER 113.
R. (Watts) v. Bedford Primary Care Trust and Another, [2003] EWCH 2228
  (Admin).
Re A (Children), [2000] 4 All ER 961.
Re B (Adult: Refusal of Medical Treatment), [2002] 2 All ER 449.
Re C (Adult: Refusal of Medical Treatment), [1994] 1 All ER 819.
Re F (mental patient: sterilisation), [1990] 2 AC 1.
Re MB (An Adult: Medical Treatment), [1997] 2 FCR 541.
Re S (Adult: Refusal of Medical Treatment), [1992] 4 All ER 671.
Re T (Adult: Refusal of Medical Treatment), [1992] 4 All ER 649.
Re W (A Minor) (Medical Treatment: Court's Jurisdiction), [1992] 4 All ER 627.
Re Wyatt, [2005] 4 All ER 1325.

S v. S, W v. Official Solicitor (or W), [1972] AC 24.

Schloendorff v. Society of New York Hospital, (1914) 211 NT 125.

Secretary of State for the Home Department v. JJ and others, [2006] EWCA Civ 1141.

Sidaway v. Board of Governors of the Bethlem Royal Hospital and the Maudsley Hospital and Others, [1985] 2 WLR 480.

State of Tennessee v. Northern, (1978) 563 SW 2d 197 (Tenn CT App).

Monographs and Articles

Armstrong, D. (1983), *The Political Anatomy of the Body: Medical Knowledge in Britain in the Twentieth Century* (Cambridge: Cambridge University Press).

— (2002), *A New History of Identity: A Sociology of Medical Knowledge* (Basingstoke: Palgrave).

Atiyah, P. (1979), *The Rise and Fall of Freedom of Contract* (Oxford: Clarendon Press).

Ballard, K. and Elston, M.A. (2005), 'Medicalisation: A Multi-dimensional Concept', *Social Theory & Health* 3:3, 228–41.

Bankowski, Z. (ed.) (2006), *The Universal and the Particular in Legal Reasoning* (Aldershot: Ashgate).

Bauman, Z. (2000), *Liquid Modernity* (Cambridge: Polity).

— (2005), *Work, Consumerism and the New Poor*, 2nd edn (Maidenhead: Open University Press).

Beauchamp, T.L. and Childress, J.F. (1989), *Principles of Biomedical Ethics*, 3rd edn (New York and Oxford: Oxford University Press).

— and — (2001), *Principles of Biomedical Ethics*, 5th edn (Oxford and New York: Oxford University Press).

Beck, U. (1992), *Risk Society: Towards a New Modernity* (trans. M. Ritter) (London: Sage).

Bennett, B. and Tomossy, G.F. (eds) (2006), *Globalization and Health: Challenges for Health Law and Bioethics* (Dordrecht: Springer).

Berlin, I. (1969), *Four Essays on Liberty* (Oxford: Oxford University Press).

Black's Law Dictionary, 6th edn (1990) (St Paul, MN: West).

Bourdieu, P. and Wacquant, L.J.D. (1992), *An Invitation to Reflexive Sociology* (Cambridge: Polity).

Brazier, M. (1998), *Surrogacy: Review for Health Ministers of Current Arrangements for Payments and Regulations* Cm 4068 (London: The Stationery Office).

— (2006), 'Do No Harm: Do Patients Have Responsibilities Too?', *Cambridge Law Journal* 65:2, 397–422.

— and Glover, N. (2000), 'Does Medical Law Have a Future?', in D. Hayton (ed.), *Law's Future(s): British Legal Developments in the 21st Century* (Oxford: Hart).

Bridgeman, J. and Millns, S. (eds) (1998), *Feminist Perspectives on Law: Law's Engagement with the Female Body* (London: Sweet & Maxwell).

Campbell, T. (1999), 'Human Rights: A Culture of Controversy', *Journal of Law and Society* 26:1, 6–26.

— (2006), *Rights: A Critical Introduction* (Abingdon: Routledge).

Christie, N. (1977), 'Conflicts as Property', *The British Journal of Criminology* 17:1, 1–15.

Christodoulidis, E.A. (1998), *Law and Reflexive Politics* (Dordrecht: Kluwer).

Cover, R. (1985), 'The Folktales of Justice: Tales of Jurisdiction', *Capital University Law Review* 14:2, 179–203.

Davies, M. (1998), *Textbook on Medical Law*, 2nd edn (London: Blackstone).

de Chadarevian, S. (2002), *Designs for Life: Molecular Biology after World War II* (Cambridge: Cambridge University Press).

Dean, M. (2004), 'Four Theses on the Powers of Life and Death', *Contretemps* 5, 16–29.

Department of Health (2004a), *The NHS Improvement Plan: Putting People at the Heart of Public Services* Cm 6268 (London: The Stationery Office).

— (2004b), *Choosing Health: Making Healthy Choices Easier* Cm 6374 (London: The Stationery Office).

Diamantides, M. (2000), *The Ethics of Suffering: Modern Law, Philosophy and Medicine* (Aldershot: Ashgate).

Dingwall, R. and Hobson-West, P. (2006), 'Litigation and the Threat to Medicine', in D. Kelleher et al. (eds), *Challenging Medicine*, 2nd edn (London: Routledge).

Dorsett, S. (2002), '"Since Time Immemorial": A Story of Common Law Jurisdiction, Native Title and the Case of Tanistry', *Melbourne University Law Review* 26:1, 32–42.

Douzinas, C. (2000), *The End of Human Rights: Critical Legal Thought at the Turn of the Century* (Oxford: Hart).

— and McVeigh, S. (1992), 'The Tragic Body: The Inscription of Autonomy in Medical Ethics and Law', in S. McVeigh and S. Wheeler (eds), *Law, Health & Medical Regulation* (Aldershot: Dartmouth).

Dworkin, R. (1994), *Life's Dominion: An Argument About Abortion, Euthanasia and Individual Freedom* (London: Vintage).

Farmer, L. (1996), 'The Obsession with Definition: The Nature of Crime and Critical Legal Theory', *Social & Legal Studies* 5:1, 57–73.

Faubion, J.D. (ed.) (2000), *Power: Essential Works of Foucault 1954–1984 Volume 3* (trans. R. Hurley and others) (London: Allen Lane).

Fisher, A. (1995), 'Theological Aspects of Euthanasia', in J. Keown (ed.), *Euthanasia Examined: Ethical, Clinical and Legal Perspectives* (Cambridge: Cambridge University Press).

Foucault, M. (2000a), 'About the Concept of the "Dangerous Individual" in Nineteenth-Century Legal Psychiatry', in J.D. Faubion (ed.), *Power: Essential Works of Foucault 1954–1984 Volume 3* (trans. R. Hurley and others) (London: Allen Lane).

— (2000b), 'Governmentality', in J.D. Faubion (ed.), *Power: Essential Works of Foucault 1954–1984 Volume 3* (trans. R. Hurley and others) (London: Allen Lane).

Freeman, M. (2002), 'Denying Death its Dominion: Thoughts on the Dianne Pretty Case', *Medical Law Review* 10:3, 245–70.

Gilmore, G. (1995), *The Death of Contract* (Columbus, OH: Ohio State University Press).

Gregor, M. (1963), *Laws of Freedom* (Oxford: Basil Blackwell).

Grubb, A. (2001), *Medical Law: Text with Materials*, 3rd edn (London: Butterworths).

— (ed.) (2004), *Principles of Medical Law*, 2nd edn (Oxford: Oxford University Press).

Gunn, M. (1994), 'The Meaning of Incapacity', *Medical Law Review* 2:1, 8–29.

Gusfield, J.R. (1981), *The Culture of Public Problems: Drinking-Driving and the Symbolic Order* (Chicago, IL and London: The University of Chicago Press).

Harrington, J.A. (1996), 'Privileging the Medical Norm: Liberalism, Self-determination and Refusal of Treatment', *Legal Studies* 16:3, 348–67.

— (2002), '"Red in Tooth and Claw": The Idea of Progress in Medicine and the Common Law', *Social & Legal Studies* 11:2, 211–32.

— (2006), 'Globalization and English Medical Law: Strains and Contradictions', in B. Bennett and G.F. Tomossy (eds), *Globalization and Health: Challenges for Health Law and Bioethics* (Dordrecht: Springer).

Harris, J. (2001), 'Human Beings, Persons and Conjoined Twins: An Ethical Analysis of the Judgment in *Re A*', *Medical Law Review* 9:3, 221–36.

Hart, H.L.A. (1961), *The Concept of Law* (Oxford: Clarendon Press).

Hayton, D. (ed.) (2000), *Law's Future(s): British Legal Developments in the 21st Century* (Oxford: Hart).

Hegel, G.W.F. (1942), *Philosophy of Right* (trans. T. M. Knox) (Oxford: Clarendon Press).

Hope, R.A. (1991), 'The Birth of Medical Law', *Oxford Journal of Legal Studies* 11:2, 247–53.

Human Fertilisation and Embryology Authority (2004), *Human Fertilisation and Embryology Authority Report: Preimplantation Tissue Typing* (London: HFEA).

Jackson, E. (2001), *Regulating Reproduction: Law, Technology and Autonomy* (Oxford: Hart).

Jacob, J.M. (1999), *Doctors and Rules: A Sociology of Professional Values*, 2nd edn (Somerset, NJ: Transaction).

Kant, I. (1949), *Critique of Practical Reason and Other Writings in Moral Philosophy* (trans. L.W. Beck) (Chicago, IL: The University of Chicago Press).

— (1997), *Groundwork of the Metaphysics of Morals* (trans. M. Gregor) (Cambridge: Cambridge University Press).

Kater, L. et al. (2003), 'Health Care Ethics and Health Law in the Dutch Discussion on End-of-Life Decisions: A Historical Analysis of the Dynamics and Development of Both Disciplines', *Studies in History and Philosophy of Biological and Biomedical Sciences* 34:4, 669–84.

Kelleher, D. et al. (eds) (2006), *Challenging Medicine*, 2nd edn (London: Routledge).

Kennedy, I. (1981), *The Unmasking of Medicine* (London: Allen & Unwin).

— (1984), 'The Patient on the Clapham Omnibus', *Modern Law Review* 47:4, 454–71.

— (1988a), *Treat Me Right: Essays in Medical Law and Ethics* (Oxford: Clarendon Press).

— (1988b), 'What is a Medical Decision?', in I. Kennedy, *Treat Me Right: Essays in Medical Law and Ethics* (Oxford: Clarendon Press).

— (1997), 'Consent: Adult, Refusal of Consent, Capacity', *Medical Law Review* 5:3, 317–25.

— (2001), *Learning from Bristol: The Report of the Public Inquiry into Children's Heart Surgery at the Bristol Royal Infirmary 1984–1995* (Cm 5207) (Norwich: The Stationery Office).

— and Grubb, A. (2004), 'Elements of Consent', in A. Grubb (ed.), *Principles of Medical Law*, 2nd edn (Oxford: Oxford University Press).

Keown, J. (ed.) (1995), *Euthanasia Examined: Ethical, Clinical and Legal Perspectives* (Cambridge: Cambridge University Press).

— (1997), 'Restoring Moral and Intellectual Shape to the Law After *Bland*', *Law Quarterly Review* 113, 481–503.

— (2000), 'Beyond *Bland*: A Critique of the BMA Guidance on Withholding and Withdrawing Medical Treatment', *Legal Studies* 20:1, 66–84.

— (2006), 'Restoring the Sanctity of Life and Replacing the Caricature: A Reply to David Price', *Legal Studies* 26:1, 109–19.

— and Gormally, L. (1999), 'Human Dignity, Autonomy and Mentally Incapacitated Patients: A Critique of *Who Decides?*', *Web Journal of Current Legal Issues* 4.

Korsgaard, C.M. (1997), 'Introduction', in I. Kant, *Groundwork of the Metaphysics of Morals* (trans. M. Gregor) (Cambridge: Cambridge University Press).

Lacey, N. (1998), *Unspeakable Subjects: Feminist Essays in Legal and Social Theory* (Oxford: Hart).

— (2001), 'Responsibility and Modernity in Criminal Law', *The Journal of Political Philosophy* 9:3, 249–76.

Lamb, D. (1990), *Organ Transplants and Ethics* (London and New York: Routledge).

Lee, R.G. and Morgan, D. (2001), 'Regulating Risk Society: Stigmata Cases, Scientific Citizenship and Biomedical Diplomacy', *Sydney Law Review* 23:3, 297–318.

Lock, M., Young, A. and Cambrosio, A. (eds) (2000), *Living and Working with the New Medical Technologies: Intersections of Inquiry* (Cambridge: Cambridge University Press).

Lord Chancellor's Department (1997), *Who Decides? Making Decisions on Behalf of Mentally Incompetent Patients* (Consultation Paper, Cm 3803).

Loughlin, M. (2000), *Sword and Scales: An Examination of the Relationship between Law and Politics* (Oxford: Hart).

— (2004), *The Idea of Public Law* (Oxford: Oxford University Press).

MacIntyre, A. (1985), *After Virtue: A Study in Moral Theory*, 2nd edn (London: Duckworth).

Maclean, A. (2001), 'Crossing the Rubicon on the Human Rights Ferry', *Modern Law Review* 64:5, 775–94.

— (2006), 'Advance Directives, Future Selves and Decision-Making', *Medical Law Review* 14:3, 291–320.

Mason, J.K. and Laurie, G.T. (2006), *Mason and McCall Smith's Law and Medical Ethics*, 7th edn (Oxford: Oxford University Press).

Mathiesen, T. (2004), *Silently Silenced: Essays on the Creation of Acquiescence in Modern Society* (Winchester: Waterside Press).

McKeith, G. (2004), *You Are What You Eat* (London: Michael Joseph).

McLean, S. (1997), *Consent and the Law: Review of the Current Provisions in the Human Fertilisation and Embryology Act 1990 for the UK Health Ministers* (London: The Stationery Office).

— (1999), *Old Law, New Medicine: Medical Ethics and Human Rights* (London and New York: Pandora).

McVeigh, S. and Wheeler, S. (eds) (1992), *Law, Health & Medical Regulation* (Aldershot: Dartmouth).

Michalowski, S. (2002), 'Sanctity of Life: Are Some Lives More Sacred Than Others?', *Legal Studies* 22:3, 377–97.

Montgomery, J. (2003), *Health Care Law*, 2nd edn (Oxford: Oxford University Press).

— (2006), 'Law and the Demoralisation of Medicine', *Legal Studies* 26:2, 185–210.

Morgan, D. (2001), *Issues in Medical Law and Ethics* (London: Cavendish).

— and Lee, R.G. (1997), 'In the Name of the Father? *Ex Parte Blood*: Dealing with Novelty and Anomaly', *Modern Law Review* 60:6, 840–56.

Nedelsky, J. (1989), 'Reconceiving Autonomy: Sources, Thoughts and Possibilities', *Yale Journal of Law and Feminism* 1:1, 7–36.

O'Donovan, K. (1998), 'Is the Patient Position Inevitably Female?', in S. Sheldon and M. Thomson (eds), *Feminist Perspectives on Health Care Law* (London: Cavendish).

O'Neill, O. (2002), *Autonomy and Trust in Bioethics* (Cambridge: Cambridge University Press).

Parsons, T. et al. (1999), 'The "Gift of Life" and Its Reciprocation', in B. Turner (ed.), *The Talcott Parsons Reader* (Oxford: Blackwell).

Pollock, A.M. (2004), *NHS, plc: The Privatisation of Our Health Care* (London: Verso).

Price, D. (2001), 'Fairly Bland: An Alternative View of a Supposed New "Death Ethic" and the BMA Guidelines', *Legal Studies* 21:4, 618–43.

Rawls, J. (1971), *A Theory of Justice* (Cambridge, MA: Harvard University Press).

Rheinberger, H. (2000), 'Beyond Nature and Culture: Modes of Reasoning in the Age of Molecular Biology and Medicine' in M. Lock, A. Young and A. Cambrosio (eds), *Living and Working with the New Medical Technologies: Intersections of Inquiry* (Cambridge: Cambridge University Press).

Rose, N. (1985), *The Psychological Complex: Psychology, Politics and Society in England 1869–1939* (London: Routledge & Kegan Paul).

— (1998), 'Life, Reason and History: Reading Georges Canguilhem Today', *Economy & Society* 27:2–3, 154–70.

— (1999a), *Governing the Soul: The Shaping of the Private Self*, 2nd edn (London: Free Association Books).

— (1999b), *Powers of Freedom: Reframing Political Thought* (Cambridge: Cambridge University Press).

— (2001), 'The Politics of Life Itself', *Theory, Culture & Society* 18:6, 1–30.

— and Miller, P. (1992), 'Political Power Beyond the State', *British Journal of Sociology* 43:2, 172–205.

Scarman, L. (1974), *English Law: The New Dimension* (London: Stevens & Sons).

— (1975), *English Law and Social Policy* (London: Doughty Street).

— (1987), *Human Rights in the UK: Time for Change* (London: The Law Society Solicitors' European Group).

Scott, R. (2000), 'The Pregnant Woman and the Good Samaritan: Can a Woman have a Duty to Undergo a Caesarean Section?', *Oxford Journal of Legal Studies* 20:3, 407–36.

— (2002), *Rights, Duties and the Body: Law and Ethics of the Maternal-Fetal Conflict* (Oxford: Hart).

Sheldon, S. (1997), *Beyond Control: Medical Power and Abortion Law* (London: Pluto).

— (1998), '"A Responsible Body of Medical Men Skilled in that Particular Art ...": Rethinking the *Bolam* Test', in S. Sheldon and M. Thomson (eds), *Feminist Perspectives on Health Care Law* (London: Cavendish).

— and Thomson, M. (eds) (1998a), *Feminist Perspectives on Health Care Law* (London: Cavendish).

— and — (1998b), 'Health Care Law and Feminism: A Developing Relationship', in S. Sheldon and M. Thomson (eds), *Feminist Perspectives on Health Care Law* (London: Cavendish).

Singer, P. (1994), *Rethinking Life and Death: The Collapse of Our Traditional Ethics* (Oxford: Oxford University Press).

Strong, P.M. (1979), 'Sociological Imperialism and the Profession of Medicine: A Critical Examination of the Thesis of Medical Imperialism', *Social Science & Medicine* 13A:2, 199–215.

— (1984), 'Viewpoint: The Academic Encirclement of Medicine', *Sociology of Health & Illness* 6:3, 339–58.

Stychin, C.F. (1998), 'Body Talk: Rethinking Autonomy, Commodification and the Embodied Legal Self', in S. Sheldon and M. Thomson (eds), *Feminist Perspectives on Health Care Law* (London: Cavendish).

Teubner, G. (1987a), 'Juridifcation: Concepts, Aspects, Limits, Solutions', in G. Teubner (ed.), *Juridification of Social Spheres: A Comparative Analysis of Labor, Corporate, Antitrust and Social Welfare Law* (Berlin and New York: Walter de Gruyter).

— (ed.) (1987b), *Juridification of Social Spheres: A Comparative Analysis of Labor, Corporate, Antitrust and Social Welfare Law* (Berlin and New York: Walter de Gruyter).

The Right Honourable The Lord Woolf (2001), 'Are the Courts Excessively Deferential to the Medical Profession?', *Medical Law Review* 9:1, 1–16.

Thomson, M. (1994), 'After *Re S*', *Medical Law Review* 2:2, 127–48.

Turner, B. (ed.) (1999), *The Talcott Parsons Reader* (Oxford: Blackwell).

Veitch, S. (2006), '"A Very Unique Case": A Comment on MacCormick's "Particulars and Universals"', in Z. Bankowski (ed.), *The Universal and the Particular in Legal Reasoning* (Aldershot: Ashgate).

Wacquant, L. (2001), 'The Penalisation of Poverty and the Rise of Neo-liberalism', *European Journal on Criminal Policy and Research* 9:4, 401–12.

Wagner, P. (1994), *The Sociology of Modernity: Liberty and Discipline* (London and New York: Routledge).

Wolf, S. (1994), 'Shifting Paradigms in Bioethics and Health Law: The Rise of a New Pragmatism', *American Journal of Law and Medicine* 20:4, 395–415.

World Health Organization (1948), *Preamble, Constitution of the World Health Organization.*

Index